# The POTUS Chronicles

To Joe,

It was a great pleasure getting acquainted with you. I wish you well in all your future exploits

Don't take politics too seriously.

Bob

Robert L. Haught

June 2, 2008

# Also by Robert L. Haught

### Now, I'm No Expert

### on Cats and Other Mysteries of Life

# The POTUS Chronicles

✦

## Bubba Between the Bushes

*Robert L. Haught*

iUniverse, Inc.
New York Lincoln Shanghai

# The POTUS Chronicles
## Bubba Between the Bushes

iUniverse books may be ordered through booksellers or by contacting:

iUniverse
2021 Pine Lake Road, Suite 100
Lincoln, NE 68512
www.iuniverse.com
1-800-Authors (1-800-288-4677)

Because of the dynamic nature of the Internet, any Web addresses or links contained in this book may have changed since publication and may no longer be valid.

The views expressed in this work are solely those of the author and do not necessarily reflect the views of the publisher, and the publisher hereby disclaims any responsibility for them.

ISBN: 978-0-595-47154-6 (pbk)
ISBN: 978-0-595-91434-0 (ebk)

Printed in the United States of America

It's a tough life, this being president and trying to please everybody —well, not exactly everybody, but enough to re-elect.

Will Rogers

# Contents

# What is a POTUS????

Washington, our nation's capital, is a city that runs on acronyms.

Only in Washington is LUST a part of the official language of government. The letters stand for "Leaking Underground Storage Tanks," a major concern of the Department of Energy in the early 1990s.

POTUS is an acronym for "President of the United States." Former *New York Times* columnist William Safire, an authority on language, became aware of the term in 1969 when he was a speechwriter for President Richard Nixon. He noticed certain telephone buttons in the West Wing carried that label.

"In current practice," Safire writes, "the acronym is not used in direct discourse with the president ... but it is a handy, sassily insidish, behind-his-back reference to the individual in that office." Similarly, FLOTUS is a shorthand identification of "First Lady of the United States." Both POTUS and FLOTUS are frequently used in White House press pool reports.

VPOTUS and SLOTUS have not come into common usage for the vice president and the second lady. However, SCOTUS has survived since the time news was transmitted by telegraphers as "wirespeak" for "Supreme Court of the United States."

*The POTUS Chronicles*—perhaps "sassily"—traces the administrations of three presidents: George Bush, Bill Clinton and George W. Bush. When the latter became president, his chief of staff, Andy Card, came up with the idea of using POTUS 41 and POTUS 43 when referring to father and son to avoid confusion. The man who served between the Bushes, POTUS 42, may be forever known as "Bubba."

This book will not be shelved in the history section of the library. The author is not a historian but rather a former editorial writer who offered humorous commentary on government and politics for more than 18 years in an op-ed page column called *Potomac Junction*. The title originated from the observation that while Washington is a crossroads of the world it also is very much like a small town in many ways.

*Potomac Junction* is a comic strip without drawings. It is populated with such characters as Senator Stump, Congressman Babble, Larry, the lawyer; Bill, the bureaucrat; Lonnie, the lobbyist; Sparky, the speechwriter; Connie, the consultant; and the like, as well as real presidents, members of Congress, Supreme Court justices, and other players in the game of politics.

In this account of three occupants of the Oval Office, readers will find highlights (and lowlights) of their terms in office, set in the context of some momentous times in the nation's history. These included wars under all three presidents, fascinating political campaigns and elections, dramatic changes in Congress, an impeachment, and the rise of a highly ambitious woman seeking the power of the presidency.

Like pages from a reporter's notebook, *The POTUS Chronicles* captures some priceless moments of one of the most memorable periods in American politics.

# POTUS 41

## George Bush

# Padding His Resume With One Term as President: "Poppy Prudently Recreating"

After eight years in the shadow of Ronald Reagan, the man with one of the longest resumes in Washington finally added "president" to his list of accomplishments.

George Herbert Walker Bush became America's 41st president by defeating Democrat Michael Dukakis, governor of Massachusetts, in the 1988 election. He took office on a pledge he made at the Republican convention in New Orleans, "Read My Lips—No New Taxes." He didn't say anything about not raising the old ones.

Bush contributed another phrase to the lexicon of the times, "A Thousand Points of Light," in describing his vision of community voluntary service. He raised hopes for making the United States "a kinder, gentler nation" and set out to establish a non-confrontational tone for his administration.

That changed when Iraq invaded Kuwait and threatened to move into Saudi Arabia. With a vow that "this aggression will not stand," Bush organized an international coalition that, in a relatively brief, low-casualty Gulf War defeated, but did not capture, Iraqi dictator Saddam Hussein. While the conflict raged, the president counseled Americans to engage in "prudently recreating" and he set an example by conducting the war from a golf cart at Kennebunkport.

Although George Bush launched some serious initiatives, including the war, he didn't always take himself too seriously. He showed he had a sense of humor when he chose Dan Quayle as his running mate. Comic Dana Carvey's career certainly benefited from Bush's trademark mannerisms and his style of talking in phrases, which he mimicked to perfection.

An advocate of traditional values, the 41st president was a dedicated family man, going by the nickname of "Poppy." Barbara Bush was a popular first lady and she played a visible role in the administration, along with first dog Millie, who became a well-known author.

In spite of a 91-percent approval rating after the war, the people were not so "kind and gentle" to Bush in 1992. Discontented by a sluggish economy, high deficit spending and other domestic worries, they turned him out of office. With a third party candidate, H. Ross Perot, getting 19 percent of the vote, Democrats reclaimed the White House after a 12-year absence.

Although he was a one-term president, George Bush definitely left an imprint on Washington during the time he was there.

## Party Time in the Nation's Capital Is Business as Usual

Nobody goes to a Washington party to have a good time. Social events are merely an extension of the day's business. The only difference is that it's harder to stab someone in the back while holding a champagne glass.

The capital's social life is always a bit unpredictable the first year of a new presidency. A certain style is set by the occupant of the White House, and George Bush is no exception.

During the early days of his term, Bush established a reputation for spur-of-the-moment, usually casual, entertaining. Such events as movie nights, complete with popcorn, were common. A big hit was *The Last Temptation of Jim Bakker*.

Big campaign contributors expecting to attend a glittery White House affair got a surprise invitation to a lawn party to dedicate a new horseshoe pit. It was sort of a black tie and sneakers occasion.

In more recent months, hot dogs and informality have given way to truffles and flourishes as the Bushes got into the swing of things. Foreign dignitaries, sports and theatrical celebrities, and even Vice President Dan Quayle have been guests for elegant affairs.

One such event was the 25th anniversary party for the American Film Institute. A highlight of the evening was a performance by comic Steve Martin, who took the stage, unzipped his fly and proceeded to produce scarves, eggs, a lighted cigarette, a telephone and bubbles. You can't say the Bush parties don't have class.

Perhaps the biggest party date of the year was the last day of September. Only in Washington is New Year's Eve celebrated on September 30, as bureaucrats hail the new fiscal year with streamers of red tape and confetti direct from the paper shredder. They drank toasts with the new "federal budget" cocktail—one drink and you're hopelessly unbalanced.

Party-giving in Washington has changed a lot since the days of Perle Mesta, Oklahoma's gift to the capital's social scene. Nowadays the "hostess with the mostest" is apt to be someone who can raise a pot full of money for a political candidate.

On the theory that fund-raising can be fun, both Republicans and Democrats hold annual dinners featuring big-name entertainers. Recently TV's Mary Hart starred for the GOP, and the Democrats billed Paul Simon as their big draw. When some contributors started begging off, they had to explain their star was the singer, not the bow tie senator from Illinois.

Sally, the socialite will be glad when the new administration is fully in place so she will know whom to invite to her power parties. The worst thing that could happen is to have someone who is "out."

She had to scratch a sub-cabinet appointee from her list at the last moment because he hadn't received the results of his drug test.

Even a party animal like Spuds McKenzie couldn't make it in this town unless he's a member of the "in" crowd.

*October 5, 1989*

## President's Press Secretary Able to Handle Snakes of All Kinds

When the President of the United States travels, the American presidency also hits the road. This was most apparent during the recent holiday break when President Bush took time out to do some fishing and hunting in south Texas.

Some of the sophisticates in the White House press corps found conditions in rural Texas to be somewhat primitive. As one reporter complained to the president's press secretary, Marlin Fitzwater, "here we are in Beeville, and we can't find the *New York Times.*"

Fitzwater managed to retain his sense of humor while catering to the whims of the fussy correspondents and keeping them informed about Bush's activities, including his daily schedule.

"The president was up early this morning, around 6," he reported, adding that he read the newspapers, had breakfast, and was hunting by 8:45. But unlike other hunters, Bush also had an intelligence briefing. And most sportsmen don't head for the mesquite brush with the secretary of state for a hunting companion.

Fitzwater conducted regular briefings in the boondocks for the elite reporters, whose newspapers went to great expense so that they could ask probing questions about major news events. An example is the following excerpt from the December 28 briefing in Beeville:

Q: Marlin, how goes the quail, and didn't this fog interfere? I mean, it's all over Texas. He went hunting in the fog?

Fitzwater: I don't know. He was out hunting when I called this morning.

Q: How's the weather?

Fitzwater: This man has eyes that can see through steel girders, let alone fog.

One reporter had an inquiry about "wholesale and wanton slaughter going on," and she wasn't referring either to Romania or Panama but rather to protests from animal rights demonstrators. This led to a follow-up:

Q: Is he hunting for food or for fun, and will they eat the quail when they bring them home?

Fitzwater: He hunts quail, and they're always dressed for consumption. Quail are excellent. I'm from Kansas, used to hunt quail as a boy, ate 'em all the time. It's a great dish.

As Fitzwater was discussing the elaborate communications system that enables the president to respond to international crises wherever he is, the telephone rang. "And there he is now," the press aide quipped.

Fitzwater's briefings sometimes produce bits of news about himself. He told reporters he thought he once had met Panamanian Gen. Manuel Noriega ("The man took one look at me and he recoiled in fear.") And it was later revealed that the press secretary had survived an encounter with a snake.

The two events were unrelated, as Fitzwater explained about his standoff with a Texas rattlesnake. "I stared that guy down," he said. "He never had a chance."

Maybe that's why Fitzwater is so good at handling the White House press.

*January 4, 1990*

## Washington Offers a Fool's Gold Mine of Comedy Talent

If it's true, as entertainment industry analysts say, that the heyday of the comedy club is over, the word hasn't reached Washington.

Aspiring amateurs, many of whom have regular jobs, are trying hard to break into the comedy field in the nation's capital, where the competition is very tough.

Just last Saturday night, three up-and-coming jokesters took their turns before a tough audience at the Gridiron Club. In this critic's opinion, all three show promise.

The leadoff comic was Tom Foley, a political satirist who poked fun at his weight and his wimpy image as speaker of the U.S. House of Representatives. "It's not easy for me to suddenly start going for the jugular, when I've spent so many years going for the potatoes," he lamented.

At a $200-a-plate fund-raising dinner, "I would eat $400 worth of food," he said.

Following Foley was Dick Cheney, whose deadpan routine about running the Department of Defense was funnier than any nuclear device. "No matter what you've heard, I'm not a relic of the Cold War," he said. "But hey, look! Somebody in this town has to worry about what we're going to do when Stalin dies." His humor was a bit too regimented, but at least he didn't totally bomb.

The final act was a monologist named George Bush, who commanded attention with his zingers about life in the White House. Referring to John Sununu, the combative chief of staff, he said that at the recent drug summit in Colombia, "We had to keep telling him: bite the taco, shake the hand."

Bush parodied a recent incident regarding a fake phone call. "Happy to take the call," he said. "Certainly worth it. Never thought I'd hear from Elvis again."

All three demonstrated adeptness at what one Washington reviewer called "self-depreciating" humor, in the style of an acknowledged master, Ronald Reagan, who is now playing the California circuit.

As standup comedians, Foley, Cheney and Bush turned in creditable performances. But none of them should quit his day job.

Two former Gridiron Club headliners, Sen. Bob Dole and Sen. Alan Simpson, are now appearing regularly on the floor of the Senate.

Dole got off one of his best lines a few years ago when he saw three former presidents—Ford, Carter and Nixon—sitting together. "There they were," he quipped. "See no evil, hear no evil, and evil."

Simpson is best known as a droll storyteller. He tells of a Wyoming rancher who got stopped for speeding. The trooper asked, "Don't you have a governor on this truck?" "Nope," said the driver. "That's manure you smell." And then there's the one about the impotent bull.

Oklahoma Sen. David Boren made his big time comedy debut last January at the Alfalfa Club. As a sample of his one-liners, he said the president told him that dealing with Congress was like his fishing trips: "hours of matching wits with tiny-brained creatures and nothing to show for it."

All in all, the capital has a respectable number of comedians. But it's safe to say there's not a Bobcat Goldthwaite in the bunch.

*April 5, 1990*

## President Calls for Budget Summit to Address Twin Peaks

The Secretary of Summits was heavily ensconced in work in his office in the West Wing of the White House. Between phone calls he could be heard softly vocalizing, "Summit time, and I'm feelin' uneasy ..."

But there was a story to be unearthed, and he agreed to fill in the details on events of recent weeks that have had many people guessing. Consulting his diary, he unfolded a creepy tale of mystery and intrigue.

It all began when President Bush returned from his Florida fishing trip to find a horrible crime had been committed. The victim: Rosy Scenario.

He immediately assembled a team of investigators, including a sheriff, a special agent and a budget analyst whose height had diminished from dancing around figures.

One misty morning they gathered in the Oval Office. After chasing out a one-eyed lady who was fooling with the drapes, they got down to business over doughnuts and hot black coffee.

"What happened to Rosy Scenario?" Bush demanded. "Growth revenues. Supposed to take care of everything. But now look where we are."

The president hauled out two charts titled Deficit and S&L Bailout.

"Budget deficit's rising to a peak of nearly $200 billion. Cost of the savings and loan bailout, climbing to a peak of $300 billion," he said. "Gotta do something about these twin peaks."

The budget midget started to speak, but Bush cut him off. "Hey, talking to you is like talking to a log," he said.

At this point Bush turned to the Secretary of Summits, who sat in on all important meetings. "Gotta have a budget summit," he said.

"I'll consult the schedule," said the SOS. "Let's see, we've had the education summit, the drug summit, and the global warming summit. Coming up, we've got the NATO summit in London July 5 and 6 and the economic summit in Houston starting July 8. And before that, of course, the summit with Soviet President Mikhail Gorbachev in Washington."

"Lotta summits," said Bush. "How about scrubbing Gorbachev? Nothing to sign anyway."

"Can't do it, sir," said the SOS. "He's looking forward to getting out of the Soviet Union for a few days."

"Can't blame him for that."

"And besides, Mrs. Bush wants to take Mrs. Gorbachev to Wellesley College to show the students she's not the only wife who's known by the company she keeps."

"Well, just gonna have to squeeze in a budget summit somewhere. Find out if the congressional leaders will be in town for any length of time. And let's order an especially large table, because everything's gonna be on it except broccoli."

The bantam budgeteer couldn't restrain himself. He burst out: "You mean everything, including the T-word?"

"Everything," said the president. "No preconditions. Got a big fish in the percolator here. Need to keep our snorkels above the water level. Have another cuppa joe."

*May 31, 1990*

## Obscurity Reaches New Height of Acceptable Standards

With the nomination of David H. Souter to the U.S. Supreme Court, "obscurity" has reached a new height of acceptable standards in Washington.

It is too early to tell whether President Bush's choice to replace retiring Justice William J. Brennan will win the right to don the black robe and join the other eight jurists on this distinguished panel. But Bush probably made a politically smart move by picking Souter over someone more well known and controversial.

For instance, if the president had decided on somebody like Andrew Dice Clay, the raunchy comedian certainly would have put some spark into the confirmation hearings. But try selling him to conservatives and women's rights groups? No way.

By being obscure, Souter has a good thing going for him. And he definitely meets the obscurity criteria. A bookish individual who lives alone in a small New Hampshire farmhouse, the 50-year-old federal judge is variously described as "a very quiet guy," "a pluperfect scholar," and "reserved almost to the point of shyness."

When Bush brought him before the television cameras to make the nomination announcement, more than one viewer might have thought he was a member of the Secret Service detail.

Obscurity is neither a new nor unusual quality to be found in politics, but historically it has been reserved primarily for vice presidents. Having served in that office, Bush undoubtedly understands its value from personal experience.

Not everyone appreciates the advantage of being obscure, however. A considerable amount of controversy was aroused earlier this year when *Roll Call*, a Capitol Hill newspaper, published its list of "The Ten Most Obscure Members" of the House of Representatives.

As *Roll Call* described members of the Obscure Caucus, "They don't hog the microphone at subcommittee hearings and hardly ever appear on C-SPAN; they just tend to business quietly and almost invisibly."

Despite its complimentary tone, the article set off a flurry of angry protests from congressmen who didn't make the obscurity honor roll and staff aides of the chosen members. The reaction was reminiscent of a situation years ago when a Washington publication singled out former Sen. William Scott, R-Va., as "the dumbest man in the Senate." The incident went without much notice until Scott called a news conference to deny that he was ... well, you get the picture.

Obscurity, as the newspaper noted, is often an admirable trait. It is not to be confused with mediocrity, a characteristic which gained notoriety in 1970 when former Sen. Roman Hruska, R-Neb., defended Supreme Court nominee Harold

Carswell by saying: "… there are a lot of mediocre judges and people and lawyers. They are entitled to a little representation, aren't they?"

*July 26, 1990*

## When It Comes to War Some Things Just Aren't That Funny

Capital dwellers, deprived of entertainment with Congress out of town, are anxiously awaiting the August 31 pre-Broadway opening of a new show at the Kennedy Center: *Shogun, The Musical*, based on James Clavell's epic novel.

If it's anything like the 1980 TV miniseries, this musical adaptation of the tale of Japanese warlords ought to be a hit, with all of the fights and head-loppings. The success of *Les Miserables* proves that Americans get enjoyment from human cruelty if the music is good.

And so it was that Sparky, the speechwriter got an inspiration for the musical revue he had been asked to put together as a community charity project. Proceeds will be used to repair a patriotic statue that was damaged when a determined protester turned a blowtorch on the bronze flag.

President Bush's decision to send U.S. troops to the Persian Gulf would be a good theme, he thought.

Never one to shy away from plagiarism, he decided to call his production *Show Guns*. He gave some consideration to the title of Naked Aggression, after Bush's description of Iraq's invasion of Kuwait, thinking it might qualify for a grant from the National Endowment for the Arts. But it just didn't seem right for a musical.

Sparky began to dash off lyrics. His opening number would feature a Bush-type character, backed by a chorus in international costumes, singing ala Eliza Doolittle:

"Just Kuwait, Saddam Hussein, just Kuwait,
"You can't take Saudi Arabia, just Kuwait."
Next a general would lead his soldiers off to war, singing:
"Come to King Khalid Military City,
"It's awful hot and the sand is gritty,
"But the people there are warm and witty,
"And that's what I like about the Sauds."
A quartet dressed in flowing white robes would harmonize:
"We're the sheiks of Araby,
"We stand for unity.
"We can't let oil get cheap,
"Saddam is such a creep."
Two oil company executives would sing a happy duet:
"We're in the money, the future's sunny,
"We've had a slump but now we're back on our feet."

While a general and an admiral sang, "We're back in the budget again, thanks to old Saddam Hussein," a band of liberals would moan:

"The Desert Shield deployment

"Spoils our enjoyment,

"Bye, bye, peace dividend."

Sparky decided to close the show with a rousing song about 24-hour news coverage of the crisis (*Iraq Around the Clock*).

Then he got word that his brother was shipping out to the Middle East. Suddenly nothing he had written seemed funny anymore.

*August 16, 1990*

## Alas It's True—Fact Can Indeed Be Stranger Than Fiction

For the past three months, Bill, the bureaucrat, has been in Eastern Europe helping one of the new democracies discover the pleasures of American-style government bureaucracy. Returning to Washington he was eager to catch up on the news. In the country where he was stationed, news reports were scarce and often garbled. One of the first questions he asked his secretary was, "How is President Bush? I heard he had lead poisoning."

"No, no. The Bush family's dog, Millie, became ill after digesting some paint that chipped off the White House."

"Where is the EPA when we need it? There's something else I'm dying to know. Why did the president get so upset because Roseanne Cash sang the 'Star Spangled Banner'?"

"That was Roseanne Barr, and she didn't sing, she screeched. A lot of Americans thought she desecrated the national anthem."

"But didn't Congress pass a law against that?"

"Congress banned burning the flag, but the Supreme Court ruled the law unconstitutional."

"Speaking of the court, is it true that the president nominated David Brinkley to fill a vacancy?"

"No, the nominee is David Souter of New Hampshire."

"I never heard of him."

"Don't feel bad. Justice Thurgood Marshall had to call his wife to ask if she knew the man."

"Marshall has to call his wife to ask for directions to get home. What about the report that Dan Quayle had brain surgery?"

"It wasn't the vice president, but his wife who had an operation."

"Too bad. I thought he might have gotten a transplant. Anything new on the civil war in Siberia?"

"There's no war in Siberia."

"Then why did President Bush send in the U.S. Marines?"

"That was Liberia."

"What about Sen. Alan Simpson's television show that's all the rage?"

"No, 'The Simpsons' is an animated cartoon about a family of dumb slobs and wisecracking juveniles who are constantly bickering. It has nothing to do with Congress."

"Are you sure? Well, I'll bet the Hubble Space Telescope has been sending back some spectacular pictures."

"Not exactly. Something to do with a flawed mirror."

"Some NASA bureaucrat is probably getting the blame. I guess Ivana Trump got a good divorce settlement."

"Not yet, and not likely. The Donald is $43.2 billion in debt and having cash flow problems."

"Well, it is obvious I've been getting a distorted version of news events. I even heard that the president had changed his mind about raising taxes and that the United States and Syria are allied against Iraq in the Middle East."

"Sir, those reports are true."

*August 23, 1990*

## Nothing Eases a Crisis Quicker Than "Prudently Recreating"

When Senator Stump returned to the clubhouse from an afternoon on the links at the Outer Banks Golf and Country Club, he was met by a clutch of news reporters eager to hear his views on the latest Mideast developments.

The senator deflected the first four or five questions with responses such as: "I haven't read the statement so I can't comment on it." "My policy is not to discuss sensitive national security matters on which I have not been briefed." "Sorry, I'm not up to speed on that."

Finally a reporter hit him with a zinger: "Senator, with Saddam Hussein holding American citizens hostage, armies massing on either side of the Iraqi border and the entire Persian Gulf region in turmoil, how can you spend your time in frivolous pursuit of a little ball around a golf course?"

"Sir, you defame a great American sport," the senator roared. "Besides, I am simply abiding by the wishes of the commander-in-chief. President Bush did not cancel his vacation just because Iraq invaded Kuwait and threatened the security of world oil supplies.

"If he can direct the largest U.S. military operation since the Vietnam war with a cellular phone in a golf cart in Kennebunkport, who am I to do otherwise? After all, he did say he hoped the rest of America would 'prudently recreate.'

"For most of August, the president has been 'prudently recreating' in Maine, the vice president has been 'prudently recreating' in Arizona, and the secretary of state has been 'prudently recreating' in Wyoming. But they are not out of touch with what is going on. I happen to know that Vice President Dan Quayle is watching very closely for any word that the Indiana National Guard might be called to active duty.

"As for me, I have spent the past few days at this gorgeous resort because I was invited to give a speech to the annual convention of the North American Machine Screw Association. From here I go to Honolulu to speak to the Orthodontists League on 'Putting Teeth into Ethics Laws.' Although I am supposed to be on vacation, I want my constituents to know that I am still carrying out the duties of my office."

"Senator, don't you think the gravity of the current situation requires your presence in Washington?"

"Certainly not. No two-bit dictator is going to force me to be a prisoner in my office. Ten years ago, we would have obtained the release of American hostages in Iran much sooner if Jimmy Carter had gone bowling two nights a week. It is important that we send a message to the world that American policymakers do their best work when they are at play. At the first sign of a dangerous conflict developing, the president, his cabinet and members of Congress should grab their clubs and head for the golf course."

"Saddam Hussein isn't out playing golf."

"Let him find his own way to 'prudently recreate'."

*August 30, 1990*

## It's a Whopper, But You Should See the One That Got Away

As pleased as a kid with a new toy, President Bush has pronounced the new Air Force One "magnificent." The fisherman president should have seen the one that got away.

An Air Force deputy assistant administrator in charge of executive aircraft and fax machines conducted a private tour of the huge whale-shaped plane and also revealed details of original plans for an even larger and more elaborate model.

The luxurious Boeing 747 jumbo jet which replaced an 18-year-old 707 is nothing to sneeze at, mind you. The two-story plane contains an elegant presidential suite complete with two beds, a dressing room and a shower-equipped lavatory (in case Millie needs a bath); a plush private office, a conference/dining room large enough for half the cabinet, and even a medical emergency room.

"The president's not likely to get a fish hook in his ear at 30,000 feet—the fishing pond option was dropped along with the tennis court," said the Air Force official, "but you never know when someone might get a thumb caught in the paper shredder. That was a nice Ollie North touch."

Planning for a new presidential plane was begun in the Reagan administration. That may account for the movie theater and all the television screens, although the horseback riding trail had to be scrapped.

Bush will have no problem finding a telephone when he wants to chat up another world leader—the plane has 85 phones, along with computers, memory typewriters, and facsimile and copying machines. It seats 70 passengers and 23 crew members and has two galleys and seven bathrooms.

"The earlier plans called for twice as much communications equipment, as well as a hot tub," said the official. "But as you know, we're on an austerity budget."

Cost of the new plane, an identical backup and a new hangar—the old one was too small—is $410 million. But that includes a tinted windshield and an anti-missile system, the official pointed out.

As for the cost of the super deluxe model that went by the boards, "Let's just say it was about the size of the annual budget of a small country. The government was hoping to sell the plans to Donald Trump, but ..."

He reached in his desk drawer and pulled out a blueprint of a plane which he said was designed to the specifications of White House Chief of Staff John Sununu. It had to be discarded for aerodynamic reasons. Close examination showed the Sununu model had only a right wing.

While he was at it, he produced plans for official aircraft proposed for use by the Democratic leaders of the House and Senate: two hot air balloons.

Then he unlocked the office safe and displayed a drawing of Air Force 13, designated for the vice president.

"This was designed by a committee of editorial cartoonists," he explained.

It was a red, white and blue beanie with a propeller on top.

*September 13, 1990*

## Budget Agreement Sparks Bull Market on Mixed Metaphors

Reaction to the new bipartisan budget agreement has come fast and furious this week, and the clichés sound as if they were drawn from a racing form.

President Bush set the tone when he commented on the compromise nature of the five-year $500 billion deficit-reduction plan. He told reporters: "I don't have the horses in the Congress to do it exactly my way."

That opened the gates for a stampede of mixed metaphors of an equestrian character.

A senior administration official, explaining why the decision was made to sign off on such a controversial proposal, said, "If the horseshoe fits, throw it."

As the months-long negotiations drew near a close, one exhausted participant was said to have pleaded, "Let's run it up the flagpole and see how fast it will gallop."

A budget office congressional liaison person expressed his frustration after spending a day on Capitol Hill trying to find a leader to help the cause. "Where do you find the horse that is ready to take up that cudgel and run with it?"

A Treasury Department legislative staffer had a more optimistic view. He reported that "certain forces on the Hill feel they have the reins in their teeth."

Senator Stump said he did not have enough information on the complex package. "We ought to know whether we've got a horse that will run, or that we can get behind and push," he said.

Lonnie, the lobbyist was not surprised that the agreement was so wide-ranging and he predicted a stiff battle among special interests. "Everyone wants a different cup of tea," he said, "and that's what makes a horse race."

Congressman Babble, who is in the middle of a tough re-election campaign, was dismayed at the thought of incumbents having to vote on tax increases and government program reductions. "It is like a Trojan horse around our neck," he complained.

Echoing his negativism, the executive director of the National Naysayers and Nitpickers League had this to say: "You can lead a horse to water, but you can't make him jump the fence."

Rep. Tom Lantos, D-Calif., can claim credit for one of the best equine analogies, but he used it up last June in arguing why the United States should stop its dialogue with the Palestine Liberation Organization.

"As an old Hungarian proverb says, 'You can't ride two horses with one rear end.' And I believe that that's really what we have been attempting to do for some time. And if you think about it, that's an awkward posture."

Secretary of State James Baker was slightly confused. Although he is from Texas, he said, "I've never seen two horses with only one rear end."

"No," said Lantos, "the rider has to have one rear end."

At that point Baker decided not to question Lantos any further about a subject on which the congressman obviously was an expert.

*October 4, 1990*

## You Can Fool Some People, But Don't Try to Flimflam Anthony

Add a new name to the list of power figures in the nation's capital.

Along with House Speaker Tom Foley, Senate Majority Leader George Mitchell and Chief Justice William Rehnquist, we now have Anthony Henderson.

Although Anthony is only eight years old and doesn't even work for the government, he is recognized as having a lot of clout. The skeptical third-grader made the President of the United States prove his identity when he visited his classroom at the Barcroft Elementary School in Arlington.

Why would anyone doubt that such a world-famous personage as George Bush was the real thing? Anthony told *Today* host Bryant Gumbel he had reason to be suspicious because the previous week a guy in tights and a beard showed up at the school and passed himself off as Leonardo da Vinci. (Photographic coverage of the Bush visit indicated he was clean-shaven and wearing a business suit.)

Fortunately the leader of the free world was prepared to document his claim. To answer Anthony's challenge, he reached into his pocket, hauled out a wallet and produced a Texas driver's license with the name, "BUSH, George Herbert."

Anthony still was not quite convinced, so the president dug a little deeper and came up with an American Express card—a plain old green one, not gold or platinum. He also fished out a photo of a grandson playing baseball.

And thus a distrustful youngster turned the tables on the chief occupant of the White House. Usually it's someone wanting to see the president who has to provide credentials.

To many Washingtonians, the most surprising thing about this experience is that Bush carries a billfold, just like every other working slob. But why does he need a driver's license? Is he allowed to drive himself in anything but a golf cart?

And why, of all things, would the man in charge of a $1.4 trillion budget need a credit card? Maybe he uses it when he and Barbara take friends to their favorite Chinese restaurant. Wouldn't you like to know what other kinds of cardboard and plastic Bush totes around in his hip pocket?

If an aging newspaper columnist had to divulge the contents of his wallet, it would be this kind of collection:

- A green American Express card, three bank cards and half a dozen gasoline credit cards, of which all but a couple are used about once a year.

- A Virginia driver's license and car titles for a 1986 Pontiac and a 1964 Chevrolet pickup truck.

- Auto and health insurance cards (which should come engraved in gold).

- A long-distance telephone card which doesn't work in those fancy airport machines.

- A membership card from the American Association of Retired (or past 50) Persons, good for a "senior discount" at certain motor inns.

- A video rental card, seldom used. (Who wants to give a snoopy investigator a record of which movies you watch?)

- Two 22-cent stamps, which have survived two postal rate increases without sticking together.

Well, that might not impress a skeptic like Anthony. But then, I'm not a president or a bearded guy in tights.

*March 21, 1991*

## Queenly Seat of Power Prompts Vision About the "King" Thing

Back-to-back visits by high-ranking dignitaries have Washington in a tizzy.

Last week it was Norman Schwarzkopf, general, U.S. Army, commander of Operation Desert Storm, grand marshal of the Kentucky Derby.

This week it's Elizabeth the Second, by the Grace of God, of the United Kingdom of Great Britain and Northern Ireland and of her other Realms and Territories, Queen, Head of the Commonwealth, Defender of the Faith.

It's a good thing the queen doesn't have to depend on taxicabs for transport. She travels with an entourage of about 40, including the mistress of the robes, the lady of the bedchamber, master of the royal household, the queen's equerry, her dresser and two assistants, two maids, a footman … well, you get the picture.

There are also tons of luggage—such essential things as her favorite tea and a silver service, a hot-water bottle, umbrellas, duck-feather pillows, and (ahem) a white kidskin toilet seat (or so the British press reports).

If she were a commoner, she'd spend her entire U.S. visit waiting in line for a taxi at National Airport.

The queen's impending arrival also set President Bush to thinking, according to a reliable source (not the one who spilled the beans about Nancy Reagan to Kitty Kelley). This tipster says Bush underwent a "vision thing" one evening after he had watched an old movie the Reagans had left behind.

It was a 1938 flick, *If I Were King*, starring Ronald Colman. Bush also had read a few pages of Macbeth from the *Readers Digest Shakespeare Bedside Companion* before dropping off to sleep.

Maybe it was all the decaffeinated coffee he's been drinking, but the president fantasized that he was delivering a soliloquy:

"If I were king, if I were king.

"I am Bush of Kennebunkport. If good, why do I yield to that suggestion whose horrid image doth unfix my cowlick and make my fibrillating heart knock at my ribs, against the use of nature?

"If chance will have me king, why, I would hence be relieved of the pain of dealing with the imperial Congress and that knave Gephardt. That dreary duty would fall to the prime minister, an occupation surely fit for John Sununu.

"I would devote my time to royal pursuits, like playing tennis and going to Orioles games.

"If I were king … neat! Or have we eaten on the insane root that takes the reason prisoner?

"Ay, when my heart quickens no longer would I have to answer questions about Dan Quayle. But forsooth, a worse fate awaits if succession be the issue. The questions would concern my son, Prince Neil.

"I have bought golden opinions from all sorts of people. But pollsters can be wrong. Is America ready for another King George? I think not. To be king stands not within the prospect of belief.

"There is room in this land for only one royal family. And the Kennedys are not yet ready to abdicate."

*May 16, 1991*

## Quayle Thinks Something Funny's Going On in the Comics

Not since Al Capp quit drawing *L'il Abner* has such a fuss been made over a comic strip. The conservative satirist outraged liberals with jabs at their heroes.

As in Capp's time, all the political commentary these days is not confined to the editorial page. Newspapers which carry the *Doonesbury* comic strip are providing cartoonist Garry Trudeau a forum to use his poison pen against the Bush administration.

A two-week series of strips depicts a fictional reporter, Rick Redfern, tracking down a story that the Drug Enforcement Administration covered up allegations of drug use by Vice President Dan Quayle while he was a U.S. senator from Indiana in 1982.

Quayle assured a high level of readership by repeated prepublication protests that Trudeau was using baseless charges to carry out a personal vendetta against him and President Bush. Indeed, the DEA stated it had investigated and found no grounds for the allegations.

By not letting the facts stand in the way of a biased opinion, Trudeau has invaded the domain of unprincipled editorial writers and columnists—yes, there are some of those still around—and may have started a dangerous trend.

What if other comic strip artists decided to devote their daily space to attacks on the White House? The possibilities should strike terror in the hearts of every member of the president's Cabinet.

Here are some examples of the kind of Bush-bashing that might turn up on the comics page:

*Blondie*—Over Dagwood's objections, Blondie joins a demonstration to protest government overregulation of small businesses like her new catering enterprise. She carries a sign reading, "Bush Caters to Faceless Bureaucrats."

*Dick Tracy*—The super sleuth takes on a case involving the Republican National Committee. He uncovers a plot by a high-ranking RNC ringleader, Trick E. Dick, to win re-election for Bush by creating mass confusion in the Democratic Party. Dick tells Tracy, "It was a great idea, but they beat me to it."

*Peanuts*—Secretary of Education Lamar Alexander visits Charlie Brown's school and explodes the "Great Pumpkin" myth, steals Linus' crying towel, breaks Marcie's glasses, kicks the legs out from under Schroder's piano and steps on Snoopy's tail, snarling "Ha, ha, kids and beagles can't vote!"

*Beetle Bailey*—Defense Secretary Dick Cheney comes to announce the base is being closed, but Beetle introduces him to Miss Buxley, the general's secretary. Cheney forgets his mission and selects her for a new recruiting poster.

*Cathy*—William P. Barr's confirmation as attorney general is placed in jeopardy when Cathy sends an affidavit to the Senate Judiciary Committee accusing him of musical harassment. She alleges he played "Hail to the Chief" on a bagpipe in her neighborhood at 2 a.m.

*Garfield*—The smart-aleck cat visits the White House and finds it infested with mice, prompting this cynical political observation: "Anyone who's dumb enough to have a dog for a house pet doesn't deserve to be president."

*November 14, 1991*

## As Time Goes By, the Presidential Campaign's a Nightmare

President Bush should have known better than to select *Wayne's World* and *Casablanca* as the two movies to watch before he retired after a long day on the California campaign trail. He had a dream that went something like this:

Chief of staff Samuel Skinner appears and says, "Good news, sir. The election is over and you have won 57 percent of the vote in a three-man race. NOT!"

"Enough of the jokes, Sam. I've got to do something to liven up my campaign. I think I need to take a trip to a foreign country."

"But you're going to Rio for the Earth Summit."

"That's just a photo op for the environmentalists. It doesn't count. I was thinking of some exotic place."

The dream fades and Bush finds himself in a Moroccan bar. Police chief Daryl Gates approaches and asks, "What brought you to Casablanca?"

"My health," Bush answers. "I came to Casablanca for the waters."

"What waters?" Gates asks. "We're in the desert."

"Hey, I was misinformed."

Skinner emerges, saying, "You've got to quit using that line, sir."

Bush is startled by the arrival of a striking couple. The barroom crowd stirs at the sight of R. Hoss Herot, the anti-establishment leader. But Bush's eyes are fixed on the woman on his arm. It is his lost love, Miss American Voter.

His thoughts flash back to a time in the past, 1988, after the election, when he happily offered her a toast: "Here's looking at you, kid." Now all he could think of was how to win her back. He could remind her of the fall of the Berlin Wall. ("The Germans wore gray. You wore blue.")

She turns to look at a longhaired metal-head wearing ripped jeans and a T-shirt listing "Top 10 Babes for Clinton." "Democratic party time," he chants, and seeing Miss American Voter, "Schwing!"

Bush collars Skinner and demands to see a new hard-hitting campaign ad that Barbara Bush had told him about. "I know you've got the tape, and here's the VCR."

"But sir, it's ugly. And you do have a weak stomach."

"You played it for her. You can play it for me," Bush says. "If she can stand it, I can. Play it!"

About that time there is a disturbance in the street—a traffic violator resisting arrest by Nazi soldiers. "Round up the usual suspects!" Gates shouts.

Herot, the jug-eared idol of the people, is off to file a petition, leaving the woman and Bush alone. He tells her about the commercial. "It's Willie Horton all over again."

"Play it, Sam," she says.

As the tape rolls, showing Desert Storm and Los Angeles battle clips, she gets excited. "Was that cannon fire?" she asks. "Or was it my heart pounding?"

With a sly wink at Skinner, Bush says, "I think this is the beginning of a beautiful friendship. My re-election problems don't amount to a hill of beans in this crazy world."

"NOT! There's one other thing, sir. Your counsel says I owe the government $3,275.50 for personal travel expenses."

"Pay it, Sam."

*May 21, 1992*

## He Went to Rio and All He Got Was That Lousy Tear Gas

President George Bush is not getting the credit he deserves as America's first "environmental president," and it's all because of the lousy reporting by the national media.

Take his recent White House news conference, for example (the one the TV networks refused to carry so they could bring viewers re-runs of *The Simpsons*, *The Cosby Show* and *Top Cops*). Bush gave a spirited defense of the administration's environmental record with his response to a question about why he was going to the Earth Summit in Rio de Janeiro:

"I want to go on the offense and say what we've done," he said. "I'm going to take a strong record, the leading record on science and technology, the leading record on oceans, the leading record on forests, the leading record on protecting the elephant ..."

*Protecting the elephant!* Now, that's news, especially since this record apparently was achieved without any band of demonstrators marching on Washington or any costly legislation from Congress. It has to be one of the administration's big successes. When is the last time you saw an American elephant being abused?

But did you read anything about it in the newspaper or hear it on a newscast? Not on your life. Those cynical reporters probably assumed he was referring to the Republican Party symbol and considered it too partisan to print.

Another Bush environmental initiative that has received all too little attention is the Cash-for-Clunkers program. As outlined by an administration official last March, the plan is to offer cash payments to owners of 1981-and-older automobiles to turn in their aging vehicles.

The idea was recycled, appropriately enough, from a 1990 experiment in Los Angeles in which an oil company paid motorists to get their old polluting autos off the road. The Bush program would reward companies buying junk cars with relief from financial obligations of federal air quality standards.

Obviously what this program needs is a hard-charging administrator. William K. Reilly, head of the Environmental Protection Agency, is a logical choice. But first he would have to get rid of his agency's fleet of gasoline-guzzling luxury cars and make top EPA officials start riding bicycles.

Other possibilities come to mind. One high profile figure from the private sector is Lee Iacocca, who could do some snazzy TV commercials on cars that pollute. As retiring Chrysler chairman, he will have some time on his hands. But he's of the wrong political persuasion.

What about former President Nixon? He could head a new agency headquartered at the Pentagon, which will become virtually vacant when Congress gets through trimming the Department of Defense. The Pentagon parking lot could even be used for temporary storage of the old vehicles.

There's just one flaw in the selection of Nixon. Can't you just see the posters with his picture and the caption, "Would You Sell a Used Car To This Man?"

But he would be great as the man in charge of elephant protection.

*June 18, 1992*

## Mr. Clinton's Neighborhood: Can You Say Mod-er-ate?

Senator Stump returned to Washington from the Democratic National Convention in a state of shock. He had witnessed a remarkable makeover by the political puppet masters to give his party a new face—the face of moderation.

Throughout his career in politics, Stump had warmly embraced the ideals and principles of the party of Franklin D. Roosevelt, Lyndon B. Johnson, George McGovern and Walter Mondale. He went down fighting to win votes for Michael Dukakis in 1988. He had lived by the party's liberal traditions.

Now, suddenly, he is handed a new script. With Bill Clinton as their nominee, the Democrats are trying to erase the liberal image. His party's rightward lurch troubled him greatly, but as a loyal Democrat he knew he had to go along. "If Al Gore can do it, I can, too," he decided.

For old-line party members like Stump, this means learning a whole new vocabulary before going out on the campaign trail. (The "New Covenant" also dictates that he must drag his wife and kids along on campaign appearances and talk a lot about home and family.)

In desperation, he canceled an important meeting of his animal rights subcommittee and enrolled in a Democrat-sponsored "Short Course in Moderate Semantics" taught by I. M. Wordy of Millard Fillmore University. The professor had won favor with Clinton by helping to flesh out the nominee's 53-minute acceptance speech.

Arriving for his first class, Stump noticed that four unfamiliar terms were written on the blackboard: moderate, centrist, mainstream and middle-of-the-road. Wordy began his lecture with an exercise in pronouncing these strange-sounding words.

"Repeat after me. Mod-er-ate. I am a mod-er-ate Democrat. The Democratic Party is a cen-trist party. Our party platform is main-stream. We are steering a middle-of-the-road course."

Stump was able to form the words, but they didn't sound natural. The next lesson was more difficult. Wordy passed out copies of the Democratic platform and called on class members to read passages. The senator almost became ill as he uttered certain phrases: "We must ... tackle spending ... require people who can work to go to work ... create an investment tax credit ... put more police on the streets ... be prepared to use military force ..."

Almost choking, Stump grumbled to himself, "This looks like something left over from the Reagan administration." Try as he might, Stump could not make himself say, "We reject ... the big government theory that says we can hamstring business and tax and spend our way to prosperity."

"That goes against everything I stand for," he said.

Somehow he got through the session. After signing a pledge that he would refrain from evoking any liberal philosophy for the duration of the campaign, Stump was awarded a "Certificate of Semantic Excellence."

"We'll be offering a refresher course in six months," said Wordy.

"No, thanks," Stump said. "After November I can forget all this nonsense."

*July 23, 1992*

## Heard the Latest? Quayle's Getting Gored, Bush Is Bleeding

Here in the hotbed of hearsay, the town's rumormongers are working overtime to meet their quota for juicy stories to ease the summertime news slump. The national news media's liberal interpretation of the First Amendment makes it unconstitutional to have a news vacuum in the nation's capital. If there isn't any news, it has to be invented.

The lull between the Democrat and Republican conventions offers a special challenge. Real news has been as scarce as congressional leaders at a Bill Clinton rally. It's no wonder rumors have been traveling faster than an Olympic runner.

Sad to say, the quality of the current spurt of speculation is quite mediocre. "Vice President Dan Quayle will be dumped. President Bush is seriously ill. Secretary of State James Baker will take over the Bush campaign." Absolutely no imagination. The work of amateurs. Easily denied.

As Texas billionaire H. Ross Perot learned from his on-again off-again independent candidacy, big league campaigning demands professionalism. The same is true for rumor spreading. You get what you pay for. One of the best suppliers of scintillating scuttlebutt is Rumors R Us, run by a former CIA agent whose job as director of Soviet disinformation was phased out.

For $29.95 you can get a "Campaign Sampler" containing some really inventive rumors:

- Quayle is in excellent health but will develop a case of prolonged laryngitis as soon as Baker starts running the campaign.

- Former Tennessee Gov. Lamar Alexander will replace Quayle on the ticket and the vice presidential debate with Sen. Albert Gore, D-Tenn., will be held at the Grand Ole Opry.

- Elvis Presley was seen on the Clinton-Gore campaign bus trying to make a drug purchase from Clinton's half-brother.

- Gore secretly chews tobacco and spits on trees.

- Independent counsel Lawrence Walsh will name former president Dwight D. Eisenhower as an unindicted co-conspirator in the Iran-Contra investigation.

- Hillary Clinton is a cross-dresser.

- Former President Jimmy Carter was overheard to say after the Clinton documentary film, "and they said my family was weird."

- Colin Powell, chairman of the Joint Chiefs of Staff, is a Libertarian.

- Perot's economic plan will be buried in a time capsule to be opened in 20 years.

- House Speaker Tom Foley takes ballet lessons.

- Chelsea Clinton is suing her parents for divorce for embarrassing her on national television.

- Marilyn Quayle bakes gun-shaped cookies.

- To win support of Reagan Democrats, Tipper Gore is having her name legally changed to Gipper.

- In his acceptance speech at Houston, Bush will again pledge "no new taxes—the old ones are still robust and growing."

- GOP campaign slogan: "Four More Years of Change."

And remember, you read it here first.

*July 30, 1992*

## Campaign '92: It's the Year of the Woman, Sweet Cakes

Don't look for Laney Spigener in the lineup of speakers for the Republican National Convention next week in Houston. He wasn't welcome at the Democrats' big show in New York last month either.

Spigener is the agent who was assigned by the Navy to investigate complaints of sexual assaults at the Tailhook convention of naval aviators in Las Vegas last year. He was taken off the case after Navy Lt. Paula Coughlin reported he had made romantic advances and called her "Sweet Cakes."

That kind of gross insensitivity, which once might have been taken as flattery, is not to be tolerated in this election year. It's "The Year of the Woman" and male politicians are emasculating themselves all over the place to win the women's vote.

Democrats had so many women on the stage at Madison Square Garden that it looked more like a Mary Kay sales meeting than a political convention. Not to be outdone, the Republicans are determined to give females prominence at the Astrodome, even if they have to import some from Mexico.

President Bush is so far behind in the polls the GOP convention planners decided to roll out their biggest gun, Barbara Bush. The first lady, flanked by five children and 12 grandchildren, will deliver a prime time speech on family values. Other women on the program will include Assistant Vice President Marilyn Quayle, three members of Congress, two cabinet secretaries and assorted lesser officials. The Republicans even made room for an unwed mother (singer Tanya Tucker) and a woman who is infected with the AIDS virus.

To show how eager the Republicans are to compete with the Democrats for the favor of women voters, a number of GOP male delegates have volunteered to give up their seats so more women may participate in the Houston gathering of the party faithful. (They will not open doors for them, however, for fear of groin injury.) Among those giving up their delegate status is Sen. Al D'Amato of New York, who is trying to keep from giving up his Senate seat to Geraldine Ferraro, the 1984 Democratic nominee for vice president.

The Republicans aren't likely to go quite as far as the Democrats, who allowed lesbian rights activists carrying signs to march on the convention floor. The GOP has laid down a strict rule against bringing placards or banners into the Astrodome. Also banned are "stakes, poles, scissors, bottles, mace and guns." (Does the National Rifle Association know about this?)

Womanpower has overwhelmed the national news media as well. In this year's campaign, political pundits have had to make way for a new wave of female television commentators, or pundettes. The networks probably had to buy more hair dryers because the anchormen were unwilling to share.

As a gesture toward equality, a Capitol Hill source says, a congressional resolution was drafted declaring 1993 "The Year of the Man" but it never got out of committee. The word is that Sen. Barbara Mikulski, D-Md., arm wrestled the chairman and won.

*August 13, 1992*

## All Heaven Is Breaking Loose Over the Presidential Race

While St. Peter was taking a morning stroll through the streets of Heaven this week, he was musing about the strange state of political affairs on Earth. It disturbed him that a candidate named God Almighty had only received 1.5 percent of the vote in a U.S. Senate race in Nevada.

Passing by the Golden Slipper Coffee Shop he heard the sound of loud voices and decided to go in and find out what all the chatter was about.

At the table just inside the door he encountered Edward R. Murrow and Eric Severeid having coffee laced heavily with cream and doughnuts covered with thick chocolate icing. (Heaven is not having to worry about calories or cholesterol.)

"What's going on here?" St. Peter asked.

Murrow took a long drag on his cigarette, blew the smoke into the air, and explained that some of the residents of the Pearly Gates Rest Home were upset about the way President Bush and Bill Clinton were conducting the presidential race.

Sevareid, sounding as wise as his neighbor Solomon, observed: "The candidates seem to be having an identity crisis."

"I'll say they are," said John F. Kennedy, who had just walked in with Marilyn Monroe on his arm. "For awhile, Clinton was me. Now he's somebody else entirely."

About that time Elvis Presley swung into view, heading for a table with a large cup of Coke. "I'm all shook up," he said. "I thought I was Clinton's idol. He knew the words to all my songs. I guess he forgot, 'Don't Be Cruel.'"

In a nearby booth, reliving old battles, sat Napoleon Bonaparte, Ulysses S. Grant and Dwight D. Eisenhower. Ike spoke up. "It's all George Bush's fault. Once I was his hero, but not any more."

"Now he's gone overboard for, of all people, Harry Truman," fumed Tom Dewey. "A Republican president wasn't good enough for him."

"Better a Democrat than me, I guess," sighed Herbert Hoover.

Savoring a jelly roll, Socrates reasoned: "When Bush decided to be Truman, Clinton did too and now they're trying to out-Truman each other."

A full-figured Eleanor Roosevelt (Heaven is not having to wear a girdle) voiced her opinion. "I think Hillary Clinton told Bill he had to reclaim Truman for our party."

A crowd had gathered and the grumbling had intensified when suddenly Harry Truman strode briskly into the coffee shop, a broad grin on his face.

"Well, I see those two fellows are still fighting over me. I haven't enjoyed anything so much since I fired Douglas MacArthur."

"So you approve of what Bush and Clinton are saying?" asked Murrow.

"That's just like the media, putting words in my mouth. Neither one of them could turn the heat on Congress like I did in 1948. If I were down there, I'd be giving both of them hell."

"You can't say that up here, Harry!" scolded Bess Truman.

"Oh, no? Who in Heaven's name is going to stop me?"

With that, a deafening thunderbolt shook the building, rattling the coffee cups, and a voice boomed: "Any more questions?"

*September 10, 1992*

## Bush's Secret Campaign Strategy Is Nothing to Sneeze At

A visit to the Bush-Quayle campaign headquarters this week was a revealing experience. Half expecting to find black crepe draped on the door, after a surge of negative national news media reports, it was surprising to see bright looks on the faces of campaign workers.

Optimism was especially overflowing in the Division of Unsavory Tactics, headed by Lotta Trix. She had just come out of a strategy session where the main agenda item was a new secret weapon to use against Democrat Bill Clinton.

"Clinton looks strong right now but he has a weakness that will do him in," she said.

"Women?"

"Worse than that. We have found his Achilles heel, and it's his nose," she said excitedly.

Trix went on to explain that the Arkansas governor has a condition known as allergic rhinitis which makes him sensitive to certain grass and weed pollens and animal hairs. Some people are so allergic that just thinking about these things makes them sneeze.

"He's had these allergies for many years. Occasionally they aggravate his vocal chords and he can't talk. There appears to be a direct correlation between his extended period of silence and his rise in the polls."

"How does that help President Bush?"

"I'll get to that. But first, I have to brag about something that happened to Clinton in Connecticut as a result of excellent work by our nasal reconnaissance unit. Wouldn't you know the only place he could get a room was a hotel where a long-haired dog show was being held? He was in such distress he told an audience a Patriot missile could find its way down chimneys."

"Enough of the shaggy dog stories. What's your secret strategy?"

"We call it Operation Ragweed and we plan to implement it for the debates. First we plan to have Barbara Bush bring Millie and sit near Clinton. And the president's opening remarks have been carefully prepared."

After reading the draft, it was easy to see how the debate might proceed:

Bush: My fellow Americans, I've made a few mistakes, but hey …

Clinton: Ah-choo!

B: I'm a quiet man, not prone to anger. But sometimes my opponent really gets my dander up …

C: AH-chooo!

B: I've sent some good legislation to Congress, but it's just up there gathering dust …

C: Ah-CHOOO!

B: Some of my proposals have been on Capitol Hill so long they're covered with mold …

C: AHH-CHOOOO!

B: It's time to separate the wheat from the chaff …

C: AHHH-CHOOOOO!

B: My opponent not only dodged the draft …

C: AHHHH …

B: … he also smoked grass …

C: … CHOOOOOOO! Bud I didda idhale!

Moderator: Governor Clinton, you have used up all but 30 seconds of your time. Is there anything you want to get out of your system?

C: AHHHHHH-CHOOOOOOOO! Bless me.

*September 17, 1992*

## Seven Days in January: A Possibility That's Debatable

Now that the presidential debates are over, the American public is fully prepared to make well-informed choices on November 3, right?

Voters who watched the three televised Q-and-A sessions, as well as the vice presidential free-for-all, learned all there is to know about how the Democrats, the Republicans or the loose cannons would run the country the next four years—unless you count such things as appointments to the U.S. Supreme Court, which none of the questioners asked about. But then, that has nothing to do with getting your brother-in-law a job and out of your house, which is the real issue in this campaign.

At the risk of offending the guy with the ponytail in Richmond who wanted everyone to "cross our hearts" and not sling mud, some observations are inescapable.

President Bush made a mistake by saying "I made a mistake" too often. Bill Clinton looked like he had eaten too many waffles. And Ross Perot showed once again that he's a quitter when he announced he would only serve one term. All this is said with "90–90 hindsight" of course, to use Bush's term.

Either Bush or Clinton is most likely to win the election, but come on, I'm supposed to be a humor writer. So, thinking the unthinkable, here's what we could expect from President Perot's first week in the White House:

Day One—He delivers the shortest inaugural address in history: "Folks, it's obvious to the brain-dead that we've got problems. We've been slow dancing too long. Are we just going to sound-bite them or fix them? As your president, I'm going to turn off the Lawrence Welk music, get under the hood and use the White House as a bully pulpit. None of these fruit-loopy inaugural parades for me. Let's go to the center of the bull's eye and stop the financial bleeding. Talk is cheap, words are plentiful, deeds are precious. Let's get on with it."

Day Two—He sells Air Force One and calls in Vice President James Stockdale to outline his duties. Stockdale has his hearing aid turned off, so no harm is done. He presents his budget in a half-hour program on all the TV networks, using charts he did himself.

Day Three—He gets a haircut and orders his attorney general, Anita Hill, to institute deportation proceedings against all registered agents of foreign corporations.

Day Four—He closes the Mexican embassy and holds a meeting of the Plan Collection Task Force, set up the day after the election to collect "all the great plans lying all over Washington that nobody ever executes."

Day Five—He calls Congress into special session and gets all 535 members to hold hands and pass his Balanced Budget, Deficit Reduction, Job Base Rebuilding and Campaign Finance Reform Act.

Day Six—War breaks out between two former Soviet republics and one of their nuclear missiles accidentally gets launched in the direction of Chicago. He holds an electronic town hall meeting to get advice from callers on what to do.

And on Day Seven—He rests.

*October 22, 1992*

## To the Victor Belongs the Spoils—and a Few Rotten Eggs

There was dancing in the streets of Little Rock and Baghdad on election night, but the party's over and it's time to get down to the serious business of analyzing the results. Pundits do have to make a living, you know.

President Bush delivered a fine concession speech. Half the country expected him to say something like, "And yes, we didn't get enough votes, but, hey, the best bozos won."

So here we have two "baby boomers" from the South elected. "Hubba Bubba," headlined one New York tabloid. The Secret Service wasted no time in assigning Bill Clinton and Al Gore new code names: "Ozark" and "Ozone."

The Democrats are still trying to figure out what they did right. Everybody from Democratic national chairman Ron Brown to Clinton's hair stylist is taking credit. The Republicans looked for someone besides the "nutty pollsters" to blame for the outcome and ended up blaming each other. Ross Perot voters are still smiling. Their candidate might have blown $100 million on a 50-state wipe-out, but he's still the smoothest dancer.

The magician-elect was criticized for being too slow in cranking up his transition, but give the guy a break. After a 28-hour jag of campaigning and partying till 3 a.m. the next night, who wants to get on the phone with Boris Yeltsin (even though he certainly knows what a hangover is like)?

The anti-Washington candidate named two Washington insiders to head up his transition team, but that's understandable for a stranger from the sticks. One of his first questions was if there is a McDonald's near the White House.

Clinton talked himself hoarse, but he had enough voice to cuss out a country club manager who let the press see him on a golf course with a cigar in his mouth. (Next thing you know, Perot will be riding in a motorcade.) Clinton told a group of churchgoers he didn't smoke the cigar. Read his nicotine-stained lips.

In the wave of post-election analysis, some pertinent questions are being asked:

In the Perot campaign, why did they call those half-hour TV pitches infomercials instead of advertorials?

Will Clinton campaign strategist James Carville remain on Earth or return to his own galaxy?

How were Perot's political enemies going to disrupt his daughter's Texas wedding? (One theory is that computer hackers were going to get into the Neiman-Marcus system and change all of her patterns.)

The Bush administration's decision to slap tariffs on certain European imports must have been shattering news to the Clinton inauguration planners. They had to scrub Ron Brown's suggestion of serving French white wine and go back to the original plan of Ripple on the rocks.

President Bush plans to go back to Texas, a state with no income tax, which gives special meaning to his most recent "no new tax" pledge.

And thousands of federal bureaucrats, harking back to another period of hard times, are seeking comfort in the thought that "all we have to fear is Hillary herself."

*November 12, 1992*

## Some Doggone Good Advice for a New Kind of Demo-cat

Socks, the Cat
c/o Bill Clinton
Little Rock, Ark.
Dear Future White House Occupant:

You may wonder why a famous best-selling author like me (nearly $890,000 in royalties from *Millie's Book*) is bothering to write a letter to someone who is about to replace me as First Pet. Well, it's because politics is a dog-eat-dog world and we so-called sub-humans have to stick together.

I see the fickle press has already turned against their favorite candidate and started beating up on the Clinton administration by picking on you.

The nerve of that *Washington Post* writer to say that cats are "preening, finicky, spooky-eyed stalkers that historically have been worshiped as gods, or hanged as witches." Now, all that may be true, but nonetheless it is not fair to prejudice First Family watchers against you even before you've had your security clearance.

The *Post* scribe obviously is not a pet lover, judging from the catty suggestion that the gold leaf Steinway might become a scratching post. But as you and the Clintons will learn, that goes with the territory—and cats know about territory.

Now, I'm aware we come from different political parties, but as one party animal to another I want to offer some advice that will help prepare you for the big move:

1.  Remember, you will be living in a fishbowl. Come to think of it, a cat might like that.

2.  The president's pet is an excellent photo op. Make sure his press flack—George Stepinalotofit, I think is his name—is aware of that.

3.  You will need to be ready to give the president a warm greeting when he returns from a trip, so plan on taking short naps.

4.  Make friends with the White House chef. You'll be sure to get state dinner leftovers.

5.  Be nice to visitors, even if you don't like them. I was tempted to bite Sam Donaldson's leg, but was afraid I might get rabies.

6.  Don't shower your affection on guests, if you know what I mean—even if the aide forgot to clean your litter box.

7.  Be careful about purring too loudly when Hollywood stars come to call. Leave that to the president.

8.  Don't scratch fleas in the presence of congressional leaders. They've got enough troubles already.

9.  If you have to spit up a hairball, don't do it while sitting in the Japanese prime minister's lap. Once was enough.

10. Don't be surprised if they put you to work catching mice. The White House seems to attract low forms of animal life.

Finally, as you claw your way to the top, don't ever forget that you are only a temporary resident in the White House. There will be plenty of new tenants available in 1996—including a little man in Dallas with a big guard dog that could eat you alive.

Sincerely,

Millie

P.S. I'm leaving a memo on what I know about foreign policy. Please pass it on to the bozos.

*November 19, 1992*

## Even Thanksgiving Will Be Different in the New Regime

Thanksgiving week usually is a quiet time around the White House, so Gus, the guard, had a moment to give some observations about recent goings-on.

"It's certainly going to be different here after January 20," he said.

"How's that?"

"We'll have a Southern governor, a pushy wife, and a teen-age girl. We haven't had a bunch like that since the Carters left."

"Will Roger Clinton be the new Billy Carter?"

"That's hard to say. He was into cocaine and songwriting. Billy just drank beer and spoke his mind."

"A president can't do anything about his family."

"That's so. But the Clintons are sure different. Their Thanksgiving dinner isn't even like most other folks'. I read that they have two kinds of stuffing because the governor likes Southern-style cornbread dressing and Hillary likes the Northern white bread kind."

"She is a woman of strong opinions, I understand."

"Their menu also includes two potato dishes and two pies."

"Clinton's opponents might say this is natural because he has more than one position on most issues."

"I don't know much about politics. But I'll bet the Clintons don't have turkey next Thanksgiving. I overheard Senator Stump say he was introducing legislation for the National Chicken Pluckers Association designating the Arkansas hen as the official Thanksgiving bird."

"That's liable to cost him the turkey producers' vote."

"That may be, but there are a lot more hens than turkeys. Which reminds me, with six women in the Senate now, I'm glad to see they're finally getting their own rest room in the Capitol."

"We're really making progress."

"But they'll have to share the spittoons with the men."

"I see."

"I met the president-elect last week."

"When he came to meet with President Bush?"

"Yeah. He shook hands with everybody in sight. We had an interesting policy debate about homosexuals in the military."

"He's for it."

"Right. But he says that under no circumstances will they be allowed to carry purses into combat."

"That's good."

"You know, I feel kind of sorry for President Bush. I think since he lost he would just like to get the heck out of here. You know what he should do?"

"What?"

"He ought to resign right now."

"And let Dan Quayle become president?"

"Yeah. That way, he wouldn't have to actually turn over the government to Bill Clinton. He would reward Quayle for being a good vice president. And can you think of any better way to annoy the media?"

*November 26, 1992*

## Hooray for Hollywood, Clinton's Government in Waiting

All those columnists who have predicted that Bill Clinton will form a government consisting of policy wonks like himself will find they have been barking up the wrong tree. Clinton is so enamored with the Hollywood types, he's more likely to get his Cabinet from central casting.

Clinton did say at a September fundraiser in Beverly Hills that he wanted actors and actresses to be a part of his administration. So here goes another round of speculation:

Although it will come as quite a shock to all those Democratic contributors, campaign workers, ex-congressmen and former Carter appointees, the country is going to be in the hands of people like Whoopi Goldberg (a prime candidate for White House Chief of Staff), Dustin (*Hook*) Hoffman (a clear choice for Secretary of the Navy) and Barbra Streisand (who can have any job she wants—except Hillary's, of course).

Robert Redford, who spends more time in Washington as a congressional witness than he does making pictures, is a natural to head up the new Department of Ecological and Environment Protection (DEEP). He will work closely with Energy Secretary Meryl (*Silkwood*) Streep, whose mission will be to replace all U.S. nuclear facilities with windmills.

Who else but Elizabeth Taylor could be chosen to direct the fight against AIDS—but only if she doesn't have to live in Washington. She found it terribly dull the last time she was here, when she was married to a U.S. senator. Life must be much more exciting with a construction worker for a husband.

Denzel (*Malcolm X*) Washington will head up an expanded Department of Health and Human Services, with Woody Allen as administrator of the Bureau of Children's Affairs. A search is on for a director of Alternative Lifestyles, which will take the place of the Defense Department. Many of the more likely choices—Liberace, Rock Hudson, Anthony Perkins—no longer are available.

Jack (*Jimmy Hoffa*) Nicholson will be appointed Secretary of Labor. Kevin (*The Bodyguard*) Costner will be head of the Secret Service. Clinton will name Gary (*Dracula*) Oldman as his budget director, with an assignment to suck the red ink out of it.

Keeping his promise to have a bipartisan team, Clinton will pick Arnold Schwarzenegger ("Conan the Republican") to administer the Office of Personnel Management. What better choice to cut 100,000 federal jobs than *The Terminator*?

Macaulay (*Home Alone*) Culkin will be Secretary of State. He ought to be able to take care of Saddam Hussein.

Clinton might even find a cameo role for his new California chum, Ronald Reagan.

*December 3, 1992*

## Somalia Rescue Mission Means Party Time in Washington

When Sally, the socialite, entertains in her Georgetown home, she always has a theme. Her "Somalia Soiree" was right in tune with the times.

"It's a wonderful party idea. Hunger is so chic," she said. "The liberals love it. And the military exercise turns on conservatives."

Sally explained that each guest was asked to bring some food to feed the starving children. The cartons of caviar, *pate de foie gras* and smoked pheasant piled around the Christmas tree were indeed mind-boggling.

"I have to confess that when I first heard about 'Operation Restore Hope' I thought it was another Bob Hope USO tour," she said. "But now I know what it is and I just can't say enough about those brave men who answered the call to duty and placed themselves in the jaws of danger."

"We can all be proud of our armed forces."

"No, I'm talking about Dan Rather, Ted Koppel and Tom Brokaw. Although I'm sorry they can't be here tonight. I had to settle for Willard Scott."

Nonetheless it was a glittering crowd, including a variety of Washington power figures. For Bush Cabinet members the party was one last twirl on the social scene before the new gang takes over in January. For prospective appointees in the Clinton administration, it was a chance to plug into the circuit that never ends.

Over near the punch bowl, Senator Stump was holding forth. "I was against Desert Storm, but I'm for this mission 110 percent. I can think of no nobler cause than for our troops to engage in hand-to-hand combat with drug-crazed Somali teen-agers carrying AK-47s."

Congressman Babble and his wife also were there. She was telling Connie, the consultant, how she would like to organize a shipment of Christmas cookies for the soldiers to have. "But then I remember what I had to go through to sell cookies to the Army a few years ago. By the time competitive bids were taken and procurement specifications were drawn, it would be next Christmas before the cookies reached their destination."

Attracting considerable attention was Larry, the lawyer, who has landed a position on the Clinton transition team. In his practice he specializes in agricultural product issues (he once represented American mung bean interests in an import case), so he was picked as an adviser on the Agriculture Department.

"The transition is organized into clusters, pods and paths," he explained. "I happen to be in the peanut cluster, the pea pod and the cow path."

Lonnie, the lobbyist, busy buttonholing all the new faces, also was the center of attention because he has been chosen to ride with President-elect Clinton on the bus to Washington for the inauguration.

"I haven't been on a bus since I played in the high school band," he said. "At least he's not coming all the way from Little Rock on a smelly, bouncy bus. Frankly, if it weren't for the honor, I had just as soon go by limousine."

Sally interrupted. "I just had a marvelous idea! I'll have a party with a bus theme. Maybe I can rent the Greyhound terminal ..."

*December 10, 1992*

## Some of These Inaugural Plans Will Tax Your Imagination

Less than two weeks before a new president will be inaugurated, the nation's capital is in a tizzy of excitement and anticipation. Washingtonians can hardly wait until the event takes place to they can get started on their tax returns.

The Internal Revenue Service, in a rare display of compassion, mailed out the form booklets early to avoid placing an extra burden on the U.S. Postal Service, which has been consumed with the heavy duty of issuing the Elvis Presley stamp.

Had the IRS delayed, the nation's mail carriers might have had the task of delivering both the tax packets and the Clinton-Gore inaugural invitations at the same time. (One inaugural planner suggested combining the mailing, but a researcher discovered that Republicans also pay taxes so the idea was scrubbed.)

The inauguration ceremonies are scheduled for January 20, 21, or 22, depending on how late Bill Clinton is in arriving. (There's always a chance of his bus breaking down en route from Virginia.)

Clinton's appointees will occupy special seating and will be easy to spot. They'll be the ones cheering the beginning of the second term of the Carter administration.

More than $20 million has been budgeted for the inaugural festivities and detailed planning has gone into making the five-day celebration a great success. The inaugural staff even includes a special assistant in charge of throat spray to make sure Clinton is able to take the oath of office and another assistant in charge of Hillary Clinton to make sure she doesn't.

Special security precautions are being taken. The Secret Service will stake out every fast food restaurant along the parade route in case Clinton is suddenly stricken with a Big Mac attack. Any woman not wearing a Hillary headband will be arrested for subversive activity.

As if to prove something or other, Clinton will have ten inaugural balls—George Bush had nine—and that's just the official count. There will be many other unofficial events, such as the vegetarian ball sponsored by an animal rights group at which bartenders and waitresses will wear only an apron that says "I'd rather go naked than wear fur." Sen. Ted Kennedy likely will represent Clinton at that affair.

Gay rights activists will hold their celebration at the Odd Fellows Hall. The word is that Clinton will put on a dress and take a turn around the dance floor with Donna Shalala, his Secretary of Homosexual Services.

The Clintons' cat will be guest of honor at a "Socks Hop" at the National Petting Zoo. Admission is free for anyone who brings a pet to be neutered. Or a senator.

Plenty of inaugural souvenirs are available for purchase. These include an autographed picture of Clinton's saxophone suitable for framing; a lifelike wood carving of the new vice president, Al Gore; a Lucite toilet seat with the official inaugural seal; and an authentic reproduction of Clinton's mother's passport (courtesy of the Bush State Department).

It's all to help the economy, stupid.

*January 7, 1993*

## Will the Last Bush Official to Leave Turn Off the Shredder?

Transition fever is rising as the Bush administration enters its final week in office and Washington gets ready to welcome a new team. It is a turbulent time of comings and goings.

Former President Jimmy Carter came to town and Ross Perot did not, but got everybody talking about him again just the same. Carter was in Washington selling autographed copies of his new book. He probably wishes he had brought his hammer to get in a few licks on the inaugural platform.

Nice guy George Bush is making the changeover so smooth for Bill Clinton that one observer grumbled that "Bush might even stick around after the oath-taking to help unload the moving van from Little Rock."

Meanwhile, Bush appointees are polishing their resumes and parachuting back to the private sector. Most of the top officials have arranged soft landings at law firms, think tanks, universities and public relations firms.

Rumors abound, but this fearless prognosticator feels safe in predicting that:

Vice President Dan Quayle will not join the cast of *Murphy Brown*.

White House Press Secretary Marlin Fitzwater will not succeed David Letterman as NBC's late-night talk show host.

Budget Director Richard Darman will not become an instructor in a charm school.

Secretary of State Lawrence Eagleburger will not open a new fast food restaurant featuring his name on sandwiches.

One upsetting development for the departing administration was a federal judge's ruling that the White House could not proceed with plans to destroy most of the records stored in its computer systems. Panic quickly spread to the Department of Agriculture where 55 shredders were standing by ready for use.

The department spent about $47,000 in the last two years to acquire the document-destroying equipment, which includes a Watergate 1000 model and a pair of heavy-duty, high-security piranhas. A skeptical Rep. Bob Wise, D-W.Va., questioned the shredder purchases. "Was there some executive order we missed directing that document mulch be produced for America's farmers?" he asked.

Obviously Wise is not aware the agency develops information on such sensitive matters as red-flowered globe mallow, computerized sow feeding systems and mosquito sterilization research. If that material fell into the wrong hands ...

No detail is being overlooked to ensure a pleasant trip for Clinton's bus caravan through the Virginia countryside Sunday with a stop for morning worship at the Culpeper Baptist Church. In what has to be the ultimate in inaugural preparations, the *Culpeper News* reports that if everything goes according to plan, the president-elect will "cruise into town on a route quite free of road kill."

"No polecats. No possums. No flattened squirrels. Virginia Department of Transportation engineer Larry Garber said that a highway crew would make a dead-animal run Sunday morning. Just in case," the newspaper said.

The Clinton inauguration may be the first in history to feature an official road kill patrol.

*January 14, 1993*

# POTUS 42

## Bill Clinton

# Bubba Comes to Washington, Along With Co-President HRC

In 1993, the man who said, "I still believe in a place called Hope (Arkansas)," settled in Washington, D.C., viewed by many cynics as a hopeless place. William Jefferson Clinton called himself a new kind of Democrat. At his side was his power-hungry wife, Hillary Rodham Clinton, or H. R. Clinton as she was identified in *Potomac Junction*.

Bill Clinton stamped an indelible imprint on the Federal City. He was the first president to have a press secretary named "DeeDee." He was only the second U.S. president to be impeached. Known in his home state as "Slick Willie," the smooth talking policy wonk was a column writer's dream.

His time in office was marked by an inordinately large number of personal and political scandals. But for all of his missteps, the "Bubba" from Arkansas demonstrated remarkable political skills that enabled him to survive the worst kinds of storms.

The Clinton years gave Americans a taste of government administered by a co-presidency. In the campaign, his wife made it clear she was not the type to stay in the background and "bake cookies." Clinton praised her abilities and promised voters they would get "two for the price of one" by electing him.

Sure enough, the first lady had her own office in the West Wing of the White House, where she channeled with Eleanor Roosevelt and developed policy, including a health care reform plan that was written in secret and doomed to failure. She made a number of cabinet recommendations that had to be withdrawn because of unpaid taxes or other law violations.

In Clinton's first term, he attempted to fulfill a campaign promise to allow homosexuals to serve in the armed forces. The "Don't Ask, Don't Tell" policy satisfied neither side in the dispute. While fighting with Congress over the federal budget and economic policy, the new president and his wife were preoccupied with investigations of their involvement in Whitewater, an Arkansas land development deal.

Problems in Eastern Europe called for attention, and Clinton sent U.S. troops to Bosnia following the 1994 elections, when Democrats lost control of both houses of Congress to Republicans. From that point on, a tug-of-war ensued over points of the GOP's "Contract With America," pushed by House Speaker Newt Gingrich.

On the strength of a booming economy, in 1996 Clinton became the first Democratic president since FDR to be elected to a second term.

Early in his administration, the saxophone-playing Baby Boomer generation president hit some sour notes.

## President Clinton Wakes Up to Find Government-in-Waiting

The Clinton presidency is in full swing following an inauguration extravaganza that seemed like it would never end. His procession to the throne began Sunday and marched forth like a transplanted Mardi Gras all week. The Japanese don't take this long to crown an emperor.

Washington was all set to start operating on "Clinton Standard Time," as close observers term the 42nd president's propensity for tardiness. But somewhere between Little Rock and the District of Columbia, Clinton found the discipline to be on time for his arrival in the nation's capital.

The man who kept members of the Supreme Court cooling their heels for an hour in November was actually early when his bus caravan rolled into town from Charlottesville, Va. News reporters had to be revived with smelling salts.

There is a plausible explanation for this abrupt change in behavior. Inaugural co-chairman Harry Thomason, a television producer, was determined that Clinton would arrive on schedule for an entertainment program at the Lincoln Memorial. Thomason, the president-elect's old friend, threatened to have military jets strafe the Clinton bus if it made an unplanned stop.

He need not have worried. Clinton is always on time for television appearances.

At Monticello, Thomas Jefferson's home, Clinton was asked whether he would appoint Jefferson to his Cabinet if he were alive today. It was a moot question since all the white male slots are already taken.

The transition went very smoothly, although there was some grumbling among the Clintonites because George Bush didn't pardon Zoe Baird for hiring illegal immigrants as domestics so she could begin her term as attorney general with a clean slate.

William Jefferson Clinton is ensconced in the Oval Office, all right, but if you want to know who's really running the government, it's Bill, the bureaucrat, and thousands like him. The Clinton team was so busy planning the five-day inauguration they didn't get around to naming any mid-level managers to take over operations of the various departments.

The Bush appointees got their walking papers and cleared out of their offices by high noon Wednesday, so the government was left in the hands of career public servants like Bill.

"There's nothing wrong with that," he said. "Bureaucrats have run things through the past several administrations."

"How does the bureaucracy manage to stay on?" I asked.

"It's called 'burrowing in.' There are 'how to' courses."

"What makes you think you can serve this president well?"

"Bill Clinton is my kind of president. He never met a policy paper he didn't like. Besides I'm a member of the F.O.B.'s."

"Friends of Bill?"

"No, Fraternity of Bureaucrats."

*January 21, 1993*

## Clinton Finds Himself Between Little Rock and Hard Place

Linda Bloodworth-Thomason's new sitcom, *The Clintons*, looks like a re-run. That's because it's a remake of *The Carters*.

*President smiles a lot. Spouse assumes a prominent role. Daughter goes to school. Brother strikes it rich. Momma makes the news. Congress seethes with hostility.*

Just about everybody in the Clinton family had a better week than the president.

It started off okay, the inaugural glow warm enough to lift anyone's spirits. Bill Clinton surprised us all by delivering a short inaugural address. He plunged into the world's toughest job with energy and enthusiasm, personally directing tourist traffic on the White House lawn and entertaining a houseful of relatives and family friends. Among the houseguests was Clinton's mother, Virginia Kelley. She wrapped up her inaugural week with a visit to a nearby racetrack where she picked three winners in the first six races.

While she was padding her income, Clinton and his economic advisers were plotting how to take it away from her and millions of others like her. Talk of tax hikes triggered a loud chorus of boos from Capitol Hill.

First brother Roger Clinton is deliriously happy. He sang with his band "Politics" at the Arkansas inaugural gala. He got a gushy write-up in the *Washington Post*. He has signed a $200,000 recording contract, made a TV video, arranged a 40-city speaking tour at $10,000 an appearance, and expects a half-million-dollar advance for an autobiographical book. Instant celebrityhood.

The president had barely laid down his saxophone before sour notes were being heard about attorney general nominee Zoe Baird, a product of Clinton's micromanagement of the appointment process. Her private servants kept her from becoming a public servant.

Twelve-year-old Chelsea Clinton, her hair and her squad of Secret Service agents skipped off to school and sneaked in the back way to avoid the press. On the second day of classes, Dad gave her $20 for lunch money. Washington prices are higher than Arkansas, but not that high!

Capital streets had scarcely been cleared of inaugural litter before 75,000 pro-life marchers filled Pennsylvania Avenue to protest legalized abortion as Clinton signed executive orders reversing restrictive actions by his Republican predecessors.

First lady Hillary Ramrod Clinton—she insists on three names—got an office near her husband's in the west wing of the White House and a highly visible job to go with it: heading a task force on health care. She'll have a chance to prove there are some brains under that goofy hat she wore in the inaugural parade.

For Bill Clinton the party's over and the hard work has begun. Gone is the relaxed environment of the Arkansas state capital and the freedom to stroll the friendly sidewalks. Welcome to the "big bubble."

The luckiest member of the Clinton household might be Socks. The Clintons decided to leave their cat behind in Little Rock until they get settled. Socks might never make it to Washington.

*January 28, 1993*

## Clinton's Governing Team Is a Bunch of Happy Campers

Reports that the Clinton administration is in retreat are absolutely unfounded. It's all a big misunderstanding. The truth is that President Clinton took all of his top officials to Camp David for a weekend retreat to figure out how to run the government.

As anyone who keeps up with the news can tell, the sessions proved to be fruitful. The Clinton White House has succeeded in being as inept as any before it. And it's all because of concentrated study and hard work. Nobody could bungle the job quite so thoroughly without really working at it.

The retreat was well organized. A fleet of buses carried members of the Cabinet and top aides to the rustic enclave in Maryland's Catoctin Mountains. Name tags were issued (Hi, I'm Al Gore) so everybody could get to know each other. Just like conventioneers.

Once there the group was immersed in policy, political and polling briefings and engaged in daylong brainstorming sessions. A lid of secrecy was clamped on the proceedings and participants were closemouthed about what exactly went on. But there's always a leak.

On Saturday night, sources said, two professional "facilitators" led a group exercise. Each person had to share a personal experience with the others, the object being to build trusting relationships. A source told the *Washington Post* Clinton talked about "how he was a fat kid … and how the other kids taunted him."

While it can't be verified, it's easy to imagine some of the other shared experiences:

Gore—"I'm ticklish."

Environmental Protection Agency Administrator Carol Browner—"I once had a tree cut down in my neighborhood."

Commerce Secretary Ron Brown—"I was a high-paid Washington lawyer, yet I didn't know I had to pay Social Security taxes for the woman who cleaned my house."

Clinton kept his appointees hopping, from early morning prayer service to late-night bowling. But he slowed down long enough to talk strategy. His remarks must have gone something like this:

"I can be a great president, but I need your help. I came to office with a great handicap. I ran a brilliant campaign and therefore I am regarded as a political genius. I also have the reputation of being a very successful governor. The pundits are greatly impressed with my leadership style and governing philosophy.

"In order to achieve our goals, we have got to lower expectations. The last thing I want to do is come across as looking too slick. We've made a good start. I raised doubts about my political judgment by giving top priority to lifting the ban on homosexuals in military service. The personnel team has done a great job in mishandling the attorney general nomination.

"If we are perceived as being something less than perfect, that is to our advantage. The public will have empathy and that translates into support. I hope I can count on you to keep this administration stumbling to bring about change.

"American deserves nothing less than our worst efforts."

*February 11, 1993*

## In Uncle Willie's World, the Budget Deficit Is Child's Play

As part of a continuing public relations campaign, President Clinton will go on television Saturday morning to communicate with the children of America. Having held several meetings with members of Congress, he has had plenty of practice for the exercise.

Someone has leaked a copy of the script for the children's show:

Announcer: Hi, kids. Welcome to Uncle Willie's Playhouse. And now here's America's favorite president, Uncle Willie!

Clinton: Goo-ood morning, boys and girls. Are we going to have fun today! I've got some wonderful stories to tell you about the budget deficit and the health care crisis, and some exciting news about a new government program that's just for you.

I'm sorry Aunt Hillary can't be here today, but she's back at the White House attending to affairs of state and doing the laundry. It's really amazing how she can handle the responsibilities of being a housewife and mother as well as the most powerful woman in the free world.

Now I want to talk to you about the deficit. I know it's a subject that's on all of your minds. (Show graphs and ad lib pitch for higher taxes.)

So you see, kids, you've got to convince your mom and dad that it's their patriotic duty to send more of their money to Washington so Uncle Willie and his friends can spend it on things that are necessary.

Since I've become president, I've learned that it costs a lot of money to run the government. You know that big airplane that presidents get to fly around in, called Air Force One? Why, I'll bet you didn't know that it cost $379,082 for me to fly to Detroit the other day to talk about cutting government expenses. And it cost $75,816 to send Uncle Al—you know, Vice President Al Gore—out to California to tell the jobless people there how we're pinching pennies.

Now kids, I know you can make your parents see why they have to make a sacrifice and pay more taxes. It's just like getting them to buy your favorite kinds of toys and breakfast cereals. Just keep pestering them until they give in.

One more thing, boys and girls. To pay for my economic program, everybody has to contribute—and I mean everybody. Here's what you can do: go get your piggy banks and empty them out—cash in your CD's if you have them—and send the money to me here in Washington. I'll put it in the big piggy bank called the U.S. Treasury. You'll be glad you did.

Now here's what I'm going to do for you. Aunt Hillary and I are concerned that some of you aren't getting your childhood disease immunizations. So we're going to see to it that every last one of you gets your shots. Won't that be great?

I'm going to ask Congress to appropriate an extra $300 million to make vaccinations available to a million more of America's children. And when that nurse jabs that needle into your arm, I know you're going to thank me.

And listen to this: After the immunization program is complete, we're going to provide all of you with birth control devices.

*February 18, 1993*

## Hillary's Guiding Spirit Has Special White House Hot Line

There it was on the *Associated Press* wire—not the *National Enquirer* or a New York tabloid, but the old reliable *AP*—a report that H. R. Clinton had revealed that she communes with the spirit of Eleanor Roosevelt.

The story said the president's wife made the startling announcement at a New York event to raise money for a statue of the woman who is her role model. She told a black-tie audience at Lincoln Center: "As I sat here this evening, I thought about all the conversations I've had in my head with Mrs. Roosevelt this year ...

"Early on as the campaign would go and things would happen, I would shake my head, and I would say, 'Why me?'" Clinton said. And the response? "Get out and do it, and don't make any excuses about it."

OK, if H. R. Clinton says she has conversations with someone who has been dead since 1962, who's not going to believe her? She's a lawyer, and we all know that lawyers never lie.

Besides, abnormal behavior is not all that uncommon in the White House. After all, Richard Nixon talked to pictures on the wall during his final days as president. And it was not so long ago that another first lady, Nancy Reagan, was said to have used an astrologer for guidance on her husband's schedule and other decisions.

The thing that's bothersome about the Clinton-Roosevelt cosmic connection is this: besides the stress of campaigns, what do they talk about? It's difficult to imagine Hillary summoning Eleanor to tell her about that wild Thursday night with the Gores, when the two couples ate at a Cajun restaurant and then went to a country night club to hear Jerry Jeff Walker. ("When he sang 'Up Against the Wall, Redneck Mother' I thought Tipper was going to have an orgasm." "I know. I felt the same way about Rudy Vallee.")

It's possible the two women might exchange views on their husbands' extra-marital affairs. ("What did Franklin see in Lucy Mercer?" "Well, she was certainly no Gennifer Flowers.")

Perhaps they trade snippets about criticism of their choices of attire. ("They're always writing about my headbands." "Yes, with me it was my fox stoles.")

They could compare notes about how they got women appointed to the president's Cabinet ("Frances Perkins never hired any illegal immigrants for household help") and about being scolded in newspaper editorials for speaking out with their opinions ("The Daily Oklahoman really gives me a hard time.")

They might gripe about White House staff ("I know some of them think I'm just meddling by chairing the task force on health care." "Harold Ickes once admonished me to stick to my knitting.")

Mutual admiration almost certainly would be indulged. ("I'm so inspired by your campaigns for civil and women's rights and your work at the United Nations." "Someday they'll erect a statue for you. It took a lot of courage to banish smoking from the White House.")

Or who knows? Maybe Hillary just wants to use the psychic hot line to get Eleanor's favorite cookie recipe.

*March 4, 1993*

## New Merchandise Galore at the Clinton Government Store

*News item: Consultant James Carville said that Bill Clinton, the man he helped elect, wants to be "a Kmart kind of president."*

"Attention, Kmart shoppers. Gigantic storewide reductions now going on. Our $16.3 billion economy fixit machine has been slashed drastically to meet the competition. Just ask any White House salesperson for the going price.

"Be sure to check the Defense Department for our giant closeout of discontinued items. You'll find some astounding bargains in everything from battleships to guided missiles. Don't miss this great opportunity to pick up a B-2 bomber. The kids will love it.

"Hurry over to the Interior Department and see the special post-Easter clearance of spotted owl eggs. Take one home today and watch it hatch. You'll enjoy seeing nature at work and help the environment at the same time.

"If you're a member of a union, you'll be treated like a VIP in our Labor Department. Leave your order for legislation and it will be filled promptly. No foreign-made products sold.

"Stop by our Justice Department and go shopping for a jury of your liking. Our attendants will cheerily validate parking tickets and invalidate federal grand jury indictments.

"In domestic wares today we are featuring a wide display of odd lots of broken campaign promises. Help yourself to as much as you can take and watch for a new stock the next time you're in the store.

"Don't fail to visit our amazing international bazaar. You'll enjoy selecting from a wide variety of policies on Bosnia, Haiti, Japan and the European Community. While you're there, sign a petition to end human rights abuses in the country of your choice.

"At this time a unique presentation is being made in our healthy living section. Store Manager H. R. Clinton is showing how health care policy can be developed in a locked, darkened room. Watch for a special announcement soon about this exciting new product.

"In the lawn and garden section, our vice president is now demonstrating the type of mower he uses to trim the White House grass each week.

"Please excuse the shortage of personnel. The store is under new management and we are having difficulty finding employees who meet our stringent ethnic, gender, geographic and political requirements. If you are interested in employment, please send a resume. Enclose a sworn statement that you have never employed an illegal alien.

"You'll note some new store policies. Democrats with approved voting records may go to the front of the line at any time. Homosexuals get first choice for any of our services. Special interests must enter through the back door. News reporters are required to take a number and wait.

"For those customers who missed our grand opening, we still have a few Clinton-Gore T-shirts left. They are available in large, extra-large, and "I Jogged With the President to McDonald's" sizes.

"Thank you for shopping the Clinton Kmart, where spending is never out of style."

*April 29, 1993*

## Fan's Lament: Will the Real Bill Clinton Please Stand Up?

Connie, the consultant, is fit to be tied. She worked very hard to get a Democrat elected president and expected all kinds of great things to happen. Instead she's seeing just the opposite.

"I have studied the events of the past several weeks and I have come to the conclusion that there is an impostor in the White House," she said.

"You mean like in that movie, *Dave?*"

"Exactly. That's the only explanation."

"How so?"

"The real Bill Clinton is a man of the people. He would never get a $200 haircut from a Hollywood stylist named Christophe. In Arkansas he could get a trim every week for a year for that kind of money.

"The real Bill Clinton disdains the perks of high office. He would not keep Air Force One on the runway, tying up the Los Angeles airport for an hour, while his wife's hairdresser fusses with his locks.

"The real Bill Clinton is dedicated to doing away with 'business as usual' in Washington. He would never put his cousin in charge of the White House travel office after firing seven nonpolitical career employees.

"The real Bill Clinton wants to clean up government. He would not allow his staff to pressure the FBI to say it was investigating the travel office for possible criminal activity.

"The real Bill Clinton jogs for exercise, not for show. He would not continue to disrupt Washington traffic by running in the streets after he had that special $30,000 track built on the White House grounds.

"The real Bill Clinton demanded more responsibility by those in government. He would not have surrounded himself with a cadre of young, brash, irresponsible staff members.

"The real Bill Clinton is a clear thinker. He would never say anything like: 'I've always felt—can you do one thing at once? I don't understand this whole—you can't do one thing at once. But anyway, that's what they say.'

"The real Bill Clinton is an articulate speaker. Unlike George Bush, he would not use phrases like, 'the health care thing' and 'that high tech stuff.'

"The real Bill Clinton is a new kind of Democrat. He would never call for the largest tax increase in history to pay for a new round of spending on social programs.

"The real Bill Clinton is a smooth politician. He would know better than to bad-mouth Democratic senators whose votes he will need if he hopes to get any kind of economic program passed.

"The real Bill Clinton has sound political judgment. He would never have filled his administration with such a collection of weirdos.

"The real Bill Clinton advocated arming the Bosnians and conducting air strikes against the Serbs. He would not wimp out by signing off on the timid strategy cooked up by the Europeans.

"I'm convinced of it. Somebody is impersonating the president. When is the last time you saw him play the saxophone?

"On second thought, I will have to say the man in the Oval Office is a lot like the real Bill Clinton in one respect. He can't salute worth a darn."

*May 27, 1993*

## If Clinton Is the Answer, Then Why So Many Questions?

"What are we doing, sending U.S. troops to Haiti?" "How soon can we get out of Somalia?" "Why do we have to pay more taxes?" "Who is Lillian Madsen?"

Why are so many questions being asked these days? Could it be that President Clinton is not "the answer" that he promised in his campaign?

When H. R. Clinton went up to Capitol Hill to sell the Clinton administration's health reform program, members of Congress were too busy fawning over the first lady to make many inquiries. But that wasn't the case with Health and Human Services Secretary Donna Shalala. Committee members pounded her with questions about the plan, particularly how it would be financed. She didn't have a clue. The five-foot Cabinet officer definitely came up short.

About the time the roof caved in on U.S. involvement in Somalia, Defense Secretary Les Aspin held a briefing for 200 lawmakers. The former college professor flunked out. Not only was he unable to provide any answers, he actually asked them to tell the administration what it ought to be doing. (As Paul Gigot of *The Wall Street Journal* observed, that's like "asking the Pamplona bulls for tourist directions.")

Some members of Congress (mostly Republicans) want to learn more about Commerce Secretary Ron Brown's dealings with a Vietnamese businessman. Specifically, did he accept a $700,000 bribe to help get a trade embargo against Vietnam lifted? Brown denies the accusation but is keeping mum about everything, including his mysterious female friend, Lillian Madsen, who sat in on some meetings and who lives in a Washington town house that Brown purchased. Inquiring minds want to know.

The Washington press is so annoyingly nosy that the Democratic Senatorial Campaign Committee barred reporters, photographers and camera crews from a $1,500-a-plate fund-raising dinner which Clinton attended. Eastern liberal newspapers questioned his behavior in hobnobbing with lobbyists at the black-tie affair at the same time he is pushing legislation to restrict special interests. As for the new closed-door policy, a Clinton spokesman explained, "We're the party of change."

The Ross Perot-Pat Buchanan-Jerry Brown-Lane Kirkland coalition has been firing a barrage of hostile questions about the North American free Trade Agreement (NAFTA). Their strategy is to create enough confusion about the accord that the public will not allow Congress to approve it. One thing that would help is to have a rule that only those who have actually read the agreement could participate in the debate.

It's not just Congress, the press and the public that have a probing curiosity about this administration. Questions are being raised in the White House itself. Nine months after the Clintons took over the operation, Chief of Staff Thomas "Mack" McLarty has sent a questionnaire to all White House staff to ascertain what they are doing. As soon as he finds out, and after they start doing what they ought to be doing, maybe there won't be as many questions.

*October 14, 1993*

## Behold the Magical Transformation of POTUS and FLOTUS

Around the White House, they're known as POTUS and FLOTUS. Those are shorthand terms for President of the United States and First Lady of the United States. But Bill Clinton and his wife are such warm and personable individuals they deserve a better identification than those dehumanizing acronyms. At least that's what the image-makers for the first family believe. And so it is that a magical transformation is in progress.

In late November, White House Press Secretary Dee Dee (My Real Name) Myers announced that Clinton was cutting back his schedule because "everybody's ready for a break." Clinton, so he keeps telling us, had been working very hard and the stress of the office was showing. He had become a sort of Southern-fried grinch.

Clinton lost his temper in an interview with *Rolling Stone* magazine and used mild profanity in blaming the "the knee jerk liberal press" for not giving him enough credit for his accomplishments. (The Society of Knee Jerk Liberal Reporters immediately demanded an apology and two new federal programs.)

"December will be an opportunity for the president to step back a little bit," Myers said. Clinton not only stepped back but did a complete Scrooge-like turnaround. He was Santa Claus personified as he schmoozed with the British author marked for murder by Iran, Salman Rushdie, authorized an American air taxi for Somali warlord Mohamed Farrah Aidid and allowed the Defense Department to lift its ban on overseas broadcasts of Rush Limbaugh.

He even conceded in an NBC interview that former Vice President Dan Quayle, a (gag) Republican, was right after all in his 1992 campaign criticism of the television sitcom, *Murphy Brown*, for its glamorization of single parenting. It is truly the season of good will.

Meanwhile, H. R. Clinton is doing her own role reversal. Within days after conducting an official tour of the Pentagon, complete with a motorcade of four golf carts, the first lady is emerging as a figure of vast feminine charm in the pages of such leading fashion magazines as *Vogue* and *Family Circle*. Gowned in a black velvet creation by Donna Karan, she looks almost sensual in a *Vogue* cover photograph. To *Family Circle* readers, she gushed about making Christmas decorations with daughter Chelsea using holly and seedpods.

It's all part of a holiday makeover for the woman accused of being a policy geek and an "iron lady."

There's nothing like riding a cherry picker to place an ornament atop the National Christmas Tree to soften a harsh image. She might not convince conservatives to stop distributing "Impeach Hillary" buttons, but she certainly has the knee jerk liberal press eating out of her hand.

With the first couple setting the pace, Vice President Al Gore is even thinking about modifying his public persona. He decided it was time to change his wooden image after a recent appearance at the White House. He showed up wearing a green suit and someone hung a string of Christmas lights on him.

*December 9, 1993*

## Mama Mia! Can That President Put Away the Pasta!

After a year in office, President Clinton is gaining recognition as a world figure who doesn't mind throwing his weight around. He has really developed a global appetite.

It's not the conference table where he excels, but the dinner table. He's all for arms reduction; just don't take away his knife and fork. He may not be the best treaty negotiator, but he can hold his own in any pizza parlor in the world.

Let's put it this way. If the Olympics had a pasta-eating event, Clinton would win sitting down. (Picture headline: "Gold Medal Goes to Pillsbury Doughboy.")

The pudgy president has been in training for quite some time. During the 1992 campaign, he had a reputation for having special radar that would lead him to a doughnut shop in the middle of the night.

One thing he learned after coming to Washington was that life is not all burgers and fries. He has expanded his gastronomical horizons (not to mention his waistline) to prove that he is an equal opportunity eater.

Remember when he went duck hunting with Oklahoma Rep. Bill Brewster right after Christmas? Afterward, he went to a lodge and ate a huge hunt breakfast of venison sausage, creamed chipped beef, scrapple, eggs, ham and biscuits. Later that day, Clinton flew back to his boyhood home, Hot Springs, Ark., arriving in time for dinner at a pizza joint.

According to a waitress, Clinton ate a pizza with the works, a salad topped with pepperoni and cheese, followed by cheesecake. After putting his wife and daughter into a limousine, he pivoted back into the restaurant for an order of cannoli.

All that gorging, no doubt, was in preparation for a high-level meeting with German Chancellor Helmut Kohl, his number one competitor for the world pig-out title. They had a face-off this week in Washington. The scene was Filomena's, an Italian restaurant in Georgetown known for serving large portions.

The 260-pound German leader loves the place and suggested dining there. Clinton, who often tips the scales at well over 200, eagerly accepted. They shared a limousine and had to pass the Pleasure Place, an adult novelty store. Clinton waved. Inside the restaurant, he greeted a woman cutting ravioli with a cheery, "Hi, Pasta Mama!" Just like old times in Little Rock.

Since Clinton recently compared Kohl to a Japanese wrestler, this mixing of politics and pasta could be known as the "Sumo Summit." The *Associated Press* filed a detailed dispatch: "Kohl and Clinton started out with a plate of hot and cold antipasto with mixed vegetables, and some squid. Clinton had Tuscan soup with white beans and spinach. For an entrée, the pair had the ravioli stuffed with veal, spinach and cheese. Mixed berries were dessert. They both drank red wine with the meal. Both ordered a huge chocolate cake—to go."

So much for the recent nutritional study that likened fettuccini Alfredo to a "heart attack on a plate." Clinton, as one Washington wag observed, "thinks diets are merely food for thought."

*February 3, 1994*

## President Felt the Heat So He Cleaned Out the Kitchen

Years from now, political science classes will be studying the manner in which the Clinton White House handled the so-called Whitewater scandal. It is indeed a classic case.

Before the roof fell in under the weight of nine subpoenas from Special Counsel Robert Fiske, President Clinton sought to convey the impression that he was carrying on a normal routine. He occupied himself with the responsibilities of his high office, which included receiving official visitors like Oksana Baiul, the 16-year-old Olympic gold medal ice skating champion from Ukraine. (Now that Nancy Kerrigan has apologized to Mickey Mouse, perhaps an American winner will be invited to the White House).

After Black Friday, when the federal grand jury summonses arrived, an operational strategy was devised, best summarized as, "We have done nothing wrong, and we won't do it again."

While Bill and Hillary Clinton flew off to Camp David to contemplate the future of their presidency, the subpoenaed administration officials were busy dialing up Hyatt Legal Services and canceling spring vacation. Spin doctors busily assembled a team from among those who didn't have papers served on them to take the message of pure innocence to the Sunday TV talk shows. Their mission: to explain why three backroom briefings by federal regulators of senior White House aides on confidential aspects of the Whitewater investigation did not amount to obstruction of justice.

Vice President Al Gore, deftly disguising thoughts of an early Gore presidency, forthrightly admitted that "mistakes were made." (In Washington, nobody "makes mistakes.") White House Chief of Staff Thomas F. "Mack" McLarty said the meetings "should not have happened" (although he arranged one of them) and senior aide George Stephanopoulos blamed everything on the Republicans.

Reflecting a Democratic affection for public works projects, Gore announced the construction of a "fire wall" to block any further contact between the investigators and the investigated. No mention was made as to whether the Clintons were being outfitted with asbestos suits so as not to get burned again.

The administration tried to create a diversion by announcing "The Giant Garter Snake Ecosystem Initiative" but for some reason reporters were more interested in Arkansas savings and loan, land development, and campaign financing activities. "There is not one shred of evidence of any wrongdoing," said Clinton—a poor choice of words, considering that former employees of his wife's Little Rock law firm say she ordered a large number of documents shredded after the Whitewater disclosures in the 1992 presidential campaign.

As the scandal threatened to engulf the presidency, heads began to roll. Among the first to go was the White House chef, who specialized in French cuisine, and the entire kitchen staff. Come to think about it, there is something immoral about *crepes suzette*.

*March 10, 1994*

## Whitewatergate's On Hold During "Be Kind to Bill Week"

President Clinton left Washington wallowing in Whitewatergate for a few days while he catches some California rays. Perhaps the president's critics will use this interlude to observe a cease-fire—a sort of "Be Kind to Bill Week."

After all, it's not nice to pick on someone who is not well, and Bill Clinton has been having trouble with his back. He can't get Republicans off of it.

Who would have thought GOP congressmen would be making such a big fuss about somebody who made a lot of money in the stock market? Maybe this would be a good time to crank up capital gains tax reduction.

As if Clinton weren't getting enough grief in Washington, his former partner in the Whitewater land deal, James McDougal, announced he is running for Congress. Just imagine having him sitting on the House Banking Committee.

And if H. R. Clinton's brother, Hugh Rodham, should win a Senate race in Florida, the president would have the worst kind of inlaw problems.

During these hectic times, it is reassuring to know that the president found time to curl up with a good book: his late mother's memoirs. And what fortuitous timing that he should find while reading the galleys a $20,000 loan that had escaped his memory.

Clinton made a valiant effort to show he was hard at work on issues other than Whitewater. He even joined 15 members of Congress in a fast to call attention to the problem of hunger in America. Clinton fasted one day, between lunch and dinner.

For a true diversion from the wicked world of Washington, Clinton traveled to Dallas to be best man for his half-brother, Roger, who married a former cheerleader who is eight months pregnant. The White House was quite secretive about details, so we can only speculate as to whether it was a combination wedding and baby shower.

One report said reception music was provided by a former member of Blood, Sweat and Tears, Bill Tillman and his Horns From Hell. Tillman said the celebration later moved to a nightclub called Fatso's Burgers and Blues. Bill Clinton must have been in hog heaven.

Actually it was the following day that the nation's No. 1 sports fan saw his beloved Arkansas Razorbacks play in the NCAA basketball tournament. The team did its best to give the beleagured president a lift, winning 76-68 over Michigan. Sports reporters noted that Clinton was the model of decorum, declining to wear a red Hog decal on the side of his face. But he did give the coach a two-handed high five and a bear hug at mid-court.

Before the game Clinton went to church in a Dallas suburb. Sitting in a sanctuary packed with conservative Republicans, he heard a sermon abut Janis Joplin, the rock singer who died in 1970 of a drug overdose.

Then on to San Diego, where the first family stayed as guests of a big Democratic contributor who just happens to be the new U.S. ambassador to Switzerland. There in his spacious ocean-front home, Clinton could relax and contemplate his next speech on family values.

*March 31, 1994*

## Worried About Finances? Take a Tip From the Clintons

With the basketball championship decided, the baseball season begun and the Easter egg roll completed, President Clinton must put behind his athletic pursuits and get back to the serious business of governing. No more fun and games—at least not until Congress gets back to town.

The *Washington Post* reports, after sending some reporters into the field, that the American people are about as interested in Whitewater as they were in Watergate at this stage of the scandal. (Well, the *Post* didn't put it exactly that way.)

What the public really is concerned about is health care, crime, welfare reform, and what Madonna said to David Letterman. Oh, yes, and taxes and what's happening in the financial markets. Anyone who had any money left after paying their taxes and followed the lure of those mutual fund ads might be just a little nervous about the price drops on Wall Street.

The president says to stay calm. But Larry, the lawyer, is so worried that he has been asking everybody he has come in contact with for advice about what to do. He has gotten some interesting answers.

His dentist said: "Just grin and bear it."

The plumber warned: "It's no time to be a plunger."

A taxicab driver suggested: "Ride it out."

His garbage collector urged: "Dump everything except junk bonds."

The supermarket cashier offered: "Bag it."

A used car salesman implored: "Sell, sell!"

His proctologist advised: "Sit tight."

With April 15 fast approaching, many two-income families are fretting about how to avoid sending one of the incomes to Washington.

There really would be no cause for worry about taxes or the stock market if everyone would just follow the example set by our national leaders, Bill and H. R. Clinton.

When the Clintons were governing Arkansas, they were a couple of modest means. They had to get by on the governor's annual salary of $35,000, a $51,000 "food fund," a $19,000 "public relations fund" and various home maintenance services valued at about $750,000 a year.

Being a good husband, Bill prevailed on a friend, James McDougal, to throw a little business to his wife's law practice to help with the family finances. She got a contract that paid $2,000 a month for 15 months to persuade Clinton-appointed state bank regulators not to close the Madison S&L for insolvency.

Even so, the Clintons took steps to trim their tax bill. For one thing, Bill donated his used underwear to charity, taking a deduction of two dollars for each pair. The Clinton family made charitable contributions of old clothes, toys and accessories valued at between $1,000 and $2,300 a year during the 1980s.

As for financial investments, anyone can make a killing by doing what H. R. Clinton did. Just find a broker named "Red" Bone, invest $1,000 in cattle futures, read *The Wall Street Journal* every day, and listen to a big poultry firm lawyer's advice. Before you know it, that nest egg will have grown to almost $100,000. And that's not chicken feed.

*April 7, 1994*

## POTUS Eschews Obfuscation and That Should Be Quite Clear

Clear communication is the prime requisite for any official who seeks public understanding and support. That is particularly true for POTUS. (That's Washington Beltway jargon for President of the United States).

To enunciate and explain his goals and policies, a president employs in his office and throughout his administration high-ranking staff members whose assignment is to communicate effectively through the news media to the American public.

Sometimes it is necessary to deal with an embarrassing incident, such as when a senior White House aide, David Watkins, along with two military officials, took a presidential helicopter to go play golf at a course in suburban Maryland.

Initially the White House said the trip was designed to scout out the course for a possible presidential visit, but a spokesperson later sought to clarify the situation, as follows (from a press briefing transcript):

"I think yesterday other staff members were giving the best—an explanation to the best of their knowledge. I think it is important that we have more information, more facts ... I don't know what the exact authority required is for use of a helicopter. I'm sure there is a specific process. I don't know exactly how it works.

"... the appropriate thing to do is for the Chief of Staff to oversee an inquiry to determine exactly what the facts are before we say anything else. It is a serious issue ... And I'm not going to discuss any more details about this." (Including the fact that two helicopters were used, which the White House first denied, then acknowledged.)

Later that day President Clinton announced Watkins' resignation and said the U.S. Treasury would be reimbursed in the amount of $13,129.66. The public is still waiting to learn Watkins' golf score.

That episode doesn't quite rank with the response given by a State Department deputy press secretary, who was asked at a March 11 news briefing if there was a "clear statement of (administration) policy on settlements in the occupied territories." He said:

"Well, I think our position on settlements is, is well known. It certainly comes up from time to time in the context of, you know, testimony and other things. We do—the briefers—also, from time to time, get those questions as well.

"As to—you know, nothing has changed on that in terms of our position and, you know, I think it's—you know, I can refer you to, you know, to probably to previous statements by officials on that. But I don't have anything—you know, I mean, you know, our—I think—I don't have—you know, I—we—usually we try to have, you know, a little bit of something on that. I'm not sure that it's going to be, you know, specifically what you're looking for.

"You know, generally speaking, our position (is) that on settlements that it's the Palestinians and Israelis have agreed that the final status negotiations will cover these issues and, you know, that's—that's also our view."

Any further questions?

*June 2, 1994*

## All the President's Menu Planners in a Stew for Royal Visit

Official Washington is all abuzz about the new book by Bob Woodward of the *Washington Post*. The author used 250 unnamed sources to produce *The Agenda: Inside the Clinton White House*. The mysterious "Deep Throat" helped Woodward expose the Watergate scandal in the Nixon administration. "Shallow Brain" is a good term for the battalion of blabbers President Clinton has working for him.

The book depicts a chaotic policymaking operation which includes four outside political advisers. It shows Clinton to be frequently indecisive, reluctant to delegate and given to ferocious temper tantrums. First Lady H. R. Clinton is said to be the *de facto* chief of staff.

Some of Woodward's sources are still eager to leak, and that's how this writer is able to report on a planning session for the visit by Emperor Akihito and Empress Michiko of Japan. Here is the way it will appear in a forthcoming book, *Things To Do: The White House Turned Wrongside Out*:

Clinton lumbered to his desk, pausing to kick the shins of his loyal aide, George Stephanopoulos. Gathered in the Oval Office were Vice President Gore, political consultant James Carville, the nominal chief of staff, Thomas F. McLarty, assorted administration officials and the new White House chef, Walter Scheib.

"This is the 14th meeting we've had on the Japanese visit," Clinton said. "I want to hear all points of view, but Hillary says it's decision time. Any more suggestions?"

Carville scooped up a handful of Fritos and drawled: "We've still got this trade problem with Japan. My daddy used to say you can't tame an alligator with a flyswatter. Here's an opportunity to turn the heat on the Japanese.

"Let's have an arrival ceremony on the South Lawn Monday. It's supposed to be hot, hazy and humid. Then let's have a formal, white tie dinner outside in a tent."

Clinton looked incredulous. "Outside? Better have plenty of bug spray. Check on that, will you Mack. Now let's talk about a menu. I want a big steak."

Chef Scheib sputtered. "But Mr. President, you know Mrs. Clinton's orders about healthy eating."

Stephanopoulos could see the "purple fit" coming. Clinton's face turned red. He climbed on top of his desk and stomped his feet. "I have to eat those ... soy burgers every day," he fumed. "This is a special occasion and I want beef!"

"Well, we sure can't serve chicken, after all those stories about Tyson Foods in Arkansas," offered David Gergen.

Clinton bounded to the floor and glared at Gergen. "I don't want to hear the word chicken ever again. I heard it enough after Vietnam," he roared.

"The emperor is into ichthyology, you know," said Gore. To a puzzled look from the leader of the free world, Carville added, "He's a fish man, man."

"Perfect," said the chef. "The main course will be farm-raised Arctic char with garlic and lime sauce."

"I had in mind catfish sushi," said Carville.

Gergen trembled visibly as Clinton fell to the carpet, tearing it into divots with his fingernails and screaming, "I'm the president and I want beef!"

At that point, Hillary Clinton entered and observed, "You people obviously aren't serving the president well. The menu is all set. Come along, Mack. There's fish to clean."

*June 16, 1994*

## Gores Set New Standards for Normalcy in Wacky Washington

Attention all weirdos, boozers and junkies: don't come rushing to Washington thinking the Clinton administration may have a job for you.

That warning seems warranted because some folks might get the wrong idea about a new policy announced at a National Press Club luncheon by Tipper Gore, leading mental health crusader and wife of the vice president. In the middle of a dry speech perfectly suited for Al Gore, she dropped a little bombshell. She said the government is revising its rules regarding federal employees to limit the amount of questioning about mental health and substance abuse treatment.

(And we thought failure to pay the "nanny" tax was the administration's biggest employment worry.)

Under current practice, she said, "the FBI investigator could go to your therapist and ask anything: 'Was it sex therapy?' 'Did you have an affair?'" Those kinds of blanket questions (the term she used) won't be allowed in the future—which should send a wave of relief through the White House.

"What is being corrected is the blanket assumption that if you have had a bout of depression, you are a security risk," she said. There was no mention of whether the policy could be made retroactive and be applicable to candidates for vice president. If so, former Sen. Thomas Eagleton, D-Mo., might have another chance at the job. He was dumped from the Democratic ticket in 1972 after disclosure he had been treated for depression and nervous exhaustion.

As understudy to First Lady H. R. Clinton, Tipper Gore seldom makes headlines. (And on that day she was competing with the Whitewater hearings and the Jordan-Israeli peace agreement. She lost.) A few years ago she was in the news campaigning against obscene lyrics in rock music. A Tennessean, she might have been the one who discovered that if you play a country record backwards, you get your sweetheart, your dog and your truck back.

Nowadays she leads a rather normal life. Her hobbies include rollerblading and playing the drums—presumably not at the same time. She is so attuned to the problems of the mentally ill, she probably never thought twice about the sicko who sprinkled tacks along her bike path some months ago.

As hostess of the vice presidential mansion, she has adapted to her husband's unique style of entertaining. According to *The Wall Street Journal*, the veep held a series of three private dinners in which selected guests were invited to listen and respond to lectures about the role of the metaphor. That's right, three evenings devoted to discussion of a figure of speech.

"Mr. Gore's rarefied philosophical conclaves," said the *Journal*, "introduce new anxieties to Washington's dinner-party circuit. Forget the usual chit-chat about, say, health care bills … Food for thought at these dinner parties ranges from Burmese language and literature to America's distrust of nature during the Industrial Revolution …"

And they said Dan Quayle was off the wall!

*July 28, 1994*

## Party Time at White House Cheers Embattled President

According to our highly placed source, the holiday spirit has arrived at the White House. First Lady H. R. Clinton gave the executive mansion a real "down home" look, with the help of designer Ralph Lauren and his "creative services team." Partridges, turtle doves, and calling birds put a smile of anticipation on the face of first cat Socks. Even the embattled President Clinton is said to have a twinkle in his eye.

What prompted his cheerful demeanor is uncertain, but it could have been any of a number of things. No doubt the 70-pound gingerbread house, a replica of Clinton's childhood home in Hope, Ark., aroused his emotions, not to mention his appetite. Maybe he perked up at that *Penthouse* magazine spread on Paula Jones, his sexual-harassment accuser, which exposed some of the finer points of her legal case. Or perhaps it was reading advance proofs of a steamy novel by his Republican nemesis, House Speaker-to-be Newt Gingrich. (Example: "Suddenly the pouting sex kitten gave way to Diana the Huntress. She rolled onto him and somehow was sitting athwart his chest, her knees pinning his shoulders.") Maybe the two have a common interest after all.

More than likely it was the round of holiday celebrations that put the president in a festive mood, despite the problems of his old Little Rock friend, Webster Hubbell, and signs of disintegration of his administration. Two Cabinet members, Lloyd Bentsen of Treasury and Mike Espy of Agriculture, are leaving, along with Surgeon General Joycelyn Elders, who had a "policy difference" with Clinton over teaching schoolchildren about masturbation.

Since the Clinton administration is economizing it was decided to have one farewell party for the departing appointees, our source said. The honorees all came bearing gifts. Bentsen brought several boxes of unopened political advice. Espy distributed buckets of Tyson Foods chicken. And Elders handed out copies of her new book, *Sex Without Partners*.

Everybody joined in singing songs of the season, led by Bentsen:
"You better watch out, you better not lie
"About a tax cut, I'm telling you why,
"Republicans are coming to town."
Espy warbled:
"Oh, Metzenbaum, oh, Metzenbaum,
"Where are you when we need you?"
And Elders belted out:
"Good King Gingrich can't look down, he's too busy strutting,
"Proud of all the plans he's made, and the jobs he's cutting."

Toward the end of the party, the president addressed the crowd, said the source. "At this time of sharing, we must remember those who are less fortunate than we," he said. "So let's all chip in and send a generous contribution to Webb Hubbell to help him pay his back taxes."

Santa Claus made an appearance and Clinton thought he recognized him. "If I didn't know better I'd think it was Dan Rostenkowski," he said. To which the jolly old elf replied, "It's just a moonlighting job to help out with my legal expenses."

*December 15, 1994*

## First Lady Will Redefine Her Image Without Newt's Help

At a time when national concerns are focused on the new Congress, the fighting in Chechnya and resettlement of Canadian wolves, some of the nation's major newspapers are devoting an inordinate amount of attention to H. R. Clinton's efforts to save her co-presidency.

A primary initiative of the first lady is to "soften a harsh image," says Marian Burros of the *New York Times*, who got the word at a chummy White House luncheon for women writers and gossip columnists. Burros, a devotee of the Connie Chung brand of journalism, front-paged a number of Clinton statements that others present understood were "just between us girls."

What was undeniably on the record were such startling revelations as, "You have to start thinking about Christmas in April"—that is, if you're the official hostess of the executive mansion or a manufacturer of Power Ranger toys.

This writer did not attend the luncheon because:

1.  He is not a woman.

2.  He does not engage in gossip (unless, of course, it is especially juicy).

3.  He avoids Washington's high crime areas.

Therefore he cannot vouch for Burros' reporting of the first lady's confession that she had been "naïve and dumb" about national politics and was to blame for the failure of the Clinton health care plan last year. Nor did he have the opportunity to respond to her solicitation of advice, as did New York gossipmongers Cindy Adams and Lisa Stasi and advice columnist Ann Landers. This writer would have suggested seeking a less controversial role, such as joining the O. J. Simpson legal defense team.

The Sunday *Washington Post* featured a lengthy profile by David Maraniss headlined, "First Lady of Paradox," which describes "her hokey form of humor." Maraniss writes: "It is not unusual for Hillary Clinton to end a conversation with a staff member by uttering, 'Okey-dokey, artichokey.'" That's hokey, all right.

Since the overwhelming rejection of their policies at the polls last November, both President Clinton and his wife have sought guidance from a variety of professionals, besides Ann Landers ("Dear Washed Out in Washington: Stop whining and get on with your life."). They hosted four New Age personal growth experts at Camp David, including Marianne Williamson, known as the "Guru to the Glitterati" by Hollywood media because she was endorsed by Oprah ("I snorted cocaine") Winfrey and officiated at Elizabeth Taylor's most recent but not necessarily last wedding.

Also on hand was Stephen R. Covey, author of *The Seven Habits of Highly Effective People*, who has coached House Speaker Newt Gingrich but presumably not the Dallas Cowboys' Barry Switzer.

Another adviser was Anthony Robbins, whose methods include having participants in his seminars walk barefoot across a bed of burning coals to help them achieve "peak personal and professional experiences." Well, if that wouldn't soften a harsh image, what would?

And to think, Nancy Reagan only had an astrologer.

*January 19, 1995*

## Why Should Clinton Praise Churchill When He Can Glorify Stalin?

Those of us who are old enough to remember World War II know that it was a time of great national unity and extraordinary presidential leadership. Sometimes nostalgia can be terribly depressing.

The clock was turned back as several events were held to commemorate the 50th anniversary of V-E Day. Television specials on the end of the war in Europe recalled some famous news reporter, such as Edward R. Murrow—prompting some children to ask, "why is that man on TV smoking a cigarette?" Murrow was good, but wouldn't it have been great to see Connie Chung ask Winston Churchill: "Do you think you can handle the Germans?"

President Clinton passed up the opportunity to go to England, where he sat out the Vietnam War, to join other heads of state in V-E Day ceremonies. He sent Al Gore instead, which was a rare treat since vice presidents usually see a foreign leader only after he's dead.

Clinton might not have been the toast of London anyway, after his warm embrace of the terrorists of the Irish Republican Army. At any rate, he opted to fly to Moscow to have a drink or two with Boris Yeltsin and hear how Russians really won the war in Europe, and maybe exchange views on how to deal with Chechen rebels and right-wing militias.

But before going to the Kremlin the president and his wife attended a V-E Day party in Washington hosted by their Hollywood friends, TV producers Harry Thomason and Linda Bloodworth-Thomason. Perhaps they talked about a plot for a new situation comedy in which a Vietnam war protester organizes anti-government demonstrations, then gets elected president and goes around scolding Americans who say, 'I love my country, but I hate my government.'" No, even a TV sitcom has to have some kind of credible basis.

Also before his departure, sources say, Clinton directed Attorney General Janet Reno to launch an investigation to determine what role G. Gordon Liddy played in the deadly Texas hailstorms and Oklahoma tornadoes.

Some Clinton critics might say a draft dodger has no business associating himself with one of the greatest military victories in history. But this photo-op president got a head start last year when he took some stones conveniently left on the beach at Normandy by White House staff and arranged them in the form of a cross. Besides, anyone who has seen Clinton jogging would know he has fought the "battle of the bulge." (And lost.)

Prior to Clinton's arrival in Russia, word leaked out that he and his wife had become separated. That's how the tabloids would headline it. Actually it was a bronze bust of the presidential pair that was split. Ukrainian sculptor Valentyn

Znoba divided his 175-pound work because, he explained, "the gift would just have been rather difficult to move about." Doesn't he know that Air Force One has no restrictions on what its chief passenger can place in the overhead compartment?)

For further discussion of First Lady H. R. Clinton's bust, please see the *National Enquirer*.

*May 11, 1995*

## New Moral Leader May Lose New York City Police Vote

When New York City cops cavort naked in a respectable Washington hotel and Sen. Phil Gramm invests in an R-rated movie, we have to ask ourselves: Have America's moral values gone down the toilet?

Around 100 visiting policemen engaged in a drunken rampage at five D.C. hotels, including the Hyatt Regency on Capitol Hill. They celebrated National Police Week by staggering around with holstered guns and little else, mooning hotel guests and groping women. Some officers even slid down a banister minus their underpants (must have been a splinter group), which from a male point of view is a pretty dumb macho thing to do, unless you aspire to be a soprano.

Observing their constitutional right to bear fire extinguishers, New York's finest sprayed each other and anyone else in range. There were reports from women of officers trying to get into their rooms. Charges of being out of uniform and impersonating a U.S. senator from Oregon are pending.

As for the most conservative Sen. Gramm, he might have recouped the $7,500 he gave his brother-in-law to back a soft porn movie if he had only hired a crew to film the night of police debauchery.

In the wake of these shocking developments, when faith in our country's institutions is being tested, there is some good news. America has a new moral leader. The bad news is, it's Bill Clinton.

President Clinton revealed himself as the national champion of all that's good and proper at—this is true—a "White House Conference on Character Building." (The second annual, no less. Guess the first one didn't take.)

The timing was a little off, coming the day after Commerce Secretary Ron Brown became the fourth administration official—including Clinton—to come under investigation by an independent counsel. It also was the same week the Whitewater scandal inquiry was reopened in the Senate.

In Clinton's speech to the conference, he took the presidential "bully pulpit" to hold forth on the nation's moral and social problems. Clinton talked of "the fundamental character strengths and traits" without saying anything about marital infidelity or avoiding the draft. He did confess to using unfair rhetoric about government bureaucrats and promised to repent. "Our political debate is too polarized," he said, while making another slur against high income earners and taking a slap at the Christian Coalition's family-oriented agenda.

The president who promised the most ethical administration in history plans to be "talking about the moral and spiritual life of the country more regularly," a spokesman says. Clinton's conversion must have had some effect on his housing secretary, Henry Cisneros. He settled a lawsuit with his former mistress for $49,000.

Clinton told the character conferees the nation's problems can be solved "in a free and open society." He made those remarks as concrete barriers were being placed on Pennsylvania Avenue, closing the street in front of the White House to cars and buses.

*May 25, 1995*

### Is a Bill Clinton Funk Anything Like a Jimmy Carter Malaise?

Bill, the bureaucrat, has been busy making plans for his annual New Year's Eve Party. Like many deskbound numbers crunchers, Bill celebrates the beginning of the new fiscal year October 1.

This year his heart really isn't in the party preparations because of the anxiety felt throughout the bureaucracy about the dreaded "train wreck" that has been predicted if the executive and legislative branches can't come together on a budget for FY 1996.

Bill's wife thought it would be clever to have party guests dress as their favorite train character, but he couldn't find any humor in the idea. Bill couldn't see Vice President Al Gore as a coal dusty engineer, although in an unguarded moment he did call House Speaker Newt Gingrich a bum for even suggesting that the $4.9 trillion federal debt limit might not be raised.

Another distraction is Bill's assignment to a key role in President Clinton's newest initiative: to eliminate the Great National Funk. As anyone who hasn't been totally immersed in the O. J. Simpson trial knows, Clinton has been jetting around the country on Air Force One laying groundwork for his re-election campaign. In his travels the president has made a significant discovery. He describes the nation as skittish and confused in a time of economic and social upheaval.

Clinton says voters are understandably anxious—"like they're lost in the fun house." (Some might argue that statement more aptly applies to Washington dwellers.) Still convinced that change is good, Clinton outlined what he sees as his task for 1996: "I'm also trying to get people out of their funk about it."

Now, if anyone ought to be in a funk, it's Clinton. He couldn't have been too happy about his brother Roger teaching a seminar this summer on "Dysfunctional Families." He's lagging so much in the polls, it has been suggested he withdraw as a candidate and allow retired Gen. Colin Powell to head the Democratic ticket next year.

But the president can take heart in the fact that Pope John Paul II dismissed suggestions by critics that he step down a few months ago. The pope said only God could end his reign. Fortunately for Clinton, his fate won't be decided by a heavenly edict but rather by someone like Ross Perot, who wants to play God.

Maybe Clinton should schedule a papal consultation while the leader of the Roman Catholic church is in the area next month, making his first appearance in Baltimore. Marylanders are making the most of the pope's visit. They're expecting a $26 million windfall from marketing products like a T-shirt on which the Holy Father, armed with a can of Old Bay Seasoning and a fistful of crab mallets, blesses a multitude of blue crabs. (The designers first had the pope holding a beer in his hand, but decided that would be sacrilegious.)

Back to Bill, the bureaucrat. He's heading a Task Force on Funk Factors, which among other things, will study how much the national funk deepens when the O. J. Simpson trial is finally over.

*September 28, 1995*

## Is Republican Candidate Bob Dole the Grand Old Party Pooper?

Now that Sen. Bob Dole has the Republican nomination in his pocket and no longer must worry about Pat Buchanan's sniping (well, no more than once or twice a week), all he has to do is convince American voters that he is not too boring to be president.

That seems to be the consensus of the Washington press corps, 89 percent of whom voted for Bill Clinton in 1992, according to a poll by the Freedom Forum Foundation. Regardless of how biased the opinion might be, Dole is stuck with the image of being the Grand Old Party pooper.

Dole is known to journalists who cover Capitol Hill and politics as a master of the quick quip and the snappy one-liner. But as his presidential campaign against Clinton moves along, many of these writers portray him in their columns as "Senator Dull."

One columnist described the departing Senate majority leader as a man "with the soul of a parliamentarian." The *Washington Post* reported a recent speech by Dole to a newspaper group left the audience "unmoved," while Vice President Al Gore "had editors laughing with recollections of his days as a cub reporter in Nashville." Whoopee-do.

*Time* magazine criticized the Dole campaign for not producing "forceful" speeches for the GOP candidate. (An address lambasting Clinton for liberal federal court appointments was prepared by an outside contractor.) And it didn't help generate much excitement when Dole was endorsed by James Stockdale, the lackluster running mate of Ross Perot in the last campaign.

In fairness to Dole, it must be said that he suffers from the same stereotyping given to Republicans in general by the Washington establishment. The *Post*, in an article last January, concluded that "Washington was a great party town" before Republicans took over Congress. The new majority is "less entertaining" preferring "strategy breakfasts, coalition lunches and working dinners" to the "Georgetown soirees, Chevy Chase cocktail parties, and playful schmoozing with traditional Washington insiders" that characterized many years of Democratic rule.

As for producing colorful candidates, Democrats often have the upper hand. Whatever else they might have done, President Clinton and his wife certainly have enlivened American politics. There's nothing dull about some of the others lining up to run on the Democratic ticket this fall.

In Nevada, Jessi Winchester seeks to become the first member of Congress to have worked at the Moonlight Bunnyranch. That's a legal bordello at Mound House, Nev., and she worked there for five years. She is quite philosophical in her campaign to be the first prostitute to serve in the House of Representatives (as an elected member, that is).

"In the world of politics, people are always so busy digging up dirt on each other," she said. "Well, they don't have to try to dig up my past. My skeletons are already out of my closet. I'm just going to go out there and kick butt and tell it like it is."

Maybe Bob Dole can hook her for his vice president.

*May 16, 1996*

## Clinton Lusts for Old Mummy, Wife Wants to Be New Mommy

America's first family is back to entertaining us again after a too lengthy moratorium on goofy behavior. Well, it's true that President Clinton has been creating some campaign mischief by playing the worst kind of dirty tricks: He's been acting like a Republican. But stealing Bob Dole's thunder by grabbing all the GOP issues for himself was getting a little monotonous.

Then he cast his eyes on a picture of a 500-year-old mummy, so well-preserved the president had this to say at a Connecticut fund-raising affair: "I don't know if you've seen that mummy. But you know, if I were a single man, I might ask that mummy out. That's a good looking mummy."

Now, former president Jimmy Carter confessed he had had lust in his heart, but not for a dead woman. What was it about this corpse that turned Clinton on? Let us count the ways. The lady known as the Maiden of Ampato in her native Peru was strikingly lifelike in her photo. "She looks sort of regal," said anthropologist Johan Reinhard, who discovered her frozen remains at the top of a Peruvian volcano.

She was a virgin, sacrificed to the mountain gods at the age of 13. Come now, Mr. President. Isn't that a little young for someone who will turn 50 in August? And how would he go about asking her out anyway—send a bodyguard to tell her she made his knees knock? That's what Clinton supposedly did with Paula Corbin Jones, the Arkansas woman who filed a sexual harassment lawsuit against him—which the president's lawyer says is a terribly unpatriotic thing to do to someone serving on active duty.

The Inca mummy is about the hottest thing going in scientific circles these days, and we may not see a find like this again. The comely maiden might be called the last of the red hot mummies—if she weren't kept frozen in a special case.

Speaking of ice maidens, First Lady H. R. Clinton has disclosed that she would like to be a mommy again. She said "it would be terrific" if she and the president could produce a sibling for 16-year-old daughter Chelsea. "We're hoping that we have another child," she said, but added: "I would be surprised." (With pro-lifers fired up over Clinton's veto of a ban on "partial birth" abortions, nothing in this presidential campaign would surprise this callous observer.)

The 48-year-old first lady said she and her husband had talked about adoption. Sounds like they could be serious. A skeptic might wonder if their motivation might be to gain another dependent, having just sent the Internal Revenue Service $2,910 in back taxes and interest on their Whitewater real estate investment.

Enough of these jabs against our nation's leader. At least, he deserves credit for looking after his health. When he had lunch with German Chancellor Helmut Kohl at Miss Katie's Diner in Milwaukee the other day, they ate barbecued chicken and ribs, steak, lemon chicken, meat loaf, hash browns and apple pie. But Clinton passed up a local microbrew and instead had a diet Coke.

*May 30, 1996*

## Campaign Matures as President Turns 50 and Perot Jumps In Again

At last, there are signs of maturity in the presidential campaign. President Clinton turned 50 and Ross "The Boss" Perot, who is rich enough to have his own political party, got into the race for the second (or third) time.

This is indeed a welcome turn of events. After all the youthful vitality displayed at the Republican convention, where Bob Dole was throwing out reckless ideas like a tax cut, it is time for serious and sober contemplation of the most important office in the land.

Having reached a major milestone in his life, Bill Clinton no longer can be dismissed as a rash, impetuous "baby boomer." With half a century of living behind him, he need not worry that Dole might raise the age issue in the campaign.

Clinton celebrated his 50th birthday among stars from the entertainment world at a big party in New York, with admission priced at up to $10,000. Next day he did penance by helping rebuild a burned-out black church. The president also took time to ponder "the meaning of it all."

"Becoming 50 gives me more yesterdays than tomorrows," he said profoundly, "and I'll now begin to think more about the long-term implications as well as the consequences of what I do." (Well, that statement ought to inspire the confidence of the American people.)

Suddenly grown up, Clinton, in an interview with CBS news anchor Dan Rather, pledged that next week's Democratic National Convention will be devoid of "snide remarks" and "negative personal asides." Guess that means Rosie O'Donnell doesn't get a speaking role.

After due consideration, convention planners decided to allow first lady H. R. Clinton to speak. It will be interesting to see how Clinton's wife attempts to top Elizabeth Dole's ringing endorsement of her husband with a unique walk on the convention floor. Maybe she will round up Gennifer Flowers and Paula Corbin Jones and give a group testimonial to his character.

Meanwhile, Perot, whose 1992 campaign theme song was "Crazy," is at it again. The Texas billionaire accepted the nomination of the Reform Party, which he organized and bankrolled, with a humble pledge: "I will be your servant ... I will only belong to you, the people."

That probably doesn't mean that the next time you have a dinner party Ross Perot will show up in a tuxedo and serve drinks. But he will do your thinking for you, because he knows what's best for America. That includes keeping all those foreigners out of the country, or else we could end up like India, Perot says.

Who can say how many votes Perot will get this time around? He didn't win the support of his political rival, former Colorado Gov. Richard Lamm, after he defeated him in an odd "straw vote" in which party members could make their selection by telephone, mail or computer. Lamm didn't even get a ballot until midway through the weeklong process.

One positive result of the Perot candidacy is that it does lend credence to the recent scientific breakthrough about life on other planets.

*August 22, 1996*

## There's No Outrage When You're All Things to All People

At the behest of Bob Dole and Ross Perot, I went looking for "the outrage" in the week before the election. Sadly, there was none to be found—at least not in the corner coffee shop where Joe Sixpack and Jill Soccermom were talking politics. Joe and Jill never agree on anything, but this year they find themselves on the same side in the election.

Both said they plan to vote for President Clinton. I asked why.

Jill: Because he will spend whatever it takes to see that my children get a good education.

Joe: And he's going to put school kids in uniform to keep them from stealing each other's designer clothing.

Q: So you're in favor of more government spending and power?

Jill: Clinton has cut the deficit to the lowest point in 15 years.

Joe: He has promised us working stiffs a tax cut.

Q: Have you forgotten he's the president who gave us the biggest tax increase in history?

Jill: All I know is, as a suburban homemaker, I'm not feeling any pain economically.

Joe: And Clinton has kept the peace after Reagan and Bush licked the commies.

Q: So what else do you like about the incumbent?

Jill: By putting 100,000 more police on the streets he's making our neighborhoods more safe.

Joe: Right. He's tough on crime, and he's also going to make those welfare deadbeats go to work.

Q: What about Whitewater, Travelgate, Paula Jones and all the other scandals of the Clinton White House?

Jill: It's just politics as usual as far as I'm concerned.

Joe: They're all a bunch of crooks in Washington. Clinton's no worse than the rest of them.

Q: But aren't you outraged by the Clintons inviting a drug dealer to the White House Christmas party?

Jill: What we talk about in our car pool is the president's efforts to keep our kids from getting hooked on tobacco.

Joe: If that guy got through the security check, maybe they'll invite me sometime, ha, ha.

Q: Doesn't it make you angry that the Democrats accepted large campaign contributions from foreign sources with an interest in U.S. trade policy?

Jill: In our church volunteer group, we are more concerned about what our children see on television. Clinton is going to help.

Joe: Hey, everybody does it.

Q: Are you voting a straight Democratic ticket?

Jill: Oh, no. My congressperson is a Republican and she does a good job of constituent service.

Joe: The guys I bowl with agree that we need a GOP Congress to provide a check on the White House.

Q: Is there any other reason you're supporting Clinton's re-election?

Jill: We'll have a first lady who will be actively involved in issues of concern to American families, like health care.

Joe: Yeah, it will be great to have Hillary to kick around for another four years.

*October 31, 1996*

# The Further Adventures of POTUS and FLOTUS in a New Century

To help "build a bridge to the 21st century," Bill Clinton made some changes in his crew. He replaced seven cabinet secretaries, not all of whom were under investigation. A top adviser, George Stephanopoulos, who once compared the White House press corps to a pack of dogs, had joined the pack, becoming an ABC-TV reporter and news anchor. The co-presidency known as "Billary" still existed, although his partner was not quite the same.

Character issues that had dogged Clinton for years presented a major challenge in Clinton's second term. As countless examples of her husband's womanizing became public, First Lady H. R. Clinton changed her mind and decided Tammy Wynette was right in saying, "stand by your man." In the strongest test of the Clinton's troubled marriage, she remained by his side even after he was exposed as a middle-aged lecher having an affair with White House intern Monica Lewinsky.

Looking suspiciously like acts designed to create a distraction, Clinton ordered the bombing of Iraq in 1998 and in response to reports of ethnic cleansing in the Serbian province of Kosovo he sent U.S. warplanes to bomb Serbia in 1999. A decline in the polls generally was followed by a Cruise missile attack somewhere.

The Lewinsky scandal triggered an investigation that saw Clinton become the first U.S. president to testify before a grand jury, during which time he dodged a question with the immortal statement: "It depends on what the meaning of the word 'is' is." The U.S. Senate decided that sin was not an impeachable offense but several senators scolded the sinner harshly in voting for acquittal.

As Clinton's vice president, Al Gore made news with various preposterous claims, such as inventing the Internet, and getting caught in questionable political fundraising activities. When he ran for president in 1999, the future Nobel Peace Prize winner was parodied on NBC's *Saturday Night Live* as a humorless, wooden candidate obsessed by a "lock box" plan to protect Social Security.

The 2000 election ended in a vote so close that recounts were held in Florida, which gave TV comedians much fodder for jokes about "butterfly ballots" and "dangling chads." The U.S. Supreme Court made the final decision, ruling in favor of Republican George W. Bush.

Bill Clinton and his wife, Hillary, who had been elected to the U.S. Senate representing New York, remained on the Washington scene and kept a high profile, highlighted by controversy, of course.

## Court Provided Preinaugural Noise, Now Bring In 'da Funk

A presidential inauguration is a very special event. Nothing—not even an important Supreme Court hearing involving alleged pants-dropping by a public official—should detract from the solemnity and dignity of the occasion.

This is especially true in the case of President Clinton's second inaugural, which organizers say will have a much more serious tone than 1993. Planners have been working hard to produce a celebration befitting the holder of the nation's highest office.

Presumably that's why they have engaged the casts of two Broadway musicals: *Chicago* and *Bring In 'da Noise, Bring In 'da Funk.* What better way to depict the symbolism of Clinton's coronation at the Democratic National Convention in Chicago and the beginning of his second term? (You won't find this kind of penetrating analysis in most editorial page columns.)

The president and his staff are looking forward to Monday's swearing-in ceremony and the American public will be glad to know they are not in the least concerned about that little old sexual harassment lawsuit before the Supreme Court. "An American Journey," the theme of the inauguration, does not include a stop at the Little Rock hotel where Paula Corbin Jones says Clinton, while governor of Arkansas, propositioned her and exposed himself.

For the sake of decorum, it is well that the court is not considering details of the case but rather the basic question of whether a sitting president is immune from a civil lawsuit until after he leaves office. It was bad enough to have six men wearing boxer shorts and trench coats carrying signs reading "Flashers Support Clinton" parading outside the nation's highest tribunal.

On second thought, it would have been interesting to hear Justice Sandra Day O'Connor ask a former Arkansas state trooper: "Is it true that the governor said this woman made his knees knock?"

The case won't be settled for some time, but one thing is clear. Paula Jones will not have a featured role in the inaugural events. She certainly was not chosen as one of the "great thinkers" who will sit in a heated tent on the frozen Mall and discuss issues with tourists. That honor was reserved for such cerebral icons as comedian/actress Whoopi Goldberg and feminist Betty Friedan.

Supposedly Paula could pay $3,000 and sit with Clinton and the first lady at an invitation-only Presidential Gala on Sunday, or perhaps find a friendly Indonesian who could book her into the Lincoln bedroom for an evening. (There might be a vacancy, because Clinton's close friend, Barbra Streisand, says she's skipping the inaugural festivities this time.) Or maybe she had just rather attend one of the inaugural balls. There are 14, not counting the Peanut Butter 'n' Jelly Inaugural Ball for kids, already held.

Truth is, the former Arkansas state employee who was branded "trailer court trash" by Clinton sympathizers, will be about as welcome at inaugural events as she would be at a meeting of women's rights activists.

*January 16, 1997*

## President Who Basks in Inaugural Glow May Get Burned

Before joining President Clinton's new crusade for sweetness and light in politics, is it all right to make a few snide observations about inaugural week? After all, before the "repairer of the breach" took his oath, First Lady H. R. Clinton got in her licks by attacking "right-wing, conservative" media organizations that she says influence news coverage.

Even the most radical of our lot can forgive her unkind accusation, however, because at least she didn't wear an ugly hat to this year's inauguration. As for her husband's speech, which even leftwing types called a dud, the best thing about it was its brevity—only 22 minutes. It usually takes Clinton that long to clear his throat.

News analysts took note that Clinton used the phrase "new promise" five times in his speech, but who should be surprised? He has built his entire political career on new promises—some of which he has even kept.

The three-day inauguration production cost $31 million, about $6 million more than 1993. But that included the expense of moving construction cranes and planting trees on one side of a federal building still unfinished after 10 years, enabling the inaugural committee to sell bleacher seats for the big parade.

Bill Clinton—pardon, William Jefferson Clinton—was indeed the star of this costly quadrennial show.

At a Capitol luncheon, House speaker Newt Gingrich, looking like a man who needed all the friends he could get, said to Clinton, "Here you're among friends." He also made this curious remark: "This capacity to transfer power ... is truly one of the miraculous events of the planet." (Maybe he meant the transfer of power from first-termer Clinton, the liberal Democrat, to bridge-builder Clinton, who talks more like a Republican.)

Vice President Al Gore echoed the speaker, saying: "In our country ... we've got something so special ... the peaceful transfer of power." (He was probably dreaming of a moment four years from now.)

Clinton is slowly defining the precise course he will take as we lurch toward a new century in a new millennium. During the first 100 days of Clinton's first term:

• He lifted a ban on fetal tissue research.

• Zoe Baird withdrew as a nominee for attorney general after admitting she hired illegal aliens and failed to pay their social security taxes.

- Clinton named his wife to run a $100,000 health care reform task force that eventually cost $13.4 million of taxpayers' money.

- He suspended the discharge of homosexuals from the military.

- Kimba Wood withdrew her name for nomination as attorney general after it was disclosed she employed an undocumented worker.

- The president halted drug testing for White House staff.

- He broke a campaign promise for a middle-class tax cut.

And that was just the beginning.

As Clinton launches his second term he can take inspiration from balloonist Steve Fossett. Although he didn't reach his goal, he did go a long way on a lot of hot air.

*January 23, 1997*

## Love Is in the Air, and Look What's in the Clintons' Closet

In this cozy new era of bipartisanship and breach repairing, love definitely is in the air in Washington. President Clinton not only has called for an end to petty bickering and acrimonious political debate, he also says forgiveness is everyone's civic duty.

Well, the president's mandate certainly worked for CIA nominee Anthony Lake. As Clinton's national security adviser, Lake had failed to sell some stocks that were a potential conflict of interest. He also urged withholding information from Congress about Iranian arms transfers. But after making a $5,000 restitution, the Justice Department declared all is forgiven. O. J. Simpson should be so lucky.

But back to the subject of love—everyone is wondering how the first couple will celebrate Valentine's Day. The president did some shopping during a visit to Annapolis this week. Wonder how First Lady H. R. Clinton will feel about getting a gift from a place called "Recapture the Past"—considering Bill Clinton's past. But it would be sort of difficult for him to shop at Victoria's Secret.

Besides, exchanging Valentine gifts does not express the true meaning of love. It's how a man and wife spend the other 364 days of a year that defines a relationship. The first lady revealed some insight about her marriage in a recent TV interview.

When she and the president are not busy running the country and changing the world, they engage in some rather interesting off-hours activities. "We do a lot of housekeeping, which is so relaxing for us," she said. "I mean, it's partly because there's a beginning, a middle and the end, so that we'll clean out closets together."

So the Clintons clean out closets together. Who would have imagined it? How romantic!

Can't you just picture the scene?

"Come on, Bill darling, there's a closet upstairs that needs cleaning out."

"All right, sweetheart. There's nothing I'd rather do. Maybe I'll see where you're hiding your Bruno Magli shoes."

"How did you know about that?"

"I read it in the paper."

"Well, I don't deny it, like you know who."

"I wonder what we'll really find in here," Clinton says, opening the closet door. The first thing he sees startles him. It's a soldier in uniform, wearing pink scuffs. "Hey, I let you guys out of the closet in 1993," says the commander-in-chief.

Next comes a well-dressed procession: a Florida drug dealer, a Russian mobster, a Chinese arms dealer, a Middle East oil broker, and a banker. "We came for coffee and got lost," says the banker. "We'll leave our contributions on the way out."

Peering further into the closet, the Clintons see several skeletons.

"There's our old Whitewater partner, Jim McDougal, and his wife, Susan," Clinton says.

"Yes, and Gennifer Flowers and Paula Jones," the first lady adds caustically.

"What's this up on the shelf?" asks the president. "It looks like a box of files."

H. R. Clinton slams the door shut.

"Honey, that's enough closet cleaning for today."

*February 13, 2007*

## Clinton Stars in 44 Videos, But Can't Hear Critics' Voices

President Clinton can't seem to make up his mind whether he wants to be Richard Nixon or Ronald Reagan.

On the one hand, the White House stonewalling of a Senate investigating committee is remarkably Nixonian. But considering what happened to that ill-fated president and his administration, it's hard to believe the similarity is anything but coincidental.

A more likely scenario is that Clinton, former governor of Arkansas, is trying to adopt the persona of the former governor of California. Earlier this year he donned the mantle of fiscal conservativism that former President Reagan wore so well. In recent days we have learned that Clinton also has a hearing problem and has appeared in a series of movies.

Washington correspondents well recall a familiar Reagan gesture, when asked an unwelcome question. He would cup his hand to his ear and shake his head, as if not understanding. Clinton, up to this point, has avoided truthful answers by saying he did not remember committing certain acts, or that he did not know what was going on in his White House.

The defense of incompetence, as Sen. Fred Thompson, R-Tenn., says, is "wearing thin." So now the president's strategy apparently will be to turn a deaf ear to media inquiries or congressional requests regarding the scandalous fund-raising practices of his last campaign.

Clinton's doctors have concluded, the *Washington Post* reports, that years of rock 'n' roll music, marching bands and campaign events have taken such a toll on his ears that they have fitted him for hearing aids. (Interestingly, the day after this was done, Clinton attended a Secret Service demonstration at which three rocket-propelled grenades were exploded, rocking the ground at his feet.)

The *Post* said Clinton will have a hidden hearing device in each ear, but will only use them in settings "where he typically has had trouble hearing, such as receptions or political fund-raisers." There could have been some embarrassing conversations:

"I like your vice president, Al Gore."

"Yeah, you're right. He is a bore."

"Are you worried about the testimony of the aide you fired, Harold Ickes?"

"No, it's been a long time since I got any hickeys."

"I hope there won't be a special prosecutor."

"Did you say prostitute? Where?"

Maybe the president also should be fitted with eyeglasses, so he will be able to see a video camera in use at fund-raising coffees held in the White House. A

Reaganesque Clinton is the star of 44 movies that suddenly were discovered and turned over to Thompson's investigating committee last weekend, without bothering to tell Attorney General Janet (See No Evil) Reno.

One of Reagan's well-known films was *Bedtime for Bonzo*. Clinton could make a sequel, *Lincoln Bedroom Time for Bonzo*, if his aides can figure out how to get a campaign contribution from a chimpanzee.

"Sir, we need a ruling from Janet Reno."

"What's the latest on El Nino?"

*October 9, 1997*

## Clinton Strains, But GOP Flush With Success on Two-Potty Issue

President Clinton is facing the biggest trial of his political career. No, not the Paula Jones sexual harassment trial—although he will have to pause in his march to the new millennium to give a deposition, with his accuser present no less. And her lawyers probably won't even let the president show the photo of him dancing with the first lady on the beach—you know, the picture he loved so much but hated the "invasion of privacy."

Problems with women are old hat to Bill Clinton, and he'll take this one in stride. The big challenge lies in the public policy arena, where he faces strong competition from the Republican-controlled Congress. Unless he demonstrates superb leadership, Clinton will lose all hope of seeing his face on Mount Rushmore.

It's not that he hasn't tried to build a legacy. The president has set noble goals, such as making Saddam Hussein behave and reconciling differences between the two White House pets, Socks the cat and Buddy the dog. In both instances, success is elusive.

Looking to the mid-term elections, Clinton has reached out to many constituencies with an activist agenda that includes child care assistance for young parents, Medicare benefits for early retirees, pension tax breaks and expanded AIDS treatment. After the Hong Kong bird flu scare, he called for tougher food inspection. And as mail bomber Ted Kaczynski went to trial, he urged Congress to ban human cloning.

All the while Clinton advocated programs that spell bigger government, he sought to outscore Republicans by promising a balanced budget next year. But the president should not get overconfident. The GOP has not been resting on its hindquarters.

As members of the party closely identified with eliminating waste, Republicans on Capitol Hill have plunged into an issue that touches every American, every day. They have launched The Great Toilet Crusade. The chief toilet plunger is Rep. Joe Knollenberg, R-Mich., who is leading a battle against a federal mandate for smaller toilet tanks.

Flush with success, Knollenberg has lawmakers standing in line to become co-sponsors of a bill to repeal a 1992 law that regulates how much water a toilet can use in every flush. New toilets are required to consume less than 1.6 gallons per flush, compared to 3.5 gallons for older commodes. But users complain the new-fangled toilets don't do the job. They require flushing two or three times instead of once, and they tend to clog more often.

Americans aren't taking the matter sitting down. Knollenberg points to an overflow of mail from irate voters across the country, some of it written on bathroom tissue, bearing the message: "Get the government out of my toilet!"

The movement, so to speak, should offer relief to Republicans who need an issue that cuts across regional, ethnic, and party lines. Thus far, Clinton hasn't got a handle on it, but when his pollsters reveal how many voters use the toilet daily, he might feel the urge. Otherwise, his future could be going down the drain.

*January 15, 1998*

## President Might Like to Put Space Between Himself and Scandals

All systems are go, as dedicated space cadets like to say, for Sen. John Glenn of Ohio, first American to orbit the Earth, to do it again next October at age 77. But as we know, after viewing the mishaps of space station Mir, anything can happen.

Politics—shock, shock—can enter into the space program. In fact, Glenn said in a recent television interview that back in the 1960s, after he had made his historic flight, then-President John F. Kennedy ordered him grounded, for reasons unclear.

The same thing could happen again. President Clinton, an admirer (and emulator) of the oversexed 35th president, might decide JFK had the right idea. He could knock Glenn off the planned space shuttle flight. Hey, with his power, Clinton could even change the mission.

The president might conclude that no more research is necessary on the durability of elderly people going around in circles in a thin air environment, considering the governmental experience of 95-year-old Sen. Strom Thurmond, R-S.C. Instead he could choose to send up a group of pioneers to establish a colony on the Moon.

That would be a great way to get rid of some scandalous baggage from his administration, and perhaps divert attention from Paula Jones, on the eve of the mid-term elections. Talk about an October surprise!

As captain of the crew, what better choice than the first lady, H. R. Clinton, who is a constant reminder to voters of the Whitewater scandal. Just last week she gave sworn testimony to independent counsel Kenneth Starr. (Then after paying a well-publicized visit to church with her freshly-deposed husband, she spent the weekend cleaning out White House closets. Who knows how many files she shredded!)

In that same week, several other Clinton friends, former associates and appointees earned tickets for the Moon mission:

- James McDougal, former business partner of the Clintons, had his conviction in the Whitewater land development scheme upheld by a federal appeals court, making him a good pick for second-in-command.

- Labor Secretary Alexis Herman came under Justice Department investigation for alleged influence-peddling when she was a White House aide. She could unionize any aliens found.

- Interior Secretary Bruce Babbitt appeared to be a target for an independent probe in connection with the rejection of an Indian casino application opposed by tribes who contributed $300,000 to the Democratic party. Put him in charge of finding water.

- Former Housing and Urban Development Secretary Henry Cisneros' ex-mistress pleaded guilty to 28 felony counts for lying about hush money he paid her to keep their affair secret. Cisneros could build moon huts.

- Mike Espy, Clinton's former agriculture secretary awaiting trial for accepting illegal gifts from agribusinesses, was back in the news when two Tyson Foods executives were charged with giving Espy $12,000 in gratuities. Let him look for plant life.

With new scandals breaking, Clinton might jump aboard himself.

*January 22, 1998*

## HRC Is Commander-in-Chief in War for State of Clinton Union

First, a denial. Although this column frequently is critical of President Clinton, this writer will look you in the eye and deny, deny, deny being part of a "vast right-wing conspiracy"—to use the words of First Lady H. R. Clinton—dedicated to destroying him.

At the most, as my editors would tell you, this is only a "half-vast" effort to destroy a president who seems bent on self-destruction.

Besides, if Clinton's chief defender is referring to those most responsible for making Monica Lewinsky a household word, that would be *Newsweek* and the *Washington Post*—aided and abetted by former Clinton confidant George Stephanopoulos. What self-respecting right-winger would want to be in that kind of company?

Whatever her misdirected motives may be, the first lady without question is in full command of a retaliatory attack to try to save her presidency. Her top general, "Mad Dog" James Carville, said flatly, "There's going to be a war."

Her first maneuver was to bring in reinforcements to strengthen the ranks of presidential advisers, drafting administration expatriates Mickey Kantor and Harold Ickes to help plot strategy. She chose not to tap such private sector resources as former Sens. Bob Packwood and Gary Hart, ex-Clinton strategizer Dick Morris, Marv (The Biter) Albert and actor Woodie Allen. Their advice on relationships with women would have been most appropriate for the current situation.

Meanwhile, Clinton polished his State of the Union speech and practiced talking about "the education of our young people" with a straight face and adopting a convincing look of sincerity when using the terms "accountability" and "responsibility."

It's anybody's guess whether Clinton will survive his latest accusation of scandalous behavior. Public opinion polls indicate wide tolerance for adultery by our country's leader, but people do like to know what mischief he is up to. The fact is, he and future presidents could prevent problems of this type by one simple act—just change the Constitution to read:

"The president and the first lady shall from time to time give to the Congress information on the State of Their Union ..."

If that change had been in effect, Clinton's Tuesday night address might have gone like this:

"Rarely have Americans lived through so much change in so short a time in so many ways. With gathering force, the ground has shifted beneath our feet. We have met the challenge. We have moved past the sterile debate.

"Because of our hard work and high purpose, the state of our union is strong.

"But we must stand up for our interests and stand against the poisoned appeals of extreme conservatism. We must combat an unholy axis of right wing conspirators: independent counsels, scorned women and hostile news media, who have unleashed their weapons of mass destruction.

"Now is not the time to walk off the field and forfeit our two-term victory. I say to our enemies: you cannot defy the will of Hillary Rodham Clinton."

*January 29, 1998*

## Titillating TV Talk Makes Some Viewers Gasp and Others Yawn

Maybe it's time to do as First Lady H. R. Clinton instructed: just take a deep breath and relax about the sordid story of the middle-aged president and the young White House intern. But isn't heavy breathing what started this whole thing?

Everybody's talking about Bill Clinton, the hot sax man, and the Spice Girls—Gennifer Flowers, Paula Jones, Kathleen Willey, Monica Lewinsky and Janet Reno (just threw that in for shock value).

Public reaction to the latest Clinton scandal has ranged on the breath control spectrum from gasping to yawning. On the banks of the Potomac, even the most callous observers have found their jaws dropping at the graphic descriptions of Monica's adventures in the federal fantasyland. There hasn't been this much prime time discussion of a president's private parts since Ronald Reagan had prostate surgery.

Her attorney, William Ginsburg, is all over the place, artfully making himself a bigger celebrity than Johnny Cochran. In one TV appearance, he joked that he, rather than his client, might accept *Penthouse* magazine's $2 million offer to pose partially nude. Wouldn't that be a violation of our constitutional freedoms? If such offers are being made, maybe someone should start a fund to pay Linda Tripp whatever it takes to keep her clothes on.

As for this notorious secret taper, who once worked for George Bush, she is said to be writing a book about sex, spanning two administrations. Wonder if she'll title it, "Bush Chastity and the Comeback Kid"?

Linda's former friend, Monica, is reported to have made 37 trips to the White House after she left her job in the West Wing. That's more after hours visits than the pizza delivery guy makes. And it's a good bet she wasn't there to help Chelsea with her homework.

If White House officials have learned anything from his experience, it's that they need an authoritative figure in charge of interns—someone like Dr. Ruth.

It's a sad time for our country, but late night TV comics don't think so. There's so much tawdry humor on the Internet some computer users fear monitor meltdown. Even regular newscasts are running parental warnings, but that's not good enough for Senator Stump. He is considering legislation to require a V-chip on sets to block the PBS Jim Lehrer Report.

That isn't to say the current scandal hasn't served to broaden our educational horizons, such as probing the question of what constitutes intimate relations. *Washington Post* columnist Tony Kornheiser entered this scholarly debate with the observation: "I also don't believe oral history is history."

So much for the "gasp" type reactions. Much of the citizenry seems to be yawning about the president and his paramours. With each new revelation, his popularity rises, making some TV news shows look silly. A graphic high-tech opener screaming, "Crisis in the White House", followed by a sober pronouncement that "the president's approval rating is soaring" doesn't make much sense.

But that's Washington for you.

*February 5, 1998*

## You Can't Fool the Original Occupant of the Lincoln Bedroom

Abraham Lincoln had a birthday wish—to return to Earth for one day and do a Barbara Walters interview. Permission was granted by the heavenly powers, on condition that he could say nothing new but only share with the current generation bits of wisdom and wit he uttered during his life in the 19th century. Here's a portion of the interview:

Q: Mr. President, I'm sure you've been following the events of the past few weeks involving the current chief executive, Bill Clinton. Did you ever find yourself in that kind of situation?

A: Others have been made fools of by the girls, but this can never with truth be said of me.

Q: President Clinton is alleged to have told a former White House intern, Monica Lewinsky, to deny having a relationship with him that involved sex in his study off the Oval Office. Wasn't that pretty foolish?

A: I never encourage deceit; and falsehood, especially if you have got a bad memory, is the worst enemy a fellow can have.

Q: Some present and former White House staffers, as well as the president's friend, Vernon Jordan, apparently have told a federal grand jury they are unaware of any improper relationship between this 24-year-old girl and her 51-year-old boss.

A: We better know there is fire whence we see much smoke rising than we could know it by one or two witnesses swearing to it. The witnesses may commit perjury, but the smoke cannot.

Q: President Clinton seems to have been caught in a lie, in saying six years ago he had not had an affair with Gennifer Flowers but more recently admitting it. What about that?

A: Reports are often false, and always false when made by a knave to cloak his knavery.

Q: What do you think about those accusing the independent counsel, Kenneth Starr, of leaking grand jury testimony?

A: I believe it is an established maxim in morals that he who makes an assertion without knowing whether it is true or false is guilty of falsehood, and the accidental truth of the assertion does not justify or excuse him.

Q: What could President Clinton do to end the slanderous attacks on his credibility?

A: Truth is generally the best vindication against slander.

Q: How important is it for the leader of the country to have the trust of the American people?

A: If you once forfeit the confidence of your fellow citizens, you can never regain their respect and esteem. It is true that you may fool all the people some of the time, you can even fool some of the people all the time; but you can't fool all the people all the time.

Q: How do you react to Clinton's use of the Lincoln Bedroom to reward big Democratic campaign contributors, saying he was forced to do it to keep up with the Republicans?

A: He reminds me of the man who murdered both his parents, and then when sentence was about to be pronounced, pleaded for mercy on grounds he was an orphan.

Q: Do you have any advice for Democrats and Clinton supporters in general?

A: Stand with him while he is right, and part with him when he goes wrong.

*February 12, 1998*

## One American Family Conversation That Shouldn't Be Taped

Mr. and Mrs. America sat down to dinner and the conversation centered on the day's events:

"How was your day, dear?"

"Well, you know, everybody at the office has been on edge since the board chairman got caught with that prostitute in his car a few weeks ago."

"I still can't believe he was dumb enough to do something like that."

"Pretty embarrassing, all right. His wife has been very supportive. She blamed it on a vast left-wing conspiracy."

"Just because he's head of a large Christian book publishing firm."

"We weren't sure how the shareholders would react. But they met today. He told them we'd had the best quarter in years. Earnings set a new high, because of record-breaking sales of our 'Modern Morality' series. And the stock price is soaring."

"The shareholders must have been happy."

"When they heard all that, they forgot all about the hooker incident. Everybody told him he was doing a great job."

"That's what they hired him for. Who cares what he does in his personal life?"

"What about your day?"

"Nothing much. The postman was right on time, in spite of the snow. I invited him in for a cup of coffee. He made a pass at me."

"I'm not surprised, what with all those extramarital affairs he has had. And then to lie about it …"

"So what? He delivers the mail, doesn't he?"

"That's true. Did you get anything done about those leaks in the upstairs bathroom?"

"Yes, the plumber came this afternoon and guess what? No more leaks."

"That's great. He's such a likeable guy …"

"A real charmer …"

"And he does his job so well. That's what people care about, not that prison term he served for raping a teen-ager."

"I know. Our plumbing is in the best shape it has ever been. But there's something I should tell you. He was still here when Veronica came home from school. She's got a mad crush on him, you know."

"They do seem unusually close. I asked him about that one time and he assured me there was absolutely nothing improper about their relationship."

"Well, I walked in on them today."

"Oh?"

"She was holding his pipe wrench and he was leering at her."

"I guess I'm going to have to talk to that young lady!"

"Now wait a minute. Remember, he is a good plumber. Almost everybody we know approves of his job performance."

"Yes, but our daughter may know something we don't."

"Oh, come on. You're beginning to sound like that guy, Kenneth Starr, who's after President Clinton."

*February 19, 1998*

## With Space Cadet Gore in Charge, Beware of Geeks Bearing GIFs

With President Clinton out of the country for an extended spring break from scandal investigations, thoughts naturally turned to the man left minding the store. It is a pleasure to note that no major bimbo eruptions occurred with Vice President Al Gore in charge.

Gore's big thing is technology, not sexology. If he and a White House intern secluded themselves in a private office, they probably would be playing computer games. Thus far no smoking tapes have emerged to blacken his Boy Scout image.

As the nation's Number One geek, Gore dreams not of carnal conquests but of technological breakthroughs. His idea of a sexy pinup is a blowup of a photo of the Earth taken by Apollo 17 astronauts, the last men on the moon, in December 1972. He is so turned on by the portrait of the sunlit planet against the blackness of space that he wants to share it with the masses.

So this man who seeks to be our nation's leader, who would assume responsibility for feeding the hungry, curing the sick and delivering the mail on time, has unveiled his great idea for the new century. Gore's plan, conceived in his sleep, is to make the "blue marble" image of the Earth continuously available through live video to all the people of the world through television and, with a GIF-type graphic, the Internet.

Because the vice president awoke at 3 a.m. one night with this brilliant inspiration, the National Aeronautics and Space Administration is embarked on a crash program to make it a reality by 2000. The project requires launching a 330-pound spacecraft, equipped with an eight-inch telescope and a high-definition color camera, to orbit the sun in a position to focus constantly on the sunny side of the planet. NASA hopes to hold the cost below $50 million.

As Lincoln is remembered for freeing the slaves and FDR for his leadership in the Great Depression and World War II, Gore's presidency—if voters are foolish enough to make that happen—would produce a different kind of legacy. Gore's place in history would be marked by a gimmick that has doubtful scientific value and is hardly more exciting than *The Weather Channel.*

The American public has decided that what an elected official does in bed is his private business. So if Gore wants to dream of space-age pie in the sky, who can criticize?

The project got off to a ragged start. When the *Washington Post* printed a front-page picture of the Earth "upside down," an agitated Gore demanded a correction. *Post* editors humored him but wondered: "in space … upside down to whom?"

The chances of this boondoggle coming off seem improbable, given the recent experience of Gore's office in matters technological. Just ask Sen. Daniel Patrick Moynihan, D-N.Y. He received an official letter from the vice president saying he was "pleased to learn about the recent birth of your twins." Moynihan, 71, hasn't had a newborn in 40 years. Sen. Orrin Hatch, R-Utah, also got one of the computer-generated letters.

Congratulations are not in order.

*April 2, 1998*

## Why Does a Turkey Cross the Road? Just Ask Bill Clinton

There seems to be general agreement that President Clinton should be punished for fooling around with a young woman—and then lying about it—when he should have been tending to business in the Oval Office. The question is whether an appropriate punishment is impeachment or something else.

A common practice in the courts, if a judge is inclined to be lenient, is to sentence a guilty party to some kind of public service. Since Clinton is not experienced in the private sector, in his case that means a government assignment to pay for his crimes.

One possibility would be to require the penitent president to spend Thanksgiving Day answering questions on the U.S. Department of Agriculture's Meat and Poultry Hotline. The hotline staff gets more than 130,000 calls a year, most of them at this season when amateur chefs may be struggling with the complexities of preparing the traditional bird. Some of the inquiries are quite bizarre, like: "Can I serve the turkey I ran over with the car?"

If Clinton were on the line today, this is how he might field some of the questions that come in:

Q: How do I thaw a turkey?

A: My best advice in dealing with this problem is that you stretch it out as long as you can, all the while denying that the problem exists. At the end of that period, if you have created a stench, ask for forgiveness.

Q: How do I stuff a turkey?

A: That all depends on your definition of "stuff." I would have to consult with my lawyers before I could give you an appropriate answer. But let me say this. I will be working hard to find a solution to this crisis that threatens the future of the children of America, as I have done throughout my administration.

Q: Is it OK to thaw a turkey in the toilet?

A: That decision is contingent on the size of your turkey. As you know, the Clinton-Gore administration counts among its greatest achievements the actions we have taken to reduce the size of America's toilets, so that a flush requires only 1.6 gallons of water. I will say this: Whatever you do in the privacy of your toilet is nobody's business but yours. It is time to stop prying into private lives and get on with our national life.

Q: Can I defrost a turkey in the attic?

A: No, but it's a good place to hide incriminating files.

Q: I would rather just cook a turkey breast for my boy friend, but my visiting brother likes drumsticks. Can you give me some guidance?

A: You'd better do a whole turkey. Obviously one is a breast man and the other is a leg man.

Q: Why does a turkey cross the road?

A: To cross the bridge we are building to the 21st century—a bridge wide enough and strong enough for every turkey to cross over to a blessed land of new promise.

Q: My husband bought a live turkey to have for Thanksgiving, but now I am concerned that the turkey is pregnant. What do you ...

A: I want you to listen to me. I did not have sexual relations with that turkey. These allegations are false. And I need to go back to work for the American people.

*November 26, 1998*

## Feeling Like a Stranger in Mr. C. J.'s New Neighborhood

Parents who worry about explaining the Clinton impeachment trial to their youngsters might find the answer in a children's story called "Mr. C. J.'s New Neighborhood.":

Mr. C. J. sat on a high perch looking out over his new playground. He was not happy.

In his old neighborhood, he had eight nice playmates. They had lots of fun together, talking about things like the census, abortion and civil rights. In this new place called the Senate, everybody was a stranger. He didn't feel at home.

He wasn't afraid. In fact, they were afraid of him, because he was so big. But he was uneasy. He could feel them looking at him, checking out the stripes on his designer robe from Gilbert and Sullivan.

He knew they had to accept him, and they had to call him "Mr. C. J." It was one of the rules of "the game." The name of the game was "impeachment." It was a strange game and it had some strange rules that all the players had to follow. And he was supposed to be running the game!

Mr. C. J. didn't find the game to be much fun, and his face showed it. Oh, how he wanted to be back home, tossing paper wads at his friend, Tony Scalia. He could hardly wait to tell his old pals about this dumb game.

Under the rules, the president of the country, Billy Clinton, was "it" and he had to try to escape. But he wasn't even there to play. There were two sides, and his friends were there playing for him.

One side was called the "House managers" and each of the players had to be called "Mr. Manager." Their goal was to catch Billy and make him pay a penalty. The other side was called "the president's counsel." They wanted Billy to be punished, too, but not as much.

There were 100 other players, called senators, and they had to be called "ladies and gentlemen," whether they acted like it or not. They had the hardest part of the game, because they had to sit on the sidelines and not say anything until the "managers" and the "counsel" had finished playing. Then they would decide how the game ended.

To start the game, a boy called the sergeant-at-arms came out and said, "Hear ye, hear ye, hear ye" and some other strange words. Then, first one side and then the other sent their players onto the field to make long speeches.

Mr. C. J. had to stand up and stretch while more than one of the managers was talking. Later he wondered why he had to sit there and look at the sour face of "Counsel" Davey Kendall when he could be hanging out with Sandy O'Connor.

Something else bothered Mr. C. J. If he was in charge of the game, why did he have to ask someone else how to rule on word fights between players? When this "parliamentarian" said they could "only object to an answer and not to a question," he felt like he was in a Dr. Seuss story.

When the game finally was over, he rushed home to tell his playmates about his experience. The first he saw was Clarence Thomas. Mr. C. J. smiled as he said, "Clarence, you'll never believe what happened in the Senate!"

*January 28, 1999*

## Love Notes From a Mighty Ruler to Queens of His Heart

We should pause and take note of the fact that the world has a new king, the product of events that shocked a nation and perhaps altered the course of history.

He lives in a great white castle in the capital city, and his name is King William. His subjects fondly refer to him as William the Rogue. He was not born to the throne but rather achieved his royal status when the people decided to abandon the principles of democracy and justice on which their country was founded and to confer supreme power on their leader.

Secure in his reign, he sat basking in his high popularity as the Minister of Female Relations answered his summons.

"How goes it, my liege?" the minister inquired.

"Great!" said the king. "I feel so good that I might issue a decree commuting the sentence of everyone serving prison terms for perjury and obstruction of justice."

"A most benevolent gesture, your majesty. Now, how may I serve you?"

"With Valentine's Day approaching, I wish to dictate some notes to dispatch to certain special women. The first is to Monica what's-her-name:

"The sex we didn't have was hot and raw,

"But I did nothing wrong. I am above the law.

"You gave good witness to the lies I didn't tell.

"No one should be surprised. I taught you very well.

"Your love still warms my heart, and though I've ruined your life,

"It could have been much worse: you could have been my wife."

"Very good, sir. Who is next?"

"This is to Lady Dianne:

"Your words of censure were rough as a cob,

"But better that than losing my job.

"You want to save face for Democrats.

"For that I send sincere congrats.

"My heart is yours, Dianne Feinstein,

"You'll always be my valentine."

"The lady will love it."

The session was interrupted by the sudden entry of Crown Prince Albert.

"A thousand pardons, your highness. Have you heard about Jordan?" he said.

"Yeah. Vernon was a terrific witness."

"I bring good news, mighty ruler. I have traveled throughout the kingdom, from Hollywood to Harlem, and everywhere I go the people love you."

"That is true. The Polling Ministry has so informed me. Now, begone," said the king. "Let's see, where were we? Who am I forgetting? Oh, yes. To Queen Hillary:

"I beat the odds, though I'll not gloat,
"Because you didn't rock the boat.
"My heart belongs to only you.
"I might mislead, but I'll be true.
"When you're in New York, I'll really be down.
"How soon will you be leaving town?"

*February 11, 1999*

## Senators Who Saved Clinton's Job Offer Odd Testimonials

Bill Clinton had enough friends in the U.S. Senate to beat the impeachment charges leveled against him. But it is interesting, if unsettling, to scan the Congressional Record and read some of the things these senators had to say about the man they wanted to continue holding the most prestigious office in the land:

"In my view, the president violated the public trust and brought dishonor to the office he holds."—Tom Daschle, D-S.D., Democratic leader.

"I am convinced that the president acted to circumvent the law."—John Chafee, R-R.I.

"His legacy will be tainted … because of his selfish and disgraceful behavior."—Patty Murray, D-Wash.

"The president is an adulterer and liar."—Joe Biden, D-Del.

"I believe the behavior of the president was wrong, reckless, and immoral."—Barbara Mikulski, D-Md.

"… what was done was clearly wrong … indefensible."—John Breaux, D-La.

"The president's conduct was inexcusable."—Patrick Leahy, D-Vt.

"He has shamed himself, his family, and the nation."—Frank Lautenberg, D-N.J.

"The president has indeed committed shameful acts, misled the American people and brought disrepute on the office."—Jim Jeffords, R-Vt.

"I condemn the president's behavior."—Barbara Boxer, D-Calif.

"… deplorable on every level."—Bob Kerrey, D-Neb.

"… shameful, despicable, unworthy, a disgrace to his office."—Paul Wellstone, D-Minn.

"Simply put, his conduct was disgraceful and possibly illegal."—Herbert Kohl, D-Wis.

"President Clinton has engaged in … conduct which has severely sullied and demeaned his tenure as president."—Paul Sarbanes, D-Md.

"All of us condemn it. He failed to tell the truth about it, and he misled the country for many months."—Ted Kennedy, D-Mass.

"His deception was calculated, politically motivated, and directed at each and every one of us."—Charles Robb, D-Va.

"He lied under oath, he sought to interfere with the evidence, he tried to influence the testimony of key witnesses …"—Susan Collins, R-Maine.

"Rather than ennobling the presidency, his behavior has been the butt of jokes and ridicule."—Tom Harkin, D-Iowa.

"The president lied to his countrymen, to family, friends, to all of us."—John Kerry, D-Mass.

"… misleading false statements to his staff, his cabinet, the country … abhorrent."—Chris Dodd, D-Conn.

"… he betrayed not only his family but the public's trust, and undermined his moral authority and public credibility."—Joe Lieberman, D-Conn.

"When the president … breaks the law himself by lying under oath, he undermines the system of justice and law on which this republic has its foundation."—Robert Byrd, D-W.Va.

"(His) conduct in this matter is unacceptable for a president …"—Dianne Feinstein, D-Calif., and other advocates of official censure.

We should all have such good friends.

*February 18, 1999*

## Gore Has Way to Go to Overcome Clinton's Lie-ability

As Vice President Al Gore officially begins his quixotic quest for the presidency, many Americans may be wondering if playing fast and loose with the truth has become a primary qualification for holding the nation's highest office.

Certainly Bill Clinton has established a remarkable record of dishonesty and that standard has been endorsed by poll-slavish politicians. Moreover, for his accomplishment, Gore has placed his White House mate in the category of "greatest presidents." It is only natural that such a faithful disciple would follow the path of his leader.

In doing so, Gore has much to learn. Clinton dances around the truth so artfully, you almost have to admire his performance and love the lie. When Gore tells a whopper, it's more like a clown's pratfall, but with less grace.

Take the claim that he and his wife Tipper were the models for the best-selling novel, *Love Story*. Author Eric Segal quickly branded the assertion false. That fib was matched by Gore's protestation of innocence when he was caught seeking political donations from orange-robed nuns. "I didn't know I was in a Buddhist temple," he said.

While the Gore 2000 campaign still has many months to go, the veep's clowning achievement thus far has to be his boast on CNN: "During my service in the United States Congress, I took the initiative in creating the Internet." A cyberspace paternity test would show the Defense Department fathered the Internet in 1969, when Gore was 21 and eight years away from being elected to Congress.

Not to be outdone, Republicans fired back. Senate Majority Leader Trent Lott announced he had created the paper clip. Rep. Dick Armey, his House counterpart, claimed credit for the interstate highway system. Steve Forbes, launching his presidential campaign on the Internet, revealed: "I am Christopher Columbus. I discovered America and wrote the Bill of Rights." Former Vice President Dan ("potato with an e") Quayle said, "If Al Gore created the Internet, then I invented the spell-check."

With such a reputation, Gore is missing a good bet by not capitalizing on it. He passed up some good opportunities in recent initiatives he has announced.

When he promised an all-out effort to ease traffic congestion, he should have mentioned that he was the inventor of the traffic light.

Gore's pledge to ensure safe and clean water with $257 million in new government spending would have sounded more sincere if he had added that he was the first to market Perrier.

In outlining more government regulations to require fair treatment of airline passengers, he should have recalled his first day of flight at Kitty Hawk, N.C.

His call for more safety in labeling of medical prescriptions should have included a reference to his discovery of penicillin.

And when he endorsed a government project to unlock the secrets of the human genetic code, why didn't he say he had cloned that sheep in Scotland?

Gore's got a way to go to be as good a liar as his hero, Bill Clinton.

*March 18, 1999*

## Is What's Happening Really True, or Is It Only April Fools?

Half of these statements are true. The rest are April Fools' jokes. Which is which?

1. President Clinton's ratings have plunged from the 70s at the height of the Monica Lewinsky scandal to the 50s after he ordered an aerial assault on Kosovo.

2. Clinton adviser James Carville recommended a "wag the dog" illicit affair to detract from the bombings.

3. Yugoslavian president Slobodan Milosevic wanted to rid Kosovo of ethnic Albanians, and that has been one of the results of the Clinton-led NATO bombardment.

4. Milosevic sent Clinton a thank you note for comparing him to Adolf Hitler.

5. The president said the U.S. "was wrong" to have become involved in a lengthy civil war that killed countless civilians. He was talking about Guatemala.

6. Margaret Thatcher protested to Clinton because he compared himself to Winston Churchill.

7. While television screens were filled with the horrifying images of war, the "compartmentalization" president played golf.

8. Cuban leader Fidel Castro was shown on TV leading a stadium crowd in singing, "Take Me Out To the Ball Game."

9. First Lady H. R. Clinton, who cancelled a foreign trip and other engagements with her husband because of a "back problem," took a jolting camel ride through the Sahara during her 12-day tour of North Africa.

10. Rev. Jesse Jackson decided not to run for president and will join Dr. Jack Kevorkian in a national effort to register death row inmates to vote.

11. Vice President Al Gore explained why he mistakenly said he had invented the Internet: "I was tired from staying up all night inventing the minicam."

12. Gore chose the one-year anniversary of the Viagra pill to unveil his presidential campaign slogan: "Stand With Me."

13. Sens. Trent Lott, R-Miss., and Robert Byrd, D-W.Va., who kept the Clinton-Lewinsky cigar incident out of the impeachment trial, each received a gift from Clinton after his Central America trip—a very large cigar.

14. Monica called Clinton a "meanie" because the Yugoslavia intervention caused the Russian publisher of her book to cancel the project.

15. Former President George Bush accepted stock in a new company in lieu of an $80,000 speaking fee, and the stock now is worth about $14.4 million.

16. George W. Bush won't have Pennsylvania Gov. Tom Ridge as a running mate—a Bush-Ridge ticket sounds too much like a housing development.

17. House Speaker Dennis Hastert ducked out of a bipartisan congressional civility retreat at Hershey, Pa., to attend the NCAA wrestling championships two hours away at Penn State.

18. Delegates to the retreat voted to take a pay cut instead of an increase in their $136,700 annual salary endorsed by Hastert and Democratic leader Dick Gephardt.

19. Zoological experts in Japan reported a decline in the sex drive of elephants.

20. Republican party symbols Bob Dole and Strom Thurmond were named honorary chairmen of the GOP 2000 campaign for president.

(Odd-numbered statements are based on actual events.)

*April 1, 1999*

## There's Nothing Like a War to Get the Media's Attention

The atmosphere was tense in the "war room" at the White House. The president had called a rare meeting of his cabinet. Nervous aides fidgeted, awaiting the arrival of the commander-in-chief. Wearing a disarming smile, Bill Clinton entered and began speaking—his remarks caught on a secretly-smuggled tape:

"Thank you all for coming. I've called this meeting because of some recent reports casting doubt on the success of our military operation in Yugoslavia. I want to assure you that this has been one of the most successful undertakings of the Clinton administration.

"First I should recognize the outstanding achievement of the secretary of state, Madeleine Albright, and the secretary of defense, Bill Cohen. They have performed superbly in their numerous interviews on all the major TV networks.

"Most importantly, I want to congratulate the White House news management team for doing a masterful job of keeping the public focused on the war in the Balkans. Through their efforts I have been able to do the work of the American people without the annoying distraction of scandal.

"I admire their skill in turning attention away from Juanita Broaddrick's charges of rape by the revelation of Chinese theft of nuclear secrets from the Los Alamos lab, and then to chase that story off the front pages of the nation's newspapers by the bombing of Kosovo. Things haven't been the same since.

"If it weren't for the war, people might be hearing more of what Johnny Chung told federal investigators about the $300,000 that the chief of China's military intelligence directed to Democrats to help re-elect me in 1996.

"Hardly anything has surfaced about North Korea's state-sponsored drug trafficking activities. It might be embarrassing if the word got out that this totalitarian dictatorship, which has become the largest recipient of U.S. aid in Asia, sold $71 million worth of cocaine, heroin and other narcotics last year—and that our government knows about it. But, as one of our officials said, 'Everything can't be priority one.'

"And right now Slobodan Milosevic is our top priority. He's even easier to hate than Saddam Hussein. And we're the good guys fighting to bring him into submission.

"As a result, the news media have forgotten all about Monica Lewinsky. Of course, that great interview I had with Dan Rather put that whole impeachment thing in the right perspective. Reporters aren't even interested in the vice president's boo-boos about inventing the Internet and shoveling hog manure on the family farm. You can thank me, and the joint chiefs of staff, for that, Al.

"If the TV correspondents weren't busy interviewing Albanian refugees, can you imagine what they'd be doing with the Susan McDougal trial? And that traitor, George Stephanopolous, and his book tour have dropped off the radar screen.

"What's best, Republicans are beating up on each other about backing the NATO attack or not.

"Who said war is hell? It's the best thing we've got going for us."

*April 8, 1999*

## Questions About Campaign 2000? Ask Political Answer Man

Rather than comment on President Clinton and NATO, the gang that couldn't bomb straight, let's peek in on a political science class at Millard Fillmore University, where Professor U. S. Polltaker, talk-radio's "political answer man," is fielding questions from students:

Q: Democrats received substantial contributions from Chinese sources for the last presidential campaign. What are the chances of that happening again?

A: As Confucius might say: "He who look at gift horse through bombsight apt to get kicked in teeth." Besides, Johnny Chung is too busy testifying before Congress to set up any fund-raising events.

Q: It appears the Democratic nomination for president will come down to a choice of Vice President Al Gore or former Senator and basketball player Bill Bradley. What are the differences between them?

A: Bradley is taller.

Q: What are Gore's biggest handicaps?

A: Clinton, Kosovo and himself.

Q: Among Republicans, Texas Gov. George W. Bush is the current front-runner. Where would he prefer to run his campaign?

A: Deep in the heart of Texas.

Q: If Bush is elected, will his father have a position in the administration?

A: It certainly won't be tax adviser.

Q: Can you suggest a campaign theme for former vice president Dan Quayle?

A: "A Man For Tomorrowe."

Q: Do you believe candidates will spend as much money in the next campaign as in the last one?

A: Even Steve Forbes, who used $37 million of his own funds last time, is starting to ask for handouts.

Q: Do you expect much negative campaigning in the 2000 race?

A: It has already begun. There was a rumor about Forbes' reaction to his first subway ride: "I never saw so many people. They were crowded in like caviar." It is being whispered that when Lamar Alexander was in college he experimented with having a personality—but he didn't inhale.

Q: Republican Rep. John Kasich of Ohio campaigns in places like pool halls and bowling alleys. Do you have any advice for him?

A: He needs to go to at least one tractor pull and a goat roping.

Q: Have we heard the last of Monica Lewinsky?

A: After that appearance on *Saturday Night Live*, not by a long shot. There will be reruns, you know.

Q: Why didn't Democratic Sen. Robert Byrd of West Virginia get a ticket when the Cadillac he was driving rear-ended a van in the Virginia suburbs?

A: He has "congressional immunity," according to the Constitution, and the senator just happened to have a copy of the document in his pocket.

Q: Dennis Hastert, who succeeded Newt Gingrich as speaker of the House, is said to be determined to stay low-key. How well is Hastert succeeding?

A: Who?

*May 13, 1999*

## Clinton's Advice to Gore Might Include Campaign Checklist

Bill Clinton must be banging on the bongos and puffing big cigars. Not since the judge threw out the Paula Jones case has he had so much to celebrate—unless you count that little old impeachment victory.

Clinton's old buddy, Boris Yeltsin, survived an attempt by the Russian parliament to impeach him. That gives the American president something to talk about, besides brunettes and booze, the next time the two leaders meet.

NATO planes haven't bombed any more embassies in Yugoslavia, and the U.S. ambassador to China, Jim Sasser, gained his freedom without any help from Rev. Jesse Jackson.

The president raised $2 million for Democrats at a Hollywood fund raiser in spite of a slap with a wet noodle at filmmakers who use violence in movies to attract audiences.

His political hero, Thomas Jefferson, was vindicated for an affair with an employee when descendants of his slave, Sally Hemings, were invited to a Jefferson family reunion.

A poll taken by the Republican party shows voters still favor Democrats the most on Social Security and education issues.

And the Clinton administration's preferred candidate, Ehud Barak, won election as Israel's prime minister with the help of Clinton adviser James Carville. Barak's defeat of Benjamin Netanyahu was viewed as a boost for Vice President Al Gore in his campaign for president in the 2000 elections.

Gore obviously needs all the help he can get. Just in case anybody didn't know the Gore campaign was off to a balky start, Clinton called up a *New York Times* reporter to share his concerns. As Gore's self-appointed campaign manager, Clinton said he had coached the veep on how to dress (ditch the blue suit), to loosen up (plunge into crowds) and to appear less rigid ("I have told him to go out and have a good time").

Who knows? Clinton even might have provided Gore with a checklist of smart things to do, based on his own 1992 campaign for president:

- Go on stage with a political rival and laugh at a dirty, tasteless joke about another candidate.

- Call your mistress in the middle of the campaign so she can tape you calling the Democratic governor of a key electoral state a thug.

• Go on national television with your wife and issue a denial, which you later will have to retract, about having a lengthy affair.

• Devise a strategy for handling "bimbo eruptions."

• Make a lot of campaign promises, aimed at various voter constituencies, that you don't intend to keep.

• Have your campaign aides unflinchingly spin the news media at every opportunity, lying if necessary.

Now that's the way to "go out and have a good time."

Gore seems to be taking at least some of the advice his boss gave him. A photographer caught him coatless and smiling at an airport rally in Iowa.

To meet an increasingly strong challenge from former Sen. Bill Bradley, maybe Gore will even go so far as to hire Carville, whose motto is: "It's hard for somebody to hit you when you've got your fist in their face."

*May 20, 1999*

## It's Back to Politics for the Clintons After Six Days in a Zoo

President Clinton is back from vacation and political junkies want to know: how did he and his wife spend their time together? The president and first lady left the campaign trail to hide out in Florida for six days last week. There was so much secrecy surrounding their getaway that even Chinese espionage agents must have been hard pressed to find out details of what went on.

The first couple holed up at the White Oak Plantation, a private complex at Yulee, Fla., covering 7,500 acres. Well, at least they could put plenty of space between them if they so desired. They stayed in a two-story, cedar-paneled five-bedroom house that overlooked a pool, tennis court and nine-hole golf course.

White Oak also is a nature preserve and is home to 400 animals, including tigers, panthers, antelopes, giraffes, zebras and rhinoceroses. The question arises, if President Clinton wanted to spend a week in a zoo, why did he leave the nation's capital?

He apparently related well with some of the endangered species—he seems to consider himself in that category after being impeached. Since the Monica Lewinsky scandal it was the only kind of exotic wildlife experience he has been allowed to enjoy.

The president told an *Associated Press* reporter he took delight in feeding pine cones to some rhinos. Aren't their horns supposed to have the properties of an aphrodisiac? Not that Bill Clinton ever needed one.

First Lady H. R. Clinton went to the retreat by way of Ireland, Macedonia and New York, and her husband flew in from Texas where he made an awkward joint appearance with Vice President Al Gore. The event called attention to Clinton's recent criticism of the Gore campaign. The veep, in a boring, 40-minute speech, mentioned his boss only in an aside.

During his week of seclusion, the only public sighting of Clinton was when he came to the plantation gate to read a statement about Yugoslavian President Slobodan Milosevic's indictment for war crimes. There were no leaked videos of the Clintons dancing on the beach in their swimsuits.

There was contact between the two, however. Clinton said he and his wife discussed her potential run for a U.S. Senate seat in New York. He didn't say whether he advised her to take back one of those tigers to help her do battle with New York Mayor Rudolph Giuliani.

Press secretary Joe Lockhart said Clinton prepared a meal for his wife one evening, but didn't provide the menu. We can only surmise it was a redneck seven-course dinner: a bag of pretzels and a six-pack. Clinton's choice for himself should have been a big slice of humble pie.

As usual, Clinton took along a stack of books to read, including some with provocative titles: *A Reasonable Faith, Sudden Mischief,* and *Lucky You.*

Another vacation pastime is catching up on correspondence. Since Hallmark doesn't make a card that says, "Sorry we bombed your embassy," Clinton might have spent some time writing notes of apology to Switzerland, Sweden, Spain ...

*June 3, 1999*

## In Search of Legacy, Clinton Eats Way Across Hunger Belt

To believe what the pundits say these days, Bill Clinton has a different kind of obsession than the one which threatened his presidency this time a year ago. He is trying to find some kind of legacy to leave behind when he ends his eight-year romp in the White House.

While the lame duck president fights to stay in the public spotlight, his toughest competition comes from close at hand: his vice president, Al (I'm No Bill Clinton) Gore, and his wife, H. R. Clinton, who is telling New Yorkers she's against some policies of the administration she helped build. The celebrity candidate stole most of the attention as she set out to get acquainted with the state she hopes to represent in the U. S. Senate.

The first lady led a pack of 200 reporters on a "listening tour" in which she outwonked both her husband and Gore on such issues as dual-use technologies, telecommuter tax incentives, and managed-care reimbursement formulas—all the buzz among Manhattan cab drivers. She also shopped for a new place to live, eyeing a $3.8 million house on 18 acres in North Salem, N.Y. Well, that beats a "carpetbagger condo."

Gore did manage to make some news when he hired as his senior media adviser a Washington lobbyist who helped the tobacco industry kill an anti-smoking bill pushed by the Clinton-Gore administration last year. That sort of makes a mockery of Gore's promise to "pour my heart and soul into the cause of protecting our children from the dangers of smoking."

The veep and wife Tipper also grabbed a headline with the birth of their first grandson, fortuitously arriving on the Fourth of July. "Clearly, he has a natural gift for timing," said Gore. "It shows his genius, really." (Who knows, he may grow up to be a great inventor like his grandpa.)

As for the president, to get any press at all he had to lay on a four-day cross-country journey to the land of the "have-nots," visiting six areas where the Democrat Great Society's "war on poverty" failed. Clinton didn't say that, of course, talking instead about his new multi-billion-dollar program of federal spending to foster employment for the poor.

(Meanwhile, in Washington a federal agency announced closing of eight supply centers, leaving 2,000 jobless—including blind vendors.)

Traveling with an entourage of bureaucrats and business heads, Clinton dispensed sympathy and hope from Appalachia to Watts, assuring those deprived of such basic necessities as food, clothing and shelter that he does, indeed, feel their pain. But he didn't deprive himself very much.

According to reporters on the trip, here are some of the places he went and what he ate:

- Hazard, Ky.: fried chicken and catfish, beef sirloin, pork tenderloin, fried apples and cornbread.

- Memphis, Tenn.: barbecued ribs, steaks and catfish.

- Clarksdale, Miss.: baby-back ribs, hot tamales, potato salad and cole slaw.

Clinton confided, "I ate too much." Guess you can really work up an appetite fighting poverty and hunger.

*July 15, 1999*

## In Rare Interview, First Lady Reveals Secrets of Marital Bed

For all of us who have been dying to know more about the relationship between Bill and Hillary Clinton (53 by last count), the new *Talk* magazine is a welcome addition to the store of knowledge about this engrossing subject.

Warming up for a high-profile race for the U.S. Senate in New York, the first lady took time out from a "listening tour" of her newly adopted state to do some talking about her marriage to the philandering president. We learned a lot from her interview in the magazine's first edition.

No more "right-wing conspiracy." She admits Clinton has a "weakness" for women, or as they say in Arkansas, he's "a hard dog to keep on the porch." (She may have to explain that expression to sophisticated New Yorkers.)

Although she barely spoke to her husband for months after learning of the Monica Lewinsky affair, she excused his infidelities, comparing herself to Jesus forgiving his disciple, Peter.

She blamed Clinton's extramarital hanky-panky on the fact that his mother and grandmother didn't get along. (Guys, don't try this at home. How many wives bought that line about oral sex not really being sex?)

If she believes all that, and can convince New York voters she's not out of touch with reality, fine and good.

But the most intriguing bit of information, at least for this columnist, was her revelation about the intimacies the Clintons share in the White House these days (when she's not campaigning in New York and he's not out across the country raising money for Democrats):

"We talk," she said. "We talk in the solarium, in the bedroom, in the kitchen—it's just constant conversation.

"We like to lie in bed and watch old movies, you know, those little individual video machines you can hold on your lap."

That sounds like a high-tech gadget no family should be without, but I'll have to confess I didn't even know Vice President Al Gore had invented it. The interviewer wasn't one to probe, so the article revealed nothing more about the device that helped save the Clintons' marriage.

Extensive research turned up an ad for a "portable DVD theater" complete with "custom carrying case" and "lightweight i-glasses," whatever that is. The ad says that with this little gem you can "watch movies anywhere"—including in bed, presumably—and the price is only $1,499.95. (Would anybody want to bet the Clintons got theirs from one of their Hollywood pals?)

Well, if the all-forgiving first lady says her husband has given up fondling women and now only holds a movie machine on his lap, who could be skeptical?

At least their marital relations won't be an issue in her Senate contest with New York Mayor Rudy Giuliani.

Since the publisher of *Talk* isn't on speaking terms with Giuliani after he denied her request to have the magazine launch party at the Brooklyn Navy Yard, we may never learn this much trivia about him.

*August 5, 1999*

## Presidential Politics Is Amusing, But It's Also Confusing

This has been a bad time for humorists. Dan Quayle dropped out of the Y2K presidential race, and John McCain got in, officially.

Poor Dan. He had as much trouble raising money for the big race as he did getting the national commentators to take him seriously. They knew they could always count on Dan Quayle for a laugh.

McCain, on the other hand, is about as funny as a crutch. You can tell he has no sense of humor when he talks about Pat Buchanan.

In addition to this dismal development, real events are providing more comedy than the one-liners crafted by late-night TV show hosts and their writers. How could they top the entrance of Vice President Al Gore at the Democratic National Committee meeting to the strains of "Love Train"? It's one thing to embrace Bill Clinton's programs, but his theme music, too?

And what about the comment by the new DNC chairman, Ed Rendell, that Gore and his opponent, Bill Bradley, don't differ much on issues? He might as well have dubbed the party's two candidates Tweedledum and Tweedledee.

Meanwhile, George W. Bush passed up a big Republican gathering in California in favor of the Ryder Cup matches. He must think he's got the GOP nomination sewed up.

Maybe Bush had better be thinking about the stiff competition he might be facing from a third party or independent candidate. Here are just a few of the potential challengers and what their candidacies might mean:

- Warren Beatty—This liberal Democrat and conservative columnist Arianna Huffington are the odd couple of the year. His role in *Bulworth* led her to promote his run for the White House. Fellow actor Charlton Heston told Beatty he'd consider being his secretary of defense.

- Cybill Shepherd—If Beatty could do it, so could she, the blonde actress decided. *Moonlighting* as president might not be so far-fetched for this member of the "Hollywood Left."

- Pamela Anderson Lee—The former *Baywatch* babe impressed actor Alec Baldwin with a speech on animal rights and he urged her to get into politics. She is Canadian, but that shouldn't be a hindrance, given the voters' apparent tolerance of "carpetbagger" candidates.

- Donald Trump—He has met one of the primary qualifications by writing a book. The wealthy developer, mulling a Reform Party bid, would bring changes to the White House, perhaps turning it into a "Capital Casino."

- Jesse Ventura—The Minnesota governor is still wrestling with a decision on whether to run.

If Gore and Bush do wind up in a November 2000 faceoff, the Texas governor should remember that a politician is only as good as his staff. John McCaslin of the *Washington Times*, chairman of the National Society of Newspaper Columnists conference in Washington next June, invited both men to speak. Gore's scheduler responded quickly, promising an answer closer to the date. Bush's delayed reply was a form letter soliciting financial support—as if he needed it.

*September 30, 1999*

## What Plays in Liberal Boston Is Not the Same in Austin

Up in Boston a wily TV interviewer thinks the governor of Texas ought to be well acquainted with certain foreign leaders. Well, maybe he's right. Imagine this conversation down in Austin between George W. Bush and his secretary:

Bush: I need to talk to the leaders of Chechnya, India, Pakistan and Taiwan.

Secretary: Why?

Bush: I just do. Please get them on the phone, starting with the president of Chechnya.

Secretary: All right. What's his name?

Bush: You mean you don't know the name of the president of Chechnya?

Secretary: No. I know the names of all the governors, every mayor in Texas, and the top officials in Mexico. But Chechnya? No, I'm sorry.

Bush: Well, I just happen to know that his name is, uh, Aslan Maskhadov.

Secretary: Thank you. Hold on a minute. I'll see if I can get him for you. (pause) Governor, I have him on the line.

Bush: Hello, President Maskhadov? May I call you Aslan?

Maskhadov: Good. And I calling you Dubya?

Bush: Sure, okay. Well, how are things in, uh, Grozny today?

Maskhadov: Blosni, blosni.

Bush: Sorry to hear that. Things are fine here. The economy is good, crime is down, the Longhorns beat Oklahoma State.

Maskhadov: But Cowboys lost to Vikings, da?

Bush: Must have a bad connection. But America could be a lot better. I'm running for president, you know.

Maskhadov: Yes, Lee Teng-hui called me from Taiwan last week and told me.

Bush: Yeah, Lee. I think he's returning my call now. So long, and hang in there.

Lee: Hello, governor. Good to hear from you.

Bush: Same here. How's everything with the Taiwanians?

Lee: Taiwanese people very interested in U.S. presidential race. Is it true the vice president, Al Gore, hired a Monica Lewinski look-alike at $15,000 a month to tell him how to be a man?

Bush: Well, I wouldn't have put it quite that way. But feminist author Naomi Wolf is advising him.

Lee: So that's where all those Chinese campaign contributions went.

Bush: Could be—hey, I've got another call coming in. Bye. (pause) Who's this?

Secretary: It's the general.

Bush: The general—oh, uh, Pervez Musharraf of Pakistan. Hello, general? I just wanted to tell you I believe your takeover holds promise for stability in Pakistan—I agree with the Clinton administration on that.

Musharraf: Except for vice president Gore, yes? Also I read in *National Enquirer* he is on diet that makes him do stupid things.

Bush: Nice talkin' to ya. Gotta run. (pause) Let's see, that leaves India's new prime minister, uh, Atal Bihari Vajpayee.

Secretary: I've got him on line one and Bill Gates on line two. Who do you want first?

Bush: What do you think?

*November 11, 1999*

## Thank Heaven For Little Pearls of Presidential Wisdom

On Thanksgiving Day in Heaven, a special table was reserved for U.S. presidents. Before partaking of a feast that included shepherd's pie, Jerusalem artichokes, hot cross buns and angel food cake, they joined in a traditional communal prayer:

"Dear Lord, we're thankful to be here, mere words can never tell,

"We hoped that Heaven would be our home, because we've already been through hell."

As the first course was being served, John Adams could not restrain himself.

"Well, Alex, what do you think of your likeness on the new ten-dollar bill?"

Alexander Hamilton bristled. "Frankly, I liked my hair better on the old one. If I were still running the Treasury department … How about you, Abe? They've given you a makeover, too, on the five."

"As I have observed," said Abraham Lincoln, "In my poor lean, lank face, nobody has ever seen any cabbages sprouting."

"Say, would somebody pass the slaw?" said Grover Cleveland, adjusting his waistcoat.

Sacajawea, leading Meriwether Lewis and William Clark on an expedition to the salad bar, paused at the presidents' table. "Did I hear some grumbling about money? You should complain. A woman only rates a dollar coin."

"I'd gladly trade places with you on the two-dollar bill," muttered Thomas Jefferson.

"Gentlemen," said George Washington, "We shouldn't spend these precious moments prattling about such minor annoyances. We have more important things to discuss, like the current presidential campaign."

"Well, I for one have a favorite candidate," said John Quincy Adams. "As the son of a former president, I like the looks of George W. Bush."

"John McCain, a war hero, is giving him a strong challenge, and I like that," said Dwight D. Eisenhower. "So do I," said Ulysses S. Grant.

"But what about his hot temper?" said Woodrow Wilson.

"What about it!" chorused Theodore Roosevelt, Harry Truman and Lyndon B. Johnson.

"Democrats Al Gore and Bill Bradley aren't very exciting," snorted Andrew Jackson.

"Who needs charisma?" said William Howard Taft, sampling some "heavenly hash."

"I don't know why, but I favor Pat Buchanan," said James Buchanan.

"Can you believe all these third party candidates?" said John F. Kennedy. "Even Warren Beatty and Cybill Shepherd are talking about running."

Lincoln cleared his throat. "I've had a bias against actors ever since that Booth fellow ruined my evening at Ford's Theatre."

Moses, at the next table, interjected: "Personally, I'd like to see Charlton Heston run."

Herbert Hoover loosened his belt and sighed. "Well, it really is an interesting time in American politics, right Cal?"

"Yep," said Calvin Coolidge.

Taking a piece of divinity from the candy tray, Franklin D. Roosevelt pronounced the meal "most delightful."

"Dee-licious!" said cousin Teddy.

A scowling Richard Nixon demurred. "I've had better," he said.

"Then why don't you fix your own dinner?" drawled LBJ.

Nixon replied: "I am not a cook."

*November 25, 1999*

## First Lady Crisis Leaves Voters Feeling Cheated

You know the Christmas season is here when the Washington-Baltimore Bare Buns Family Nudist Club kicks off its annual holiday clothing drive. The 235-member group's president, Gary Brown, said the event "gives us a good feeling." (Goose bumps, even.)

But on to matters of more pressing importance.

Once again, the Clintons have grossly misled the American people. We all remember that in 1992 when Bill Clinton was running for president, he tried to convince voters that his wife, Hillary, would be a great asset to the White House. He went so far as to say that if he were elected, "you'll be getting two for the price of one."

Now look what's happened. The first lady has quit "exploring" a candidacy for the U.S. Senate in New York and announced that she does, indeed, "intend" to run. What's more, she said she will take up residence in the house in Chappaqua, N.Y. that the couple purchased, and that she will be in Washington "from time to time." (When Bill least expects her, no doubt.)

In other words, half of the governing team that the Clinton election gave the nation will be gone from the White House, leaving poor Bill to run the country all by himself. Another broken promise, another breach of faith.

Well, as any government professor will tell you, our present system simply cannot function without a first lady in fulltime residence at 1600 Pennsylvania Avenue. Only once in history has that occurred: during the 1857–1861 term of James Buchanan, the only bachelor president. His niece, Harriett, served as official hostess.

First daughter Chelsea Clinton can't fill in because she's knee-deep in studies at Stanford.

Choosing his words carefully, to preclude a panic on Wall Street, President Clinton publicly acknowledged, "we will have to make some accommodations."

So what are we to do about the vacancy in the Office of First Lady?

The Constitution wisely provides a backup for the chief executive, specifying that in the event of the president's "inability to discharge the powers and duties" of his office, that responsibility falls on the vice president. Although the founding fathers were silent on the subject, it follows that if the first lady is unable to fulfill her traditional role, the wife of the vice president shall perform that function.

That's not likely to happen. First, Sen. Robert Byrd, D-W.Va., would challenge the constitutionality of the action. Second, Vice President Al Gore wants no connection with the Clintons if he is to win the Democratic nomination for president. Third, Tipper Gore has a heavy schedule of her own, advising on mental health and debating Bill Bradley's wife, Ernestine, on the campaign trail.

Here's one possible solution to the first lady crisis: Roger Clinton. The president's half-brother seems an ideal choice to fill the vacuum when H. R. Clinton curtails her travels overseas to go handshaking in Brooklyn. She has been an active emissary for the U.S. in international relations, as in her recent joint appearance with the wife of Palestinian leader Yassir Arafat.

Roger Clinton is poised to have an equally effective impact on American foreign policy. He already is scheduled to display his talents as a rhythm and blues singer at a "Peace and Friendship Concert" in North Korea next month. Cuba could be his next stop on a world tour of communist countries that hate the United States.

On second thought, the country might have to hobble along with only one Clinton in the White House.

*December 2, 1999*

## Forgotten But Not Gone Clinton Returns To Spotlight

Let's hear it for Bill Clinton! Like Mighty Mouse, he has saved the day for journalistic political observers everywhere.

Despite all his notoriety of the past few years, the president who has inspired headlines from the *Christian Science Monitor* to the *National Enquirer* virtually disappeared off the national political radar screen as the 2000 presidential election campaign got underway.

Clinton's disappearance from the nightly news prompted *Washington Post* columnist Tony Kornheiser to mourn, "I keep thinking I'm going to see you on a milk carton."

The capital city's biggest newsmaker had faded into the background so far that he didn't even rate a sketch on *Saturday Night Live*. He did make a few feeble attempts at staying in the public eye, like vetoing Republican tax cuts and approving a medal for ailing Cardinal John O'Connor. But Kathie Lee Gifford got more attention by terminating her talk show partnership with Regis Philbin.

Kornheiser sized up the situation for the lame duck president: "Here's the problem. You're forgotten, but not gone."

Boy, was he wrong! Tony the K is primarily a sports writer, so what does he know about politics? Not that that is an essential requirement to make humorous comments. If that were true, how to explain Jay Leno and David Letterman? Tony just didn't take into account the big early primaries, which eliminated any suspense about the Gore-Bush run for the White House, thus creating a huge vacuum in political news. The Washington news media took it especially hard when John McCain parked his "Straight Talk Express" bus and suspended his campaign.

*Post* media critic Howard Kurtz opined that "press types fear a tough slog through a dull preseason with two less-than-scintillating candidates." That might be true if the sitting president hadn't found himself on the hot seat once again because of past indiscretions. Just as capital correspondents were searching desperately for stories to justify their expense accounts, Whitewater reared its ugly head with the decision by independent counsel Robert W. Ray to release a series of reports on his findings.

So the first bombshell, on misuse of FBI files, had a wet fuse. Three more are coming, spread out over the next several months, and that's got to be uncomfortable for the presumptive Democratic presidential nominee, Al Gore, second in command of the Clinton-Gore administration.

Clinton also grabbed the headlines by openly feuding with the National Rifle Association, whose president, actor Charlton Heston, accused him in a TV ad of violating one or more of the Ten Commandments. Clinton said in an interview that he personally owned a rifle, so maybe the way to resolve the dispute is for him and Heston to go hunting together.

As if he hadn't done enough to reclaim the news spotlight, the president ignored security warnings and insisted on making a visit to Pakistan next week as part of a long-planned trip to South Asia. He'll be accompanied by his daughter Chelsea, who apparently decided it was safer in that part of the world than in New York, where her mother is campaigning for the U.S. Senate.

Political writers definitely owe Clinton a debt of gratitude for taking up the slack when the excitement of the primary season ended so abruptly. Until Gore and George W. Bush get their circus acts perfected to take on the road to the national nominating conventions, Clinton has shown he is a reliable performer for the press.

Maybe that will be his legacy.

*March 16, 2000*

## Presidential Interviews Are Becoming Just Child's Play

On "Earth Day" ABC is performing an extraordinary public service by presenting an hour-long news special featuring Bill Clinton, president of the United States, and Leonardo DeCaprio, star of *Titanic*, in the role of a TV journalist.

The program has stirred controversy because many news professionals say the twenty-something actor has no business interviewing the nation's top leader, and many Americans say Clinton has no business being president. Others believe that if anyone should be interviewed about the environment, it is Vice President Al Gore. But advocating the end of combustion engines might not sit well with big sponsors from Detroit.

When ABC drew criticism for not giving the assignment to a genuine, impartial newsperson like *20/20* correspondent Chris Cuomo, son of the former New York governor and brother of Clinton's housing secretary, ABC News president David Westin weaseled out. He claimed that DeCaprio, chairman of "Earth Day 2000", only went to the White House for a "walk-through" to look at the weatherstripping, and it was Clinton's idea to answer questions.

But the president and his staff insisted that ABC had requested an interview, and Westin was shamed into 'fessing up. Clinton rubbed it in at the Radio and Television Correspondents annual dinner when he said: "Don't you news people ever learn? It isn't the mistake that kills you, it's the cover-up."

And so it is that Americans will have a chance to see a teen-agers' heartthrob sit down with a middle-aged lecher and explore ways to make the world better for future generations—truly a remarkable milestone in TV journalism.

Commercial television being what it is, no doubt the other networks will follow suit in order to remain competitive. Just consider all the copycat shows that popped up after the success of ABC's *Who Wants To Marry a Millionaire*. Don't be surprised to find these programs in the TV listings:

*DC Decision Day*—This special CBS News presentation will provide a penetrating analysis of the presidential primary in the District of Columbia. President Clinton sits for an interview by Haley Joel Osment, 12-year-old star of *The Sixth Sense* on the meaning of voters' choices in the nation's capital. Nominated for an Academy Award for his role as Cole, a child who sees dead people, Osment is highly qualified to add his own observations about Al Gore.

*Salute to Science*—NBC is devoting two hours to an absorbing discussion ranging from laboratory to laptop, climaxing "Science and Technology Week." The live event, featuring field reports from Cal-Tech, MIT and Bob Jones University, will be hosted by Cassidy Gifford, the six-year-old daughter of Kathie Lee and Frank Gifford. A highlight of the program will be Cassidy's one-on-one with

President Clinton examining the accomplishments of the recent Critical Infrastructure Assurance Summit. She also will endeavor to seek a scientific explanation for the disappearance of White House e-mail messages.

*Mother's Day in the New Millennium*—Theme of this production by Fox-TV is "Diapers and Dollars—Wiping Away Debt." President Clinton is interviewed by the infant daughter of actor and political activist Warren Beatty and his Oscar-nominated wife Annette Bening. The baby, making her first journalistic appearance on national television, brings a unique perspective to the subject, having just assumed a proportionate share of a national debt totaling $5,757,083,549,106. Clinton is expected to explain how he plans to make her and her parents debt-free.

*April 20, 2000*

## Lieberman's a "Good Joe"—So How Did Gore Get Him?

We may never know the full story of what led to Al Gore's choice of a running mate, but it might have gone something like this:

Deep inside the Democrat war room at Nashville, the vice president's campaign strategists sat around a table looking glum after analyzing polls showing the Republican ticket of George W. Bush and Dick Cheney with a double-digit lead. A Gore pollster led off a frank discussion.

"Our guy's got to do something dramatic to turn this thing around. We've tried everything else—changing positions, trying new clothing, reinventing history—and nothing seems to work. But we've still got a chance with the vice presidential nominee."

"We've narrowed the list after Dick Gephardt turned us down. He's not dumb enough to risk losing a chance to be House speaker some day. There would have been some shock value in naming a Republican like our defense secretary Bill Cohen, but he went on national television and said he's voting for Bush.

"So we've got Sen. John Kerry of Massachusetts, but voters might get him mixed up with Sen. Bob Kerrey of Nebraska, who has called President Clinton 'an unusually good liar.' There's Sen. John Edwards of North Carolina, but with only 18 months in government he's still wet behind the ears. We have Sen. Evan Bayh of Indiana, but that's a no-brainer."

"Why is that?"

"Can't you just see crowds shouting 'Gore-Bayh', 'Gore-Bayh', with hands waving? Too much fatalistic symbolism there. That leaves only one person that Gore can pick and draw some attention to the Democratic ticket: Sen. Joseph Lieberman of Connecticut."

"But he said worse things about Clinton than Kerrey did."

"Okay, he said the president's sexcapade with Monica was 'disgraceful' and 'harmful' but that will help counteract Gore's ill-advised reference to him as 'one of the greatest presidents in history.'"

"Didn't Lieberman vote to acquit Clinton of impeachment charges?"

"Sure, but nobody remembers that."

"Lieberman's an Orthodox Jew."

"So he can't campaign on Friday night or Saturday. Somebody else will have to handle the football crowds."

"Well, I guess being Jewish won't be a problem unless he gets crosswise with Hillary."

"I don't know. He seems too nice to be Gore's attack dog."

"As if he needed one. It might be good to have at least one guy on the ticket who can smile. Although most of the time he has that pained expression, like he's got a bad case of hemorrhoids."

"Look, Clinton's immorality is killing us in the polls. Democrats are in danger of losing Connecticut and the Jewish vote. We need Lieberman. It would be a bold stroke for inclusiveness. The Republicans have just about pre-empted every other minority. And would you believe he's got a granddaughter named Tennessee?"

"All right. We're all agreed. Let's go tell the candidate. And we'd better alert the Democratic party chairman."

"Yeah, Ed Rendell is a loose cannon. It would be just like him to go on a TV talk show and say something like, 'If Joe Lieberman were an Episcopalian, it would be a slam dunk.'"

*August 10, 2000*

## Democrats Usher In the Age of the "New Gore-ality"

And so it came to pass that in the year of our Lord 2000 the Democrats gathered in the City of the Angels to choose a new leader. And lo, Los Angeles was ready for the multitudes of Democrats who descended for their quadrennial convention which was to be "not for show, but for substance."

Yea, it was the age of the New Morality, or more precisely, the New Gore-ality, as declared by Albert, the Baptist, and Joseph, the Prophet, who saith unto William, the Conqueror, "thou art immoral and harmful to the values of our civilization."

And on the eve of the meeting, William went before an assembly of ministers and repented of his sins with the young woman, Monica, with whom he had shared adulterous intimacies. He bareth his soul at length, to the dismay of Albert, who had hoped to banish that tawdry episode from the minds of voters with his choice of the publicly religious Joseph at his side and his angry denunciation of a fundraiser scheduled in the *Playboy* mansion. Party chiefs, in the name of family values, forced a move of the Hispanic-American event.

Prior to Albert's arrival, William celebrated the end of his reign with a round of hedonistic feasts attended by hordes of the Hollywood celebrities so fiercely condemned by Joseph for their wickedness on the movie and television screens. William and his wife, Hillary, reveled in the adulation of the smut-and-violence peddlers, who know they have no fear from a Democrat White House. And so they dip deeply into their pockets to keep a good thing going, as William implored Americans so to do.

The delegates were blessed by the presence of the first child Chelsea, the most-traveled daughter of a U.S. president, who arranged her schedule of foreign trips to be front-and-center on family night. Hearts were warmed as she and her mother flashed many unscripted smiles.

The familiar smirk of George, the Younger, which was lost in Philadelphia, was found on the face of William as he boasted of progress and prosperity and reproached his enemies for their faithlessness in his policies. He adorned Albert and Joseph and the sainted Hillary with praise and bade his followers farewell.

Alas, the passing of the torch to Albert was fraught with danger of the anointed successor being burned by William's transgressions and his reluctance to leave the stage. In the words of a certain wise man, Franklin, the Professor, of the College of Charleston, it is "like the passing of a painful kidney stone that just won't pass."

Those with allegiance to Albert were sorely pleased with William's leaving and the farther away from their man the better. Maybe he could rescue the Russian submarine at the bottom of the Barents Sea.

Then came Edward, the Kennedy, and his kin to evoke images of a martyred leader, followed by Harold, the Keynoter, who indeed was no match for Colin, the Republican.

While orators on the podium cursed "big oil" and other corporate interests, guards outside the arena used nightsticks and rubber bullets against uncredentialed demonstrators carrying the same message in the streets.

Verily, Joseph faced a mighty challenge in going before the throng. He had to reach deep within his soul to convince loyal party activists that his Republican-like positions on school vouchers, affirmative action, privatization of Social Security and cultural pollution by the entertainment industry were not written in stone.

With faith that God will remain neutral through November 7, let the crusade begin.

*August 17, 2000*

## Summer Love Is a Many-splendored Bipartisan Thing

Along with politics, love is in the air and it's not even Valentine's Day.

It's all Al Gore's fault. He really got the juices flowing with that X-rated kiss he laid on Tipper at the Democrats' convention, shortly before he declared, "I am my own man" (a phrase he no doubt borrowed from Attorney General Janet Reno.)

That moment of unexpected passion may be all many voters remember from the evening. Surely nobody can recall the entire laundry list of big government programs that make up his "fresh start" campaign agenda—even if you stayed awake through his speech.

Pundits weighed in on "the kiss", of course. While liberal columnists swooned in ecstasy over the "humanizing" gesture, conservative Robert Novak rated it "disgusting." Maureen Dowd of the *New York Times* said the kiss "was more suited to a third date than the fourth night of a convention," and she said it caused "a chain reaction with Joe and Hadassah (Lieberman) starting to lip-lock."

Gore, who once said he was the inspiration for the novel and movie, *Love Story*, and claimed undue credit for the "Love Canal" expose, insisted his un-Gore-like action was "spontaneous." Asked if he meant to tell the public something about himself, he said, "Actually, I was trying to send a message to Tipper." E-mail from the lonely campaign trail just doesn't do it, we suppose. (That's said with tongue in cheek.)

The "big smooch" set the tone for an explosion of affection at the convention windup, which even included hugs for Albert Gore III from parents who had been infuriated by their son's arrest for driving at almost 100 miles per hour on a beach highway in North Carolina on the eve of the convention—a story the *Washington Post* and other sympathetic newspapers tried to keep under wraps. Green Party candidate Ralph "Unsafe At Any Speed" Nader might have found himself an issue to run on.

Cupid proved to be bipartisan by shooting arrows into the Republican camp, where former House Speaker Newt Gingrich found wedded bliss with Calista Bisek, the young congressional staffer with whom he admitted having had a six-year affair before divorcing his wife of 19 years. The happy couple were joined in marriage at a ceremony at an elegant inn in Old Town Alexandria, Va., where the wedding bower included a U.S. flag.

The union had been blessed by Gingrich's mother, who threw a shower at her Harrisburg, Pa., nursing home. (That must have been a good House cloakroom story.) "Newty is in love," she beamed. And this time it's not just with himself.

During the honeymoon period, Newt was spotted shopping in a local bookstore.

Meanwhile, President Clinton, try as he might, just can't seem to keep himself out of the news spotlight, especially when it comes to the opposite sex. While vacationing in upstate New York, he graciously stopped to autograph the T-shirt of a pretty young woman, and what did she do but strip to the waist to show her gratitude.

Clinton probably wasn't expecting that kind of present for his 54th birthday. Alert officers quickly subdued her before she could compromise the Philanderer-in-Chief any further.

Love is not forever, and to show his concern Clinton, according to a senior White House source, "reached out" to actress Anne Heche and her ex-lover Ellen DeGeneres after they ended their 3-year relationship last weekend, which sent Heche to a hospital.

It's reassuring to know that our president hasn't forgotten his promise to "feel your pain."

*August 24, 2000*

## Candidates Are Just Going Through a Phrase

With all signs pointing to one of the closest presidential elections in years, what will be the deciding factor? It could be that the winner in November will be the candidate who has the best phrase writer.

In today's made-for-television campaigns, a snappy phrase is important because it translates into a sound bite, which means exposure on the evening news and weekend talk shows.

As the race moves into the homestretch, as political observers with no imagination like to say, Al Gore is ahead by a nose over George W. Bush in the phrase-making derby. While holding forth on his plan to help senior citizens pay for prescription drugs, Gore worked himself into a near frenzy tweaking Bush about his lack of a proposal. The oratorical climax came when he challenged his opponent to—are you ready?—"put up or shut up."

What a novel expression! For originality it ranks right up there with "read my lips", those memorable words from 1988 that Dubya's daddy later had to eat when he joined ranks with Democrats in Congress to raise taxes.

"Put up or shut up." Those are fighting words from Alpha Male Gore. Whoever on his staff came up with that phrase already has earned a big bonus. (So has the aide who whispered to Bush, "class warfare.")

Bush did not respond in kind to Gore's dare, saving his harsh comments for *New York Times* reporter Adam Clymer. Bush said Gore's statement didn't sound "very presidential."

Both candidates must have had a stable of phrase composers at their national conventions. Who could forget Bush's ringing declaration to "leave no (fill in the blank) behind" or Gore's somewhat unconvincing "I am my own man."

Dick Cheney, the Republican vice presidential candidate, drew the assignment to repeat several times in his speech attacking the Democrats in the White House, "It is time for them to go."

Gore's running mate, Sen. Joseph Lieberman, must write his own stuff. He's still bubbly about being the first Jew on a national ticket. Lieberman never skips an opportunity to say how fortunate he feels to be running for vice president. He may be the first politician ever to thank God for the prospect of holding a do-nothing job. But when he gets carried away and says, "Only in America!"—it makes you wonder about those elections in Israel.

At the Democrats' convention, Gore introduced what he undoubtedly hopes will be a winning phrase combination. "Let others argue the case for the 'old guard,'" he said. "We're the 'new guard.'" Well, it worked for J. Howard Edmondson in Oklahoma back in 1958 when he got elected governor by running against the "old guard." Many politicians before and after Edmondson have borrowed the expression, which was used as early as 1844 as a description of the Whigs in a newspaper editorial.

And so the cliche-ridden campaign rolls on. Bush says there's a need for some "plain-spoken folks" in Washington, and Gore argues that "working people" deserve to be told "the unvarnished truth." Both candidates have promised a "fresh start" and each is entitled to refer to the other's solution to a problem as "too little too late." That's in the public domain.

As Ronald Reagan, a president who knew how to turn a phrase, might say: "There they go again."

*September 7, 2000*

## Listen Up Candidates: Here's How To Win the Next Debate

Democrat Al Gore and Republican George W. Bush put on dark suits and red ties and attempted to show voters how different they are in the first presidential debate. Each tried hard to make a strong case for his election, but both candidates missed chances to take vote-winning stands on certain key issues. If the right questions are asked, the next debate might go like this:

Q: Governor Bush, a 79-year-old woman from Des Moines, Iowa, Winifred Skinner, told your opponent she has to collect cans to pay for groceries because of the high cost of her medicines. What would you do for her?

Bush: First let me say I respect her choice to pick up cans, as she has done all through the Clinton-Gore administration. What I would not do is exploit the woman and call for federal aid. Rather, I would mobilize the resources of the private sector. I am tonight launching a nationwide campaign to "Send Cans to Winifred" and I call on all citizens to join me in this effort. That includes the vice president and his arthritic dog, Shiloh. Save those empty dog food cans and send them to Winnie so she will be able to make ends meet. That designer jacket she wears must strain her budget. And despite this dear lady's request not to tell the government about how much she earns selling scrap metal, I urge her to be an honest citizen and pay her income taxes.

(This would put Gore on the defensive as condoning tax evasion.)

Q: Mr. Vice President, you and your running mate, Sen. Joseph Lieberman, strongly condemned the entertainment industry for the quality of television programs, among other things, but softened your criticism at big-dollar fundraisers for your party. What will you do to convince voters you are really serious about cleaning up what children see on the screen?

Gore: I have formulated a new initiative that begins with the denunciation of the shocking decision by ABC to postpone the Miss America pageant from September to October. The network decided to air this wholesome show that is so instructive both to young women and young men in mid-October, rather than compete with the Olympics. The ugly profit motive that is behind so much of what passes for entertainment these days has deprived millions of viewers of the opportunity to greet the autumn season by enjoying an evening of culture from Atlantic City, a classic display of charm and talent. Miss America is beloved by all Americans ...

(On second thought, Gore wants to distance himself from Bill Clinton, who once had an affair with a former Miss America.)

Q: Governor Bush, you said you quit drinking when you turned 40. Have you ever regretted that decision?

Bush: Not really, although I'll have to say I have been tempted in recent days by the announcement that Wal-Mart is going to begin selling its own private-label wine. To think that in the future you can go to one of their stores and stock up on cookies, toilet paper, motor oil and wine, all at a discount price—well, that's what makes America great.

(That ought to get the redneck vote.)

Q: Vice President Gore, after 8 years in office you claim everything is better than ever. But what do you say to criticisms like these, and I quote: "Millions of Americans lack adequate health insurance." "More than one-half of America's nursing homes don't have the minimum staffing levels necessary to guarantee quality care." "Our children are forced to go to school in trailers, overcrowded classrooms and crumbling buildings."

Gore. That's just President Clinton's opinion. I am my own man.

*October 5, 2000*

## Flexible Florida and "Fuzzy Math" Confuse Election Results

This was supposed to be a penetrating analysis of a winning campaign and the potential offered by the newly-elected president for amusing commentary. But no-o-o! Blame it on "flexible Florida" and "fuzzy math", but the picture couldn't be more confusing. Any time now so-called experts might attribute the closeness of the vote to alligators eating the absentee ballots.

It's good that Florida has "controlling legal authority" to require a recount or perhaps Judge Judy would have to decide the outcome. If one candidate won the popular vote and the other had the highest tally in the Electoral College, she might very well order a co-presidency. (Well, it worked for the Clintons, didn't it—up to a point?)

Al Gore could be president Monday, Wednesday and Friday, and George W. Bush could run things Tuesday, Thursday and Saturday. Joe Lieberman and Dick Cheney could mind the store on alternate Sundays.

If you think that sounds wacky, just consider the campaign America has endured for the past 96 months—or did it just seem that long?

It was a campaign that cost an estimated $3 billion, but worth every dollar in providing merriment to a complacent citizenry—and think what all that spending on political ads and voter turnout operations did for the economy!

It was a campaign based both on issues and personalities, and Gore had many of both. Bush used the same stump speech from Seattle to St. Augustine.

It was a campaign that introduced words like "lockbox" and non-words like "subliminable."

It was a campaign that saw Gore endorsed by President Clinton, who said he would be "the next best thing" to a third Clinton term. The Bush campaign cheered. Then Ross Perot, whose campaign song was "Crazy", came out for Bush, making it a draw.

It was a campaign in which Gore gave his wife Tipper an X-rated kiss on national television and Bush gave his wife Laura a peck on the cheek on his campaign plane. (It was her birthday.)

It was a campaign with the usual flubs—Colin Powell, a former general, was introduced as Adam Clayton Powell, a former congressman, at a Michigan rally, and Gore's running mate was identified as Bob Lieberman at a campaign stop in St. Louis.

It was a campaign that produced the defeat of a live U.S. senator (John Ashcroft) by a dead Missouri governor (Mel Carnahan), and the first $60 million senator (former financier Jon Corzine of New Jersey spent that much of his own money to win).

It was the campaign that didn't want to end, even when Gore made that post-midnight call to Bush to concede, only to retract later. It was his prize flip-flop.

But once it's officially over, maybe we'll find out how Bush debate preparation materials got into the hands of Gore's debate coach.

One thing is for sure: First Lady H. R. Clinton now is Senator-elect Hillary! Let's hurry up and get this mess straightened out so her 2004 presidential campaign can begin.

Maybe sometime soon we'll have a better idea of whether Spot, Bush's English springer spaniel, or Shiloh, Gore's arthritic black Labrador, will take Buddy's place as first dog in the White House.

Historians are waiting for that defining moment.

*November 9, 2000*

## Why Not End the Vote Deadlock By Pulling a Wishbone?

Over the beaches and through the swamp to Florida's courts we go.
It was too close to call, and they had a ball.
The vote count went to and fro.
In Tallahassee the high court ruled to maintain the status quo.
The hand count goes on, and on, and on.
Democrats are all aglow.
Meanwhile, in D.C. in bitter chill to Al Gore's house we go.
He won't relent. He did invent
The dimpled chad, you know.
Over Red River and through the mesquite to George W.'s ranch we go.
Although you can't tell, he's madder than hell.
He's really been dealt a low blow.
Over the breadth of the Sunshine state to K. Harris' place we go.
She enforced the law, but opponents got raw.
Her makeup offended them so.
Under the palm trees and on the sand to Palm Beach County we go.
The voters feel punk. They're all punch drunk.
That butterfly ballot must go.
Over the oceans, throughout the world to military bases we go.
It's so sad to see, to vote absentee
And then be called a no-show.
Up in Cook County in Illinois to Bill Daley's house we go.
The Daley machine will keep the vote clean,
As pure as Chicago snow.
Over on K Street in Washington to big law firms we go.
There's nobody there, their offices bare.
They've all gone to Orlando.
At the state capitol where Jeb Bush lives to the governor's house we go.
His brother just called. He's really appalled.
The wind chill was 20 below.
Into the state of Connecticut to Lieberman's house we go.
He's learned to whine the new party line.
He's just not the same old Joe.
Up at the Capitol under the dome to Congress' House we go.
They're fit to be tied. They may have to decide
Just how to end this woe.
Across the Potomac and by the Mall to Bill Clinton's house we go.

He likes the delay, he's ready to stay
For eight more years or so.
But perish the thought. That just cannot be.
Let Bush and Gore go toe to toe,
With a gentlemanly tone, and pull on a wishbone.
Who gets the short part, it's no-go.

*November 23, 2000*

## Before the Ruling, Some Disorder in the Court, Perhaps?

We may never know what really went on in chambers when the nine justices of the U.S. Supreme Court were in deliberations over the presidential election dilemma. The all-powerful jurists probably were not in the best of moods. After all, the tornadic situation in Florida had cut into their weekend and threatened to spoil the court's annual Christmas party. And one of the attorneys had called two of the justices by the wrong names.

In this saga of unimaginable scenarios, the discussion might have gone like this:

Chief Justice Rehnquist: Well, here we are. It looks as if it's up to us to decide who will be president for the next four years.

Justice Stevens: I'm 80 years old and I've never seen anything like this. I can't believe it's a choice between these two bozos. Any one of us is much more able to lead the country than "Dimples" Bush or "Chad-face" Gore.

Justice Breyer: We've got supreme power, haven't we? What's stopping us from choosing a member from our exclusive circle to be president?

Rehnquist: There's a little matter of the law.

Justice Souter: The Florida Supreme Court took the law into its own hands. Why shouldn't we? We can say it's for the good of the country.

Justice Kennedy: I'm game. The American people don't care who is president—they just want the election to be over. Modesty forbids me from offering myself as a prospective selection, although the country might welcome having another Kennedy in the White House. I nominate the chief justice.

Rehnquist: Oh, no, no, no! A president has to work with Congress. I had a belly full of those jokers when I presided over Clinton's impeachment trial.

Justice Thomas: You know, we could really make history here. We have a splendid opportunity to give America its first black president.

Justice O'Connor: You've got a point, Clarence. But I'm not sure the country is ready for that. On the other hand, a woman president would be history-making and also very timely. Why wait and allow Hillary Clinton to be the first woman to sit at the desk in the Oval Office?

Justice Ginsburg: You're absolutely right, Sandy. But there's something else to consider. With the impressive showing made by Joe Lieberman in this election, maybe voters are saying they want a Jewish president. And a Jewish woman would be a two-fer.

Justice Scalia: Well, if we're going to go the ethnic route, I think the country needs a leader of Italian heritage. Anybody got a problem with that?

Rehnquist: All right. Let's decide. Everybody write a name on a piece of paper and we'll have a clerk tally the votes. (Pause) Has everyone voted? Very well. The clerk will announce the results.

Clerk: Stevens 1. Scalia 1. Breyer 1. Kennedy 1. Souter 1. Thomas 1. Ginsburg 1. O'Connor 1. Rehnquist abstains. It's an eight-way tie with one abstention.

Several justices: Are you kidding? This can't be! You voted for yourself? So did you! I demand a recount! And I want a recount of the recount! The votes have already been counted. We must discern the will of the people! No one should be denied to have his vote counted! Don't be a sore loser. Who's a cry baby? You pull my hair and I'll ...

Rehnquist: Ladies and gentlemen! Please! Let's have order in this court! Thank you. Now, as to the matter of Bush v. Gore ...

*December 14, 2000*

## Dear Santa: Please Bring Al Gore a Life

From: Executive Office of the President
To: Santa Claus
Subject: Christmas
Dear Santa,

I am a little boy 54 years old. I live in a big white house in Washington, D.C., our nation's capital.

I have a dog named Buddy and a cat named Socks and lots of playmates.

I have been a good boy this year and I hope by now you have forgotten about the years before that.

I hope you will come down my chimney this year. I am still at the same house, the one with a big iron fence around it, but I will not be living here next year. Another little boy named George is moving into my house in January. His daddy used to live here before I did.

I might be in New York or Arkansas next Christmas, but I'll have to let you know.

I will leave you some milk and cookies, along with security clearance for you and your reindeer.

Here is what I want for Christmas:

I would like to have a big black car with a driver that will take me anywhere I want to go.

Also, I want an airplane—a Boeing 747 with an executive suite and a kitchen and dining room and all the latest electronic gadgets and a flight crew that can fly me any place on a moment's notice.

Please bring me a military band that will play every time I enter a room.

I also want some soldiers to play with in places like Haiti and Bosnia.

I don't want to be greedy, but there are a few more things I really would like.

I want a gift certificate to McDonald's—and yes, I'd like to have fries with that.

Please bring me a big box of Cuban cigars. My friend Fidel Castro could help.

If I go to live in New York, I'd like to have a membership in an exclusive golf club.

I would like to have a $10 million dollar book deal. If the Pope can get $8.5 million and Hillary $8 million, that's not too much to ask, is it?

Since I am going to have to start buying my own clothes, maybe you could bring me a supply of boxer shorts. Also, I would like some new ties to replace those that Monica gave me.

I could use some cash. I need about $5 million to pay my legal bills.

I don't want to be too selfish. I hope you have some goodies in your bag for my family and friends.

Please bring Senator-elect Clinton some good committee assignments. Also a multi-million-dollar house in Georgetown and something pretty to wear instead of those awful black pants suits.

I would like you to bring my daughter Chelsea some travel books so she can read all about the places she traveled with me at taxpayers' expense this past year.

Please bring my friend Al Gore a life.

Let's see, what else? A Middle East peace settlement before January 20 would be nice. Oh, and could you change the Constitution so I could run for president again?

Santa, I just thought of one more thing to put on my list—a pardon. And if it's not too much to ask, I would like for you to give me a legacy.

*December 21, 2000*

# POTUS 43

## George W. Bush

# "Dubya" Does It His Way, Telling Terrorists "Bring it On"

With the confirmation of the Republican election victory, Democrats almost had to be pried loose after eight years of controlling the White House.

The Clintons were in no hurry to leave Washington, and with Hillary Clinton starting a term in the Senate, she had a reason to stay awhile longer.

Although he followed another southern governor, George Walker Bush ("Dubya" for short) brought a sharply different style to the Oval Office—no interns tucked away in the private study, a commander-in-chief who knew how to salute. He preferred an early-to-bed, early-to-rise routine, and threw meeting planners off guard by showing up on time. About the only thing he and Bill Clinton had in common was jogging, but as Bush matured in office he switched to a mountain bike for exercise.

As the first son of a former president to be elected since John Quincy Adams, POTUS 43 took some jibes for bringing a few figures from his father's administration back to Washington. The most prominent of these were Condoleezza Rice to be his national security adviser (and later secretary of state) and Donald Rumsfeld to be secretary of defense. They joined a former colleague, Dick Cheney, who occupied the vice president's office—when he wasn't out shooting quail or lawyers.

"Dubya" also brought a new language to Washington, featuring such words as "tacular" and "misunderestimate." He spoke eloquently about "the haves and the have mores" and putting "food on your family," and implored skeptics to "give my chance a plan to work."

Bush faced many major crises in his presidency: the worst terrorist attack in history, Hurricane Katrina, a pretzel that could have made him a very short-term president.

During his first term George W. Bush teamed up with an unlikely Senate ally, Ted Kennedy, to pass a major education act. He got a $1.35 trillion tax cut through Congress, rejected a number of international treaties, signed into law the largest expansion of Medicare since it was created, launched a war on terrorism, ordered invasions of Afghanistan and Iraq, and brought T-ball to the White House lawn.

But first, he had to get the Clintons out of the way.

## Clintons Don't Want To Leave the Scene of Their Crimes

It's not enough that Washingtonians will have to get used to a new Redskins coach as well as a new president. They're going to have to keep putting up with the Clintons, too.

While George W. Bush is fighting for approval of his cabinet selections and Marty Schottenheimer starts rebuilding a once-powerful football team, the news spotlight continues to follow the first couple.

Although their White House lease is up next week, the current White House occupants apparently have enjoyed their eight-year roller coaster ride so much they're sticking around for some more thrills.

Normally, when a new chief executive is sworn in, his predecessor boards a government plane and flies off into the sunset. Not so with Bill Clinton. More than likely he'll hop into a limousine and motor up to new digs on Embassy Row.

Now that Hillary Clinton is a member of the U.S. Senate, she needed a place to catch a few winks when she's not at work on Capitol Hill for her New York constituents. From all indications, she's allowing hubby Bill to bunk there, too, despite rumors of a split after he left office. It seems the only tomcat facing expulsion is Socks.

Not just any house would do for the celebrity senator, of course. The Clintons will be living in a two-story brick Georgian with six bedrooms and seven bathrooms costing $2.85 million. There's also a garage and swimming pool. With 5,500 square feet of space, there's enough room for power sharing at home as well as at work in the Senate.

The couple still have a $1.7 million Dutch colonial in Chappaqua, N.Y., which they bought last year to establish residency before the election. The combined mortgages total almost as much as their legal bills, but with Sen. Clinton's $8 million book deal, who's to worry? (That is, if she can find a suitable ghostwriter.) Her $145,100 Senate salary and his $157,000 pension will help keep food on the table.

Somebody had better get busy and give the Clintons a housewarming, however. They've lived in public housing so long, with everything furnished, they don't own so much as an easy chair or an electric mixer. (Bill might want to bake some cookies in his spare time.)

He and his wife and daughter Chelsea drove up to Frederick, Md., over New Year's and went antique shopping. News reports say they spent $3,000 on such things as Chinese straw baskets and wooden marriage boxes, 100-year-old German wagons, a ladder and a breadbox. Nice knickknacks, no doubt, but not even a futon to sleep on.

Speaking of antiques, 98-year-old Sen. Strom Thurmond, R-S.C., was the center of attention on opening day of the new session of Congress. When Hillary came to the Senate floor to be sworn in, Thurmond grabbed her and held her in a prolonged embrace. Maybe it was the aqua pants suit that turned him on, or perhaps the ice lady has sex appeal after all.

Sen. Clinton had not one, but three, swearing-in ceremonies: the official oath-taking, another in the old Senate chamber where photographs are permitted, and a third which the *Washington Post* described as "a swinging, swaying, celebrity-studded, standing-ovation-flooded affair on the stage of Madison Square Garden's theater." The latter was sponsored by the Democratic party with proceeds going to the Clinton campaign committee.

As president of the Senate, Vice President Al Gore had to participate in all three of these ego-centered events, and you can imagine what was running through his mind as he crowned the Democrats' new star and a potential opponent in the 2004 election.

*January 11, 2001*

## Education, Bush Style: Learning the ABC's of Dubya

It's about education, stupid!

That's the message George W. Bush sent to the nation as he settled in as president and set about convincing Congress and other professional jokemakers that he's not as dumb as they might think.

Bush launched his presidency with "Education Week"—a time to focus on learning in America. As survivors of a historic transition, we have learned a lot of lessons in the past several days.

1.  Bush can indeed deliver a mighty good speech. In his inaugural address, he strung sentences together rather eloquently, and didn't mispronounce a single word. And it was mercifully brief.

2.  Bill Clinton is still around. He told you so himself in one of his many farewell addresses during his tasteless prolonged departure from the nation's capital for New York, one of his many homes. The former "Comeback Kid" became the "Nevergoaway Brat."

3.  Rev. Jesse Jackson, leader of the Rainbow Coalition, showed his true colors, admitting that while he was counseling Clinton about his infidelity he was engaged in an adulterous relationship that produced a child. He pulled out of the "Moral Outrage" demonstration, but bounced back after the world's fastest rehabilitation to criticize the new administration.

4.  As a dancer, President Bush is no Al Gore (surprisingly good), and he admits it. He must remember that when dancing with a daughter who is wearing a strapless gown, be careful when giving her a vigorous twirl.

5.  Some Clintonites do have some class. After enduring what must have been a most painful experience on the inaugural platform, Gore performed his last duty as vice president, shook hands with his victorious opponent and exited quietly to return to private life.

6.  Juvenile behavior in the White House marked both the beginning and the end of the Clinton administration. Outgoing staffers removed the letter W from the keyboards of computers in offices of the Old Executive Office Building.

7.  A president can stay on schedule. No more "Clinton Standard Time." While his predecessor persisted on running late and keeping people waiting, the 43rd president practices punctuality. On his first day of work, Bush arrived in the Oval Office at 7:28 a.m.

8.  A first lady can show respect for a partisan opponent in Congress. Upon arrival at the White House for the traditional ride to the Capitol Hill inauguration ceremony, Laura Bush extended a proper greeting: "Good morning, Senator Clinton."

President Bush is bound to liven things up in the capital if for no other reason than being from Texas. One of our most colorful presidents was a Texan—no, not Dubya's daddy ("wouldn't be prudent"). Everybody remembers the fun of the Lyndon B. Johnson years. But don't expect this Texan to hold his dog up by the ears or show us his scar.

Meanwhile, Washington society is learning the ABC's of a new era:

A is for Austin, armadillos, amigos, the Alamo, action, angus, ability, Aggies, Ari Fleischer, authenticity, Artesia mineral water, across-the-board tax cut, and awl (oil).

B is for Bushes (the whole family), beef, barbecue (not pork), baseball, Blue Bell ice cream, bass fishing, boots, Bevo, Bo Derek, bluebonnets, and big everything.

C is for Cheney, chipotle grills, compassionate conservatism, chili, Crawford (the new presidential retreat), cow chips, cowboy hats, change, character, courage, and class.

*January 25, 2001*

## A President Also Can Get a Lot of Nuisance Calls

Don't you hate it when you're right in the middle of something and the phone won't stop ringing? Just imagine what it must have been like when President Bush was trying to work on his budget speech to Congress.

Ring, ring.

Hello. Oh, hi, Mom … Yeah, yeah, I know I goofed when I said I was looking forward to having dinner with "he and Mrs. Blair." It's ladies first, I know that … Bad grammar? Look, I'm taking care of that in my education bill. I'm declaring war on dangling participles … Okay, okay. How's Dad? … Oh, that's right. He's on that overseas trip. Well, give him my love. You know I wouldn't be here without you and he.

Ring, ring.

Jeb, hey. How's the governor of Florida today? … You say you've got some election results that show me beating Al Gore in Miami-Dade County? … Well, that's really great news, little brother. Why couldn't you have told me that on election night?

Ring, ring.

Laura, honey, I'm working on my speech … Yes, I know we've got to do something about the dog … Yes, I heard you say on television that he's not completely housebroken yet and that's why we're not replacing the carpets right away … Listen, I'll get him trained. But first I have to get Tom Daschle and Dick Gephardt trained. Need to find some good nicknames …

Ring, ring.

Dad? Where are you? … In a plane over Kuwait! You're not going to make another one of those parachute jumps, are you? … Good. Are you having a high old time over there with the two generals? … Well, I'm glad you called. I'm putting the finishing touches on my budget address … No, "read my lips" is a phrase I'll never use. But what do you think about this: "My fellow Americans, we will have plenty of money to run the government and also have a tax cut. And we would have $48 million more in the treasury if the Clinton administration had forced Marc Rich to pay his taxes."

Ring, ring.

*El Presidente Fox! Buenas dias, senor. Como esta?* … Thanks for returning my call, Vicente. I just wanted to tell you again what a great job you're doing as Mexico's new president … Had a great time on my visit. And those pills you gave me really did the trick with that little intestinal problem … Good to talk to you. By the way, did anyone ever tell you that you look like Victor Newman on *The Young and the Restless?*

Ring, ring.

Yes, Ari ... When do I want to schedule the next formal news conference? Would you believe never? ... I know, I know. I'll tell you one thing. If I have to endure another lecture from Helen Thomas on faith-based initiatives, I say it's time to take her down to the ranch and find a mean bull for her to ride ... I think Jesse Ventura might have the right idea in issuing press credentials that identify reporters as jackals. Except that I might use another word.

Ring, ring.

Bill? Well, good morning, Mr. President. Ooops! I'm the president. How're you doing? Never mind. What can I do for you? ... No, I don't believe anybody came across a box of presidential pardons labeled "big givers" after we moved in ... There was some pizza in the refrigerator, but we ate that ... Oh, and a pair of thong underwear in one of the closets ...

*March 1, 2001*

## Foot-in-mouth Disease Plagues Washington, D.C.

An outbreak of foot-in-mouth disease has been sweeping the nation's capital and authorities seem powerless to control it.

The new treasury secretary, Paul O'Neill, was too blunt for his own good when he described Wall Street traders as people who "sit in front of a flickering green screen" all day and were not the sort "you would want to help you think about complex questions." Other offhand comments by the former business executive triggered market dives.

At the height of the pardon scandal and while many Americans were glowing about Ronald Reagan's 90th birthday, Sen. Hillary Clinton, D-N.Y., advised her party colleagues in a closed-door meeting: "We should say, 'What we don't want is Reaganomics; we want Clintonomics.'" The reaction was stunned silence, reports say.

Not only politicians and bureaucrats are affected. Media mogul Ted Turner caught flak from many directions when he noticed CNN staffers with ashes on their heads in observance of a religious holiday and referred to them as "Jesus freaks."

Hollywood diva Barbra Streisand's hard-hitting memo advising Democrats on Capitol Hill to quit whining and start pounding the GOP contained a curious sentence. Stressing the need to reclaim the White House and gain a majority in both houses of Congress, she wrote: "Unless we win, we'll be consistently on the defensive with our fingers holding the dyke against the Republican revolution." Did she mean "dike" or was that a Freudian slip?

President Bush, by his own admission, is a leading exponent of grammatical gaffes. In a news conference last week the originator of "Hispanically" coined a new word, "misunderestimate." He quickly caught the error and joked to reporters, "just making sure you were paying attention." At a luncheon for baseball greats, including malaprop master Yogi Berra, Bush quipped, "Some in the press corps here even think he might be my speechwriter."

When the president spoke at the Radio-Television Correspondents Association annual dinner, he devoted most of his remarks to his free-wheeling syntax. To the delight of the audience, he shared some of his classic quotes:

"I know the human being and fish can coexist peacefully."

"I understand small business growth; I was one."

"More and more of our imports come from overseas."

Bush explained that when he went on record stating, "We ought to make the pie higher," he was making "a complicated economic point." He added, "But believe me, what this country needs is taller pie."

He also gave an analysis of what might be his most widely known quote: "Rarely is the question asked, is our children learning." Daring to step into rhetorical quicksand that trapped his predecessor, Bush said, "If you read it closely, you'll see I'm using the intransitive plural subjunctive tense. So the word 'is' are correct."

After reeling off a long list of "Bushisms", the president smiled and chided his critics. "And you know what? Life goes on," he said. "My wife and my daughters still love me. Our military still protects our shores. Americans still get up and go to work.

"I don't think it's healthy to take yourself too seriously. But what I do take seriously is my responsibility as president to all the American people."

And that's no joke.

*April 5, 2001*

## Here's the Real Skinny On the First 100 Days of Al Gore

Never mind the first 100 days of President Bush or Sen. Hillary Clinton. What Americans crave to know about is the first 100 days of Al Gore as Mr. Nobody. Or maybe we should say the first 100 pounds.

The president-reject, as one parody Web site calls him, had to make a rather rapid adjustment to civilian life after spending most of his adult life on the payroll of the federal government. After the election results were final, he suddenly found himself out of a job and forced to vacate the roomy vice president's residence and move back into the modest home in the Virginia suburbs where he and his wife Tipper had lived previously.

Gore's circumstances were markedly different from those of his White House partner for eight years, Bill Clinton. (Has anyone done a report on Clinton's first 100 $100,000 speeches?) An ex-president, no matter how bad he was, is in much higher demand on the lecture circuit than a former vice president ever could be.

As a newsmaker, Clinton is unbeatable. Who else would go to an orphanage in India and sing a hymn at the tomb of Mother Teresa, then cuddle babies and dance with children? Al Gore wouldn't do that. He might jingle his pockets in a Buddhist temple ...

Poor Al. He barely made the top 10 list of America's most foolish people. Clinton led in this annual poll for the second straight year. Gore came in ninth, just ahead of Jesse Ventura.

On the positive side, Gore did not have to feel the heat of the public spotlight as Clinton did because of the scandalous way he left office. In fact, tracking Gore's activities since last January 20 presented a strong challenge. The man simply has not been making much news. But it's not quite true to say he is a shrinking figure on the national stage.

Gore virtually dropped off the radar screen when he chose academia as his post-politics profession, electing to teach at UCLA, two Tennessee institutions and Columbia University in New York. His Columbia professorship at the graduate school of journalism has produced the most visibility, partly because of the celebrity guests he has brought to his class on national affairs reporting.

If you overlook the anomaly of journalism being taught by a guy traveling in a motorcade and in a class where everything is off the record, it's possible to see that students might benefit from exposure to such people as media mogul Rupert Murdoch or Federal Reserve Chairman Alan Greenspan. But David Letterman? Wonder what my old OU J-school prof, Jack Whitaker, would have to say about that?

It's a sad state of affairs when we have to look to a gossip columnist to get the real skinny on Al Gore. Here's what Liz Smith wrote in the *New York Post*: "Do any of you remember a guy named Al Gore? He ran for president and almost won. They said the election was his to lose and he lost it.

"As for the disappearing candidate Mr. Gore, all I know about him is that he was mighty buffed up for the presidential race. But the minute it was over, he started eating and filling himself up with instant gratification. They say he's pretty chubby these days."

It sounds as if he's been hitting the burgers and fries. Who does he think he is, Bill Clinton?

Tipper might have to let out those earth tone suits he wore in the campaign.

What is he doing, auditioning for a new Bill Cosby TV version of "Fat Albert"?

That book he's supposed to be writing must be a high-calorie recipe-tested cookbook.

*April 26, 2001*

## Senate Changeover Brews Trouble for Some Jobholders

Vice President Dick Cheney's worst nightmare might have gone something like this:

"Thank you for coming in, Mr. Cheney. Please be seated.

"We realize that when an employee receives a call from the White House personnel office, there might be some apprehension. Let me assure you at the outset that we have no complaints about your job performance. The only abnormality in your record to this date is an above-average number of sick days. But overall you have an excellent rating.

"However, in view of recent developments, we feel it is necessary to reexamine your work assignment and, if I may be candid, to reassess your pay scale. It is clear that you brought to your current job some exemplary qualifications. Your experience both in the federal government and in private industry, as well as your intelligence and maturity, filled a genuine need in the Bush organization.

"None of that has changed. But one aspect of your role as vice president and president of the Senate has been transformed drastically. With the Senate evenly divided between Democrats and Republicans, you had the power to cast a tie-breaking vote. Because of the Democrats' successful recruitment efforts, they now control the Senate. You no longer have that power. Consequently, your value to our operation has diminished considerably.

"The Constitution defines only limited duties for a vice president. In fact, it says all you have to do is preside over the Senate—and as you well know, the senators prefer to do that themselves—and to take over for the president if necessary. Without that tie-breaking vote, it comes down to this: you are being paid $181,400 a year for doing almost nothing. I think you will agree that is an intolerable situation.

"In cases where a salary reduction becomes necessary, we make every effort to soften the impact on an employee and his or her family. We want to work with you to achieve that goal. We can provide counseling if necessary.

"I see from your personnel file that you are drawing some retirement benefits from your previous employment and that you derive a certain amount of income from investments. I also understand that your wife has job skills that enable her to supplement the family income. And of course, if your income should fall below a certain level, you might become eligible for a wide array of government benefits.

"In the near future, you may be receiving a check for your share of the tax cut that President Bush recently signed into law. That ought to help ease the transition to a lower pay grade. If you have any questions, I will try to answer them. Mr. Cheney? Hello?"

That's a flight of fantasy, but what about those Republican Senate committee staff members who suddenly found themselves out of work when the changeover occurred? More than one GOP senator tried to lay a guilt trip on Sen. James Jeffords, R-Vt., when he turned independent, blaming him for staff job losses when Republicans lost committee chairmanships.

It's too bad these staffers couldn't get the same kind of severance pay as workers at Ireland's most popular brewery. When Guinness fired 140 employees at its Dundalk plant the company gave them 10 years of free beer as part of an innovative compensation package. Not that dedicated, hard-working Capitol Hill jobholders like the suds ...

If the Senate tried to copy the Irish plan, the best a fired staffer could expect would be a supply of pencils and note pads, or perhaps a desk pen set or a pair of bookends—all bearing the imprint of "U.S. Senate." It's not quite the same as Guinness stout.

*June 21, 2001*

## Letter To a Vacationing President Out In the Heartland

Dear Mr. President 43:

Your critics are giving you a hard time for spending August in Texas. Here's some advice: don't let them give you heartburn for going to the heartland. The jalapenos will do enough.

The criticism is highly unfair. Every working person deserves a break, and if you prefer Texas heat over Washington heat, enjoy it.

You're smart not to copy your dad, President 41, who gave himself an image he didn't deserve when he decided to run the Persian Gulf war from Kennebunkport. A golf cart is not the best choice for a command post.

True, you don't have an armed conflict on your hands, unless you count that pesky Israeli-Palestinian dispute. But clearing brush in your blue jeans does send a strong signal to would-be troublemakers overseas: don't mess with Texas—or the guy with a chainsaw who calls that Godforsaken place home. (Sorry, a bit of friendly Oklahoma rivalry coming through.)

You've got every right to pick your vacation spot. You are the man. If that 1,583 acres of dust you call the Prairie Chapel Ranch is where you want to be, then Crawford, Tex. is the current world capital.

The worst bellyachers are the traveling White House press, mostly a bunch of East and West coast sophisticates whose closest association with the Southwest lifestyle is free taco night at the National Press Club. As Maria Antonio might say, let 'em eat cactus.

As for the whiners who complain that a president shouldn't be away from his desk, why do we have a vice president if not to serve as a summer temp? Dick Cheney is filling in nicely running the country just as well as when the boss is in town. Cheney did arouse some controversy over a scheduled trip to Salt Lake City for the Utah Republican state convention.

Cheney's Secret Service agents had the audacity to demand that nobody be allowed to tote a gun during the veep's appearance. The Utah Gun Owners Alliance angrily protested, claiming "Self-defense is a right." They apparently feel threatened by a mild-mannered 60-year-old man with a heart condition. Well, he was secretary of defense, after all, and he does know how to launch a missile. Packing a .45 might make them feel safer.

Besides Cheney, Federal Reserve Chairman Alan Greenspan also is on the job. And everybody knows he's the real power in Washington.

So you don't need to hurry back, Mr. President. Congress won't be in session until after Labor Day. Just ignore all that yapping about the length of your vacation. At least you're not frittering away your time floating over the ocean in a balloon.

And look at Tom Brokaw. He's taking 10 weeks off! If somebody that important to the well-being of the people of this nation can be away, certainly a president can have a little leisure time. By relinquishing his NBC anchor post for such a lengthy period, Brokaw did risk missing the biggest news story of the summer, which could be running on the next TV newscast:

"Rep. Gary Condit suffered a heat stroke while playing touch football on a beach during a family outing. His public relations adviser said the congressman had spent part of the day fighting forest fires. She said he recovered quickly, in time to rescue a female constituent from a shark attack. The victim tested negative for the West Nile virus but she has some side effects of a cholesterol drug. Rumors circulated that Condit had invited the woman to his Washington apartment, but he declined comment to anyone but Connie Chung."

*August 23, 2001*

## Some 9-11 Reactions Show How To Tickle a Terrorist

The president says—commands—everybody get back to work.

The masters of terrorism must be watching with diabolical joy at how some Americans reacted in the chaotic days that followed the horrible disaster of September 11.

Perhaps a bemused smile crept across the Satanic face of Osama bin Laden as Sen. Hillary Clinton, D-N.Y., spoke approvingly of President Bush, knowing that bipartisanship often is transitory.

More than likely he flashed a wicked grin at the picture of former president Bill Clinton and his vice president, Al Gore, oddly reunited by the destruction of the World Trade Center towers. Clinton invited the stranded Gore to stay overnight at his Chappaqua, N.Y. home, then fly to Washington on a government plane. (It must have been Gore's birthday call to his old boss that broke the ice.)

Iraqi tyrant Saddam Hussein surely clapped his hands in exhilaration at the *Washington Post* headline: "Nation Reels." He probably danced with devilish glee at *Post* columnists Mary McGrory and David Broder's implied cowardice of the commander-in-chief because he prudently delayed returning to the capital following a credible threat to Air Force One. McGrory said Bush "flunked" his first test in the crisis, and Broder wrote that the president "seemed to be seeking a hideaway from both unknown enemies and his own nerves." *Post* TV critic Tom Shales also kicked the nation's leader, labeling him "ineffectual, neither reassuring nor forceful enough."

Terrorists planning future attacks no doubt delighted in the *Post*'s publishing of details of how flight attendants are trained to thwart hijackers from entering the cockpit.

Mad bombers cowering in their caves could take fiendish pleasure in the media's obsession with the idea of removing the ban on assassinations of monsters like bin Laden, as if to say, "he must be read his Miranda rights."

America haters everywhere must have been cheered by the absurd statement of Gar Smith, editor of the Earth Island Institute's journal, that the terrorist strikes were "an attack not on U.S. citizens but an assault on U.S. foreign policy."

They must have loved hearing the Rev. Jerry Falwell's opinion that the tremendous loss of life and property was "probably what we deserve" for harboring feminists, homosexuals and civil rights groups—with televangelist Pat Robertson chiming in.

Reports of merchants hiking prices of gasoline and the U.S. flag might have been music to the ears of madmen bent on disrupting the American economy.

If such thoughts ran through the twisted minds of those who would destroy this country, they should wipe the smiles off their faces. Americans quickly united against a common enemy. Blame seekers recanted their remarks, including Falwell and Robertson. Some columnists began to write admiringly of Bush's onsite visits to the Pentagon and New York and of his leadership in rallying the nation from a devastating blow and pointing the way toward victory over evildoers. Retailers bowed to public protest.

Maybe it was just a coincidence, but unquestionably fortunate timing, for the Postal Service to pick the day after the disaster to announce it will seek a 9 percent increase in postage rates. The story was buried on an inside page.

Americans are going back to work, restoring a shaken society and seeking a return to normalcy. But perspectives have been forever changed.

*September 20, 2001*

## President's Pretzel Incident Produces a Lot of Bad Chokes

There is no hard evidence that the White House chief of staff made the following remarks in a staff meeting, but he might have:

"As you all know, extraordinary measures have been taken to protect the life of POTUS, especially since September 11. White House tours were cancelled. Streets were closed to establish a security perimeter. Concrete pollards block vehicular passage on Pennsylvania Avenue, Jersey barriers are massed at the 15th and 17th street entrances, and chain link fencing surrounds the Ellipse. Air force jet fighters stand ready to provide cover for Air Force One and to intercept any aircraft threatening Washington, D.C. Increased security accompanies POTUS when he travels. His Secret Service detail is always on alert wherever he goes—well, almost everywhere. The president and the first lady are afforded some privacy in the family quarters.

"In a word, George W. Bush probably is the most heavily guarded president in American history. Yet we are faced with a most serious breach of security, an event which could have been disastrous. Immediately upon learning last Sunday that the president had fainted and fallen on the floor, suffering an ugly facial abrasion, I ordered an internal investigation. It was ascertained that the president was alone, except for Barney and Spot, the family dogs. His wife was in an adjoining room talking on the telephone. He said he awoke to find the two dogs looking at him curiously.

"We checked out one suspected cause of his fainting—a column in a liberal newspaper absolving the Bush administration of blame in the Enron scandal—but no evidence was found. We ran down a rumor that Senate Majority Leader Tom Daschle had sent word that he no longer opposed our tax cuts, and it proved to be untrue. Our final conclusion was that in spite of all precautions, a deadly substance came within close proximity of the commander-in-chief. Not realizing its dangerous potential, and in a moment of distraction while watching the NFL football game between the Baltimore Ravens and the Miami Dolphins, he momentarily forgot his mother's advice and swallowed without chewing. I refer, of course, to what is now known as the presidential pretzel incident.

"Fortunately, because of the president's superb physical condition—which doctors say could have caused him to choke—the incident resulted in no serious harm. But it is imperative that such an occurrence must not be repeated. Therefore, I have issued a series of directives.

"1. I have given strict orders that no items on a "dangerous substances" list that has been prepared shall come within reach of the president. The list includes pretzels, potato and corn chips, peanuts, popcorn, cheese puffs and oyster crackers, among other things. Special procedures will be in effect in the event of a visit by POTUS 41 to prevent covert delivery of pork rinds to the residential area of the White House. Soft tortillas and other snack foods certified to be safe will be permitted.

"2. It has been determined that the Bush family dogs must be replaced. As lovable as they may be, they pose too great a risk to the president's health. Their docile reaction to the sight of their owner lying passed out on the floor is unacceptable. The selection process will involve testing for alertness, responsiveness and bark-ability.

"3. A sign has been ordered for the president's desk which reads, "Chew Slowly."

"4. Serious consideration is being given to adding Dr. Harry Heimlich to the White House physician's staff.

*January 17, 2002*

## President Is Keeping Very Strange Company, Indeed

President Bush might not be totally up to speed on American pop culture (a new biography jeers that he had never heard of actor Leonardo DiCaprio), but he certainly knows about Bono, the lead singer of Grammy-winning rock band U2.

In fact, the president had the Irish rocker participate in a White House meeting with him, national security adviser Condoleezza Rice and Treasury Secretary Paul O'Neill. Afterwards Bono rode with Bush in the presidential limousine to an Inter-American Development Bank confab where the president praised his efforts to fight Third World poverty.

Certainly the nation's chief executive is entitled to obtain advice from whatever source he deems appropriate, but it makes one wonder if a regular briefing by his appointments secretary might go something like this:

"Mr. President, I'd like to go over your appointment schedule for the day. At 9 a.m. Attorney General John Ashcroft will give you an update on potential terrorist threats and share his views on the deeper meaning of *The Simpsons*. It's one of his favorite TV shows, you know, and his son and daughter-in-law recently gave him a set of the series on DVD.

"Next you will welcome visiting college athletes. This will be an opportunity for further elaboration of your remarks to another such group last week in which you said the 9-11 terrorists must have drawn the mistaken conclusion that the United States is a weak nation from watching *The Jerry Springer Show.*

"You will have lunch with Bo Derek for further discussion of her twin roles in your administration as a Kennedy Center trustee and as the national chairwoman of Department of Veterans Affairs Special Events. The first lady will be in attendance, at her request.

"In accordance with your desire to broaden your experience as a wartime president, Secretary of Defense Donald Rumsfeld has arranged for you to meet at 2 p.m. with two experts in hand-to-hand combat. This conference with Tonya Harding and Paula Jones will be in the White House gymnasium, where they will demonstrate the techniques they used on their 'Celebrity Boxing' special on TV.

"The secretary also wanted you to be able to expand your knowledge about offensive tactics by talking to Mike Tyson, but the Secret Service made it clear there was no way he would get anywhere close to you. As one of the agents commented, 'that man is more dangerous than a pretzel.'

"At 3:30 p.m. in the press briefing room you will announce your new family values initiative to promote strong marriages. A photo opportunity is scheduled and you will be joined by Liza Minelli and her new husband, David Gest.

"Between 4 and 4:30 p.m. your 2004 advisory team will present an analysis of the political significance of Al Gore shaving off his beard prior to Tipper Gore's announcement that she would not run for the U.S. Senate from Tennessee.

"You will have a half hour of time to handle phone calls and other desk work, work out, and play with the dogs.

"Then at 5 p.m. you will go by helicopter to Andrews Air Force base to fly to Florida. The purpose of this trip is not to campaign for your brother, Jeb, but to spend the weekend with Rosie O'Donnell, at her invitation, to become better informed about alternative parenting issues.

"That is a pretty full schedule, Mr. President, but if I may say so, it is all high quality time."

*March 21, 2002*

## Did the President Really Say What They Said He Said?

Some purists have been complaining that President Bush's words are not being properly preserved for posterity. They insist he be quoted verbatim for the sake of historical accuracy.

What a lot of hooey! They seem to forget that it has been a longstanding White House practice to clean up a president's language before it gets printed in an official transcript. ("Clean up" might be the wrong term to use, except maybe in the case of Richard Nixon or LBJ.)

In past administrations, it has been perfectly acceptable to correct small mistakes and smooth out grammatical goofs. One of Bill Clinton's press secretaries, Mike McCurry, has said White House stenographers were given the go ahead to restore the "g" to words ending in "ing"—to repair the damage wrought by a southern accent.

But critics like Joe Lockhart, McCurry's successor, contend that the Bush handlers are "rewriting history." (As if Clinton didn't do that by usually giving his own version of the truth.)

It's true Bush has made some misstatements—like calling Connecticut Lt. Gov. Jodi Rell "Judi Kell." What president hasn't gotten somebody's name wrong? Oklahomans will recall that when the former governor and senator, Henry Bellmon, was campaigning with Rep. Page Belcher in the 1960s, on more than one occasion a visiting Republican dignitary would heap the highest praise on "my good friend, Page Bellmon."

When Bush told a Missouri audience he wanted to make "the death tax permanent," the transcript of his speech added an asterisk and a footnote explaining that it should read "death tax repeal." But such words as "misunderestimated", coined by Bush, remain untouched, said a White House spokeswoman.

So what if a president's remarks don't read the same way he uttered them? Making minor revisions before they are printed is no worse than what members of Congress do. When tempers flare on the floor of the Senate and harsh words are spoken, it is not uncommon for such an exchange to be stricken from the official proceedings—or at least modified considerably. Members of the House of Representatives customarily "revise and extend" their remarks for the *Congressional Record*.

Having laid the foundation of a strong defense for Bush and his staff, I'm now curious to see the transcript of the president's speech to the White House Correspondents' Association dinner last Saturday night. I wasn't in attendance, and couldn't watch it on C-SPAN because a thunderstorm knocked out satellite dish transmission. All I have to go on is the *Washington Post* and the *New York Times*—newspapers that we know aren't always 100 per cent accurate.

These dinners always have some high-profile guests, and this year's major celebrity was Ozzy Osbourne, the aging British rocker with magenta-brown hair and pink shades who is currently starring with his family in the hottest show on TV. On *The Osbournes*, the lines he speaks are a mix of mumbles and bleeps. In his heavy metal concerts he has bitten off the heads of a bat and a dove. He was at the Fox News table.

Both the *Post* and the *Times* report that Bush singled out Osbourne in his speech. The papers quote him as saying, "he's made a lot of big hit recordings", mentioning such titles as "Party With the Animals", "Sabbath Bloody Sabbath" and "Bloodbath in Paradise." Then he added: "Ozzy, Mom loves your stuff."

Or so the papers say. Let's see how the transcript reads.

As for Osbourne, the *Post* had this quote from him: "I hengh heenth hunh president denngh hmmhmme heng!"

*May 9, 2002*

## Congressional Hindsight Committee Upstaged By Security Plan

One thing Congress does well is investigate. It's the fun part of the lawmaking process. Who wouldn't rather glare down at a nervous witness and demand to know what he knew and when he knew it than to sit through monotonous appropriations hearings or try to get support for a bill nobody is interested in?

So you might say these are fun times in Washington. The Congressional Hindsight Committee got in gear and settled in for a long run—at least until the next election—while the Joint Task Force on Fingerpointing and Faultfinding staffed up for an equally lengthy pursuit of truth and publicity. Meanwhile, there were calls in both the House and Senate for a Blue Ribbon Blamecasting Commission with an annual budget the size of Finland's.

But the executive branch of government was not about to let Congress have the only circus in town. The Bush administration launched a counteroffensive by doing what the bureaucracy enjoys doing the most—government reorganization.

In a bold move that knocked congressional investigators out of the spotlight, at least for the moment, President Bush unveiled a plan cooked up in secret in the White House basement to establish a Department of Homeland Security.

Now some citizens might have thought we already had one of those, headed by Bush's good friend, Tom Ridge. But Ridge's operation is only small potatoes. Texans tend to think big, you know, and Bush has put forth a Texas-sized proposal to combine 22 agencies into a giant bureaucracy of 170,000 employees who will come to work each morning, as the president said, "knowing that their most important job is to protect their fellow citizens." Right now these employees probably come to work with one thing on their minds: how to protect their own turf.

When Ridge was quizzed about the initiative on NBC News' *Meet the Press*, he stressed the importance of getting and sharing information. He said that "trying to discriminate between rumor and speculation and misinformation and fact and everything else that's in the clutter of information and noise out there is a critically important process."

The president himself established the criteria for handling information and addressing issues in a way that solves problems. In a speech to the 14th Annual World Pork Expo in Des Moines, Bush told of how he dealt with a specific issue: "I went at it in a way—the only way I knew how, which is in a straightforward, plain-spoken way."

Well, the secretary of defense, Donald Rumsfeld, must not have gotten the message. Here's part of his response to a reporter at a press conference at NATO

Headquarters in Brussels last week. The question was about intelligence information and terrorist threats:

"The message is that there are no 'knowns.' There are things we know that we know. There are known unknowns. That is to say there are things that we now know we don't know. But there are also unknown unknowns. There are things we don't know we don't know.

"So when we do the best we can and we pull all this information together, and we then say, 'Well, that's basically what we see as the situation,' that is really only the known knowns and the known unknowns. Each year, we discover a few more of those unknown unknowns."

Rumsfeld went on to clarify further:

"There's another way to phrase that and that is that the absence of evidence is not evidence of absence. Simply because you do not have evidence that something exists does not mean that you have evidence that it doesn't exist."

Is that plain enough for you?

*June 13, 2002*

# Now We Know All About Saddam Hussein's Weak Spots

With President Bush determined to bring about a "regime change" in Iraq, it's presumed that orders have been issued to find out everything that can be learned about Saddam Hussein. You have to know your enemy in order to destroy him, as the international regime-changing experts might say.

The Central Intelligence Agency no doubt has provided a great deal of, well, intelligence. But the president should not overlook other sources of information about this villainous ruler. We earnestly hope he has got wind of the ABC News program about Saddam's former mistress.

Our early-to-bed president might have missed the primetime broadcast featuring Claire Shipman's interview of Parisoula Lampsos, who said she was Saddam's mistress off and on for 30 years. She also claimed she saw him almost daily and shared his innermost thoughts.

So what did she tell ABC? She said he liked to look in the mirror and say, "I am Saddam. Heil Hitler!" He enjoyed watching videos of his enemies being tortured, and he once tried to get his son killed, she added.

Well, we already knew he wasn't a nice guy. It's Saddam's personal habits that might be his undoing.

Lampsos told Shipman her ex-lover enjoyed relaxing with a cowboy hat on his head. Maybe Dubya could send him one of his castoffs. That ought to drive him up the wall, especially if a few Texas cockleburrs were stuck inside the crown.

Another thing he liked to do was listen to Frank Sinatra. Bush could send in a Special Forces team armed with boom boxes and drive him crazy with Barry Manilow tapes.

The former mistress also revealed that Saddam sometimes used Viagra to enhance their sexual encounters. Remember several years ago when some genius in the national security apparatus dreamed up the idea of sending Fidel Castro an exploding cigar? What about implanting an explosive device in one of Saddam's pills? Ouch!

Perhaps the piece of information that could be the most damaging to the Iraqi leader is the fact that he raises gazelles—and that he has them slaughtered for his dinnertime meals. When People for the Ethical Treatment of Animals finds that out, Bush might not even have to think about using U.S. troops to do away with him. PETA is a force to be reckoned with.

That Saddam has had contacts with Osama bin Laden should come as no surprise, but Lampsos confirmed it. After all, the two tyrants have a lot in common. Both enjoy the company of a large number of women, it seems.

One of bin Laden's wives spoke to a London-based Arabic weekly, Al-Majallah, and said that carrying out terrorism made him irritable. The woman, identified only as "A.S.", said the al Qaeda leader suffered from kidney and stomach ailments.

On his weekly visits, taking turns seeing his different wives, bin Laden "was constantly worried and looked tired and exhausted due to the lack of sleep," she said. "Most days he was taking medicine and sleeping pills to help him go to sleep." She made no mention of any other kind of pill.

Most people wouldn't have a problem with a woman wanting to stand by her man, but if these two women think they can generate any sympathy for the two murderous thugs they shared beds with, they don't know Americans very well.

All they have done is shed more light on the men's weaknesses, which ultimately could lead to their downfall. May that day be sooner rather than later.

*September 19, 2002*

## Bush Can Blame His Problems On Bad "Chi" in the Office

If everything doesn't always go the way President Bush wants it to, he can always blame it on bad "chi" in the Oval Office.

That's "chi", not "Cheez Doodles"—reported to be a favorite snack of the nation's chief executive.

Bush's workspace simply is not conducive to high performance, according to Sara Schroerlucke. She is a 22-year career employee of the federal government and currently is an Internal Revenue Service official. But that's got nothing to do with White House furnishings. She is not in charge of tax code regulations on home offices.

Schroerlucke is a voice of authority because she is a certified practitioner of feng shui (pronounced "fung shway"), which is not a type of Oriental cooking but the ancient Chinese art of placement. The idea is that a person's environment should be in balance and in harmony with nature.

In an interview with the *Federal Paper*, Schroerlucke shared some interesting findings of her audit of the layout of the president's office. As her interviewer, A. B. Stoddard, reported, "the president experiences trouble getting people to listen to him because the Oval Office suffers from poor feng shui."

So what's the problem?

"Unfortunately for the nation's boss, and his predecessors," Stoddard wrote, "the president sits with his back to the window, robbing him of essential 'chi', or energy, which diminishes support for administration policies.

"There are also too many doors in the Oval Office, providing multiple escapes for chi."

Well, then, what's the solution?

"Schroerlucke recommends that Bush reposition his desk with his back against a wall."

All presidents surely have had days when they feel like that. So before Dubya calls in Dick Cheney and some other guys with muscle to start shifting furniture around, consider what else the energy-efficient interior designer advises.

Wearing lots of purple and red (yang colors) would boost confidence and authority, she suggested.

"She also recommends that he surround himself with symbols of strength, compassion, motivation and wisdom," the article said. That's Laura Bush, but she can only be in one place at a time. Besides, the first lady has better things to do than be a floor lamp.

One suggestion might not be too hard for Bush to follow. The "chi" consultant, a Las Vegas native, seems to believe in luck—not from a rabbit's foot but from a small green elephant. She has one next to her telephone.

"The elephant who puts his ear to the ground hears for miles and miles," she counseled. The Republican party symbol wouldn't be out of place on Bush's desk—say, close to the hotline.

Skeptics might ask, does feng shui really work? Schroerlucke can point to her own experience as a government bureaucrat as a testimonial. After 18 years of federal service, she was still a GS-13. She redesigned her living room, getting rid of a statue of Hamlet holding Yorick's skull, and is now a GS-15 managing a multimillion dollar information technology project.

If Al Gore learns about that kind of success, he might try to hire her as a campaign adviser for 2004.

*October 17, 2002*

## Snow Time at White House May Be Good for Ooching Economy

Who says President Bush doesn't have a sense of humor? He really got into the spirit of the winter holiday season when he picked a man named Snow to shovel out of an economic drift.

The new treasury secretary, CSX chairman John Snow, became an instant target for wisecracks. *Kansas City Star* columnist Bill Tammeus said Bush should have chosen Apple computer CEO Steve Jobs as the new White House economic adviser. "Fiscal policy then could be officially Snow-Jobs," he quipped.

Bush probably did a smart thing by choosing a railroad man to put the economy back on track. At least Snow ought to be more popular on Wall Street and Capitol Hill than Paul O'Neill, who was pink-slipped along with chief economic adviser Lawrence Lindsey.

The blunt-speaking O'Neill once characterized currency traders as "not the sort of people you would want to help you think about complex questions." He termed the House Republican economic stimulus package "show business" and publicly pooh-poohed the president's tax policies.

Still, it seemed a rather cruel deed to kick out the economic teammates right before Christmas. To show there were no hard feelings, Bush probably should have given them a pleasure trip on the newest Disney cruise ship, the Nausea.

O'Neill must have naively assumed that what came out of his mouth didn't matter all that much, considering some of the utterances of his boss. There was that time last August, for instance, when the president said in Waco, Tex.: "There may be some tough times here in America. But this country has gone through tough times before, and we're going to do it again." How's that for creating optimism?

The difference is that the market didn't go crazy when Bush made remarks like this one in Boston last Oct. 4: "Let me tell you my thoughts about tax relief. When your economy is kind of ooching along, it's important to let people have more of their own money."

So his marching orders to his new team are apt to be something like: "I want you to take this ooching economy and get it to mooching—or moving, or whatever it takes to see us through the tough times."

Bush's grammatical gaffes may, in a small way, be helping one segment of the economy—the Christmas toy industry. The "talking President Bush doll" is a hot selling item among Internet shoppers, according to its creator, John Warnock. The foot-high Bush miniature, which sells for $29.99, is programmed with "17 powerful and patriotic phrases," Warnock's Web site explains. Press a button on the back and the doll says, "I will not hold this nation hostile," or "I will put food on your family."

The Dubya doll is not the product of a devilish Democrat. Warnock is a California Republican and says he's a big fan of Bush. That should be a big thrill for the president.

Bush was not at a loss for words when country artist Roy Clark had an embarrassing moment at the White House national tree-lighting ceremony. Clark, who was this year's Santa Claus, was in the spotlight and while the president and first lady and thousands of viewers watched, his red pants slowly slipped to below his knees. Washington TV station WJLA reported Clark was wearing sweatpants under his suit. Bush told the audience: "I appreciate Santa coming. It looks like he needs a belt for Christmas."

And we thought pants-dropping at the White House went out when Bill Clinton left.

*December 12, 2002*

## Democratic Candidates Say: "Vote For Me—I'm Different"

With nine Democrats in the field already and others thinking about running for president next year, voters are asking themselves: "Who are these people? Why should I vote for any of them?"

News reports tell us there are four U.S. senators, two members of the House of Representatives, one governor, and a former senator in the race for the Democratic nomination. And proving this is a free country where any native-born American over 35 who has lived here 14 years can seek the presidency regardless of how unqualified he is, Al Sharpton is a candidate.

There's more than one "Joe Millionaire" in the group, but they all need huge amounts of money to mount credible campaigns. Some of the party's biggest contributors, from New York City to Hollywood, are holding back, waiting to see the candidates "distinguish themselves," the *Associated Press* reports.

That poses a challenge to the "gang of nine" to show how they are different from one another. Voters appreciate candor, so it's in their best interest to be brutally honest.

In their campaign appearances around the country, here's how each of the candidates' self-introductions might go:

"I am Sen. Joseph Lieberman of Connecticut and I'm Jewish. I should have been vice president. I am sponsoring legislation to honor America's military working dogs."

"I am Sen. John Kerry of Massachusetts. I'm an Irish Catholic, but my grandparents were Jewish. I am a veteran and I have good hair. I recently had prostate cancer surgery after telling a reporter I was in good health."

"I am Sen. Bob Graham of Florida, a former governor of that state. I had recent heart surgery which was more extensive than previously disclosed. I have a habit of making daily entries in color-coded notebooks about what I eat, how I dress and other mundane details."

"I am Sen. John Edwards of North Carolina. I am a trial lawyer who has made lots of money from personal injury lawsuits. I've got good hair. I was caught on national television popping and chewing gum at a dinner marking the 30th anniversary of the Supreme Court's Roe v. Wade decision."

"I am Rep. Richard Gephardt of Missouri. I should have been speaker of the House. I'm not the flashiest candidate around. I have no eyebrows. I love organized labor. My goal is the enactment of a global minimum wage."

"I am Rep. Dennis Kucinich of Ohio. That's K-U-C-I-N-I-C-H. I have weird eyebrows and strange hair. I'm an FDR Democrat with ties to Big Labor. I'm an anti-war demagogue. I am running my campaign on the Internet."

"I am Gov. Howard Dean of Vermont. I am the only governor in the race. I am a physician. I have even lower name recognition than Kucinich. I'm the official underdog."

"I am Carol Moseley-Braun. I'm a former senator from Illinois. I am an African-American. I am a woman. I was accused of dipping into campaign funds for personal use. I am the only candidate with a hyphenated name."

"I am the Rev. Al Sharpton of New York City. I was supposed to be the sole black contender in the race. I have perfected the art of being obnoxious, according to the *Washington Post*. I have faced tax evasion charges, had to pay damages to a man I wrongly accused of rape and was blamed for inciting an arson attack on a white-owned Harlem business. Well, everybody in politics has baggage."

*March 6, 2003*

## Byrd Shots Wound Democrats Running for President

If Sen. Robert C. Byrd finds a pair of crosses burning on his lawn he might have a momentary nostalgic memory of his days in the Ku Klux Klan. But such an event, if it were to occur, more likely would be race-related only as it applies to the 2004 race for president.

The Democrats who are running no doubt would like to send a graphic message accusing Byrd of a doublecross. The West Virginia Democrat did his party and its candidates a great disservice by his pompous attack on President Bush for his visit to the USS Abraham Lincoln to greet homebound troops and declare a combat victory in Iraq.

Byrd took to the Senate floor to lament the anguish he felt "as I watched the president's fighter jet swoop down onto the deck of the aircraft carrier." Amid quotes from the Bible and reminiscences of "the tobacco barns of my youth," the self-styled "Dean of Congress" pulled out all the oratorical stops. He found Bush guilty of "self-congratulatory gestures," using the ship "as an advertising backdrop for a presidential political slogan" and the uniformed troops "as stage props." It was "an affront" to those killed or injured in battle, Byrd said, for Bush to "exploit the trappings of war ..."

In a classic example of pot-and-kettle rhetoric, he charged Bush with an act of "flamboyant showmanship." What gall, considering that Byrd flaunts his image as "pork barrel king" by putting his name on more highways, buildings and other taxpayer-financed projects in West Virginia than Saddam Hussein ever thought of doing in Iraq.

The dramatic fly-in by the commander-in-chief was so well received by the 5,000 troops aboard the ship and the public in general, Byrd had few allies by his side. Rep. Henry Waxman, D-Calif., a fellow big spender, called for an investigation into how much it cost for the president to pay tribute to the men and women who liberated Iraq in just 21 days. Another California Democrat, Rep. Maxine Waters, was outraged that Bush wore a "custom-fitted flight suit."

Byrd, who may be more comfortable in a white sheet than camouflage clothing, said he questioned "the motives of a deskbound president who assumes the garb of a warrior for the purposes of a speech." Someone should tell Byrd and Waters that Bush was dressed quite appropriately since he flew the Navy S-3B Viking jet part of the way. A former pilot in the National Guard, Bush also knows how to salute, unlike his predecessor.

Byrd calls himself a historian, but he ignores the fact that every president since John Tyler in 1844 spent time on a Navy vessel. A Democrat, John F. Kennedy, was the first to visit a carrier. Even Bill Clinton, who said he "loathed" the military, traveled on a warship from Britain to Normandy for the 50th anniversary of the D-Day invasion. Talk about exploiting "the trappings of war" for political purposes!

By his clumsy, ego-driven assault, Byrd actually did Bush and his party a big favor. Every time he or another Democrat takes a potshot, those images of a triumphant wartime leader flash across the TV screen. The stupidity of Byrd's speech drove the liberal *Washington Post* to editorialize about "the Democrats' tone-deaf handling of this episode."

After Byrd's jibes about "props" and "backdrops", what Democratic candidate would dare climb into a tank as Michael Dukakis did in 1988? Not even Sen. John Kerry, D-Mass., who wants to make sure everyone knows he is a Vietnam veteran, would be that dumb.

*May 15, 2003*

## Savior of the Democrats Must Be Wearing a Disguise

When word was received that Saddam Hussein was running around Iraq in disguise, two thoughts came to mind:

1.   He's safe. Who would arrest someone who looks like Captain Kangaroo?

2.   What kind of disguise has Al Gore been wearing?

With his frequent radio reports, the Iraqi leader gives some evidence he's still alive.

But the former leader of the Democratic party hasn't been heard from in months—well, not until this week. A spokesman for the anti-war organization MoveOn said Gore called and asked to speak to its members at a meeting at New York University. He had dropped out of sight after his appearance on *60 Minutes* last December to announce he wasn't running for president in 2004.

Before he resurfaced, Gore might have been "hiding in public", just like Saddam. The former vice president got plenty of experience in remaking his image when he was campaigning in the last election. After losing to George W. Bush he grew a beard and mustache. He was clean shaven when he emerged as a book promoter and potential candidate last fall. Who knows if he grew facial hair again, and if he looked more like Osama bin Laden or Charlie Daniels?

With the media buildup for Howard Dean, a flaming liberal who stands about as much chance of being elected as Kobe Bryant, the party bosses probably would love for Gore to change his mind about making another run.

The Democrats who did put their careers on the line to seek the White House are having all kinds of problems. Sen. John Kerry of Massachusetts and Sen. John Edwards of North Carolina had that pesky little matter of late payment of their taxes. Rev. Al Sharpton was tardy in filing a quarterly campaign finance report, the least of his transgressions. Sen. Joseph Lieberman of Connecticut got a sore arm from trying to steer the party toward the center.

And Rep. Dick Gephardt of Missouri was dizzy from dodging questions like what he intends to do about "the chicken problem." That challenge came from a New Hampshire eighth-grader who complained about school lunches. "Every day we have chicken," he said. "We're sick of it." Gephardt told the boy, "If you don't eat chicken, you won't be successful in politics."

The Democratic field is so dismal, TV talk show hosts were thrilled at the prospect of Sen. Joe Biden of Delaware making a run for the presidency. Biden, or any other candidate entering the race now, faces three problems: raising enough money, finding a vacant time slot on the Leno or Letterman show to announce his candidacy, and getting a celebrity endorsement to match the one Rep. Dennis Kucinich of Ohio got from Willie Nelson. (With his past tax problems, wouldn't Willie be more in tune with Kerry or Edwards?)

Jerry Springer would be a good campaigner for the Democrats, but he's got his eye on the Senate. What he really should do is move to California and run for governor.

If Gore stays out and no better candidate comes forth, Democrats don't have to lose all hope. A presidential exploratory committee has been formed for former Rep. James Traficant, D-Ohio, who is doing time in a Pennsylvania prison on a bribery and racketeering conviction. A Traficant campaign spokesman is quoted as saying, "Someone buy the Washington establishment a bottle of Maalox."

*August 7, 2003*

## Who's Running for President? Voters Don't Have a Clue

You have to feel a little sorry for the Democrats running for president this year. Despite all the money they've spent and the miles they've traveled, most voters don't know who they are—much less what they stand for.

A poll taken just before Labor Day—the traditional campaign season kick-off—showed that two-thirds of the people who were surveyed could not name any of the candidates seeking the Democratic presidential nomination.

In the CBS poll of 775 registered voters Connecticut Sen. Joe Lieberman had the highest name recognition, but that was only 14 percent. You would think the Democratic candidate for vice president in the last election would have made a bigger impression. Ah, how soon we forget! But then, some candidates are just remarkably forgettable.

Close on Lieberman's heels were Missouri Rep. Dick Gephardt at 11 percent and former Vermont Gov. Howard Dean at 10 percent. Nobody in the rest of the field could do any better than 5 percent of voters who ever heard of them.

You have to wonder if Lieberman and Gephardt would have made as good a showing if they hadn't come up with some ideas to get attention—such all-American ideas as baseball and apple pie.

Lieberman appealed to New Hampshire voters with a campaign to "See Joe's Car and Go See Nomar." Anyone spotting the candidate's "JoeMobile" could win a chance for free tickets to see Boston Red Sox star shortstop Nomar Garciaparra in a game with the Chicago White Sox.

Gephardt's campaign announced a "pie challenge" in the important caucus state of Iowa. Citing the candidate's "deep dish support", the announcement called on Iowans to help him find "the tastiest, flakiest, fruitiest, creamiest, most scrumptious slices of pie" in the state.

Dean, who is a doctor, used a different kind of gimmick. At a Fourth of July parade in New Hampshire, he handed out tongue depressors stamped with his Web site address. The things some candidates will do sort of makes you want to gag.

It's really hard to believe Massachusetts Sen. John Kerry did so poorly in the name recognition poll, considering some of the stunts he's pulled to get attention. Kerry surely must have known he would get wide publicity when he went into Pat's Steaks in Philadelphia and ordered a cheesesteak—with Swiss cheese. As anybody knows, Philly cheesesteaks come with Cheez Whiz, or maybe American cheese, or provolone. Even Al Gore knew that much.

In Wisconsin—Harley-Davidson country—Kerry campaigned riding his own bike. He got photos of himself windsurfing in *Vogue* magazine. Maybe these efforts to project a macho image were supposed to offset his reputation for $75 haircuts, expensive shirts and long well-manicured fingernails. (He needs to have long nails to play classical guitar, says his staff.)

Former Illinois Sen. Carol Moseley Braun registered with only 2 percent of the voters in the poll, and Ohio Rep. Dennis Kucinich was at the bottom of the list with zero. Maybe if they changed their names to Jennifer Lopez and Ben Affleck ...

The state of mind of the American voter, as seen by this and other polls, would do nothing to discourage the late entry of another candidate with low name recognition—someone like retired Gen. Wesley Clark. Skeptics might ask how a nonentity from Arkansas could expect to be elected. Well, in 1992 that description fit Bill Clinton, and it didn't keep him from going to the White House.

*September 18, 2003*

## Long-running Senate Talk Shows Provide Entertainment

By staging a 39-hour talkathon, the U.S. Senate proved what most voters already know: senators are longwinded, and they will go to almost any length to make a point.

Senate Democrats also demonstrated their ability to make light of what the Republicans considered a serious issue—blockage of President Bush's judicial nominations.

The extended debate produced some memorable moments, such as when Sen. Charles Schumer, D-N.Y., said the stalled nominees were "so far out of the mainstream they would take America back to the 1930s—or the 1890s." Sen. Edward Kennedy, D-Mass., reached farther back in history, saying that Democrats will "continue to resist any Neanderthal that is nominated by this president." You might say Teddy "went ape."

All the while, Bush stayed above the fray, occupying himself with taping a pre-Britain trip interview with *The Sun*, a Fleet Street tabloid that features daily photographs of nude women and articles about freaky human behavior.

Speaking of which, anyone watching the Senate spectacle on C-SPAN had the pleasure of seeing cots being rolled through the majestic halls of the U.S. Capitol for senators like Barbara Mikulski, D-Md., and Hillary Clinton, D-N.Y., to get their beauty rest. Seventeen cots were set up in a room named for the late Sen. Strom Thurmond, R-S.C., who set a still-unbroken record for a one-man filibuster in 1957, holding the floor for 24 hours and 17 minutes in opposition to a civil rights bill.

That's not to mention the display of visual aids carried by such senators as Pat Leahy, D-Vt. ("I voted to confirm 97 percent of Bush nominees and all I got was this lousy T-shirt") and Tom Harkin, D-Iowa, who stomped out of the session with a crudely lettered posterboard saying, "I'm going home to watch *The Bachelor*." Harkin might have taken his cue from fellow Democrat Dennis Kucinich, who is trying to pump up his presidential campaign by a public appeal for a wife to accompany him to the White House.

The non-stop session was the longest since 1988, when senators debated for 57 hours on campaign finance legislation. And to think, the Republicans mounted this marathon mouth exercise without Thurmond, who died last June at 100 years of age.

Even more ironic, the two-day debate came on the heels of a nearly nine-hour solo filibuster by minority whip Harry Reid, D-Nev., against an appropriations bill, which GOP Senate leaders had criticized. During his time on the Senate floor, Reid passionately spoke of such compelling topics as where his hometown of Searchlight, Nev., got its name and which desert cacti are "rabbit-proof."

With the long-running talk shows behind them, the senators got back to work on important business, including what to do about a $400,000 hole in the ground. After a year of construction, an underground capitol visitor center and tunnel system has followed historical government precedent in expanding far beyond its original $71 million cost estimate.

Taxpayers no doubt will be reassured by reports that lawmakers have installed "new fiscal checks" to control costs.

*November 21, 2003*

## The Big Question Is: Can God's Vote Be Counted?

Scrap the Iowa caucuses. Cancel the New Hampshire primary. Howard Dean and the rest of the pack can fold their tents. It's all over. President Bush is a shoo-in for reelection.

That's the word from no less an oracle than the Rev. Pat Robertson, who claims that God told him Bush would win a landslide victory next November.

"I really believe I'm hearing from the Lord it's going to be like a blowout election in 2004," said the politically-attuned televangelist. "It's shaping up that way."

Robertson said on his *700 Club* program on the Christian Broadcasting Network, which he founded, that Bush "could make terrible mistakes and come out of it" because "God's blessing him."

In spite of this holy messenger's unequivocal and confident prediction, the president might be well advised not to halt his fundraising nor to take anything for granted. To do so would be to totally disregard the wide range of opposition he faces.

It's a common notion that Bush is running unopposed. Well, maybe the news hasn't reached the precincts in Heaven, but there are 14 Republicans on the New Hampshire presidential primary ballot, in addition to the current occupant of the White House.

Thanks to the comprehensive election coverage by the *Washington Post*, voters can be informed of the views of Robert Haines, Michael Callis, Dick Bosa and John Rigazio, to name a few. A top issue for Haines, serving time for a parole violation, is "the deliberate attempt by the Dark Side to infiltrate the church." (Why wouldn't he merit a blessing from on high?)

Callis, a bricklayer, is sounding the alarm about Max Hugel, CIA deputy director under President Reagan. Bosa, an Italian ceramics company sales representative, has traveled widely over the state campaigning against the man he calls "a silver-spoon kid who's never had a real fight." Rigazio is a former Democrat who says in newspaper ads and on his Web site that he has "the answers to America's greatest problems."

Before dismissing these challengers as "fringe" candidates who don't matter, Bush and his advisors should remember some of the third party and independent campaigns of the past that did make a difference.

Take Ralph Nader, for instance. Some say he cost Al Gore his chance at winning the presidency. The *Post* quoted a Nader associate as saying that while the well-known consumer activist will not run again as the Green Party candidate, he is contemplating a race as an independent.

A recent article in the online *Salon* magazine by Micah L. Sifry raises the question of whether Ross Perot might be planning a return to presidential politics. Says Sifry: "Judging from a well-written 95-page book proposal making its way through the New York publishing circuit ... the crazy aunt in the basement wants to sing again."

And then there's Hillary Clinton, a self-proclaimed non-candidate who could always change her mind and tell Pat Robertson: "The devil made me do it!"

*January 9, 2004*

## John Kerry Suffers a Political Candidate's Worst Fate

John Kerry's campaign advisors must be of hardy stock. Consider the shocks they've had to endure since the liberal Democrat from Massachusetts began his quest for the presidency.

It was bad enough when they had to defend his Botox treatments and $75 haircuts, not to mention his incredible act of ordering swiss cheese on a Philly cheese steak. But those were small things. And what else could his imagemakers expect from a Boston Brahmin born rich and married wealthier.

The fact is, Kerry's entire campaign has been one gaffe after another. Some of his actions would make even the most seasoned political strategist weep:

- In early March Kerry said in an Urban Radio Network interview: "President Clinton was often known as the first black president. I wouldn't be upset if I could earn the right to be the second." That remark brought protests from civil rights groups and jeers from editorialists.

- On March 16, attacking a Republican campaign ad that chastised him for voting against a defense bill for aid to troops in Iraq, Kerry argued: "I actually did vote for the $87 billion before I voted against it." The image of the flip-flop candidate continued to build.

- Then the presumptive Democratic presidential nominee took a week's vacation at a Sun Valley ski resort, where he went snowboarding and lost his cool when he fell on a slope. He blamed the tumble on one of his newly-assigned Secret Service agents. "That (blankety-blank) ran into me," he said, adding sharply: "I don't fall down."

The latest shock to hit Kerry campaign headquarters came when the candidate decided to have elective surgery to repair a torn tendon in his right shoulder. It wasn't the fall on the Idaho mountain, Kerry insisted, but an incident that occurred last January in Iowa. When his bus braked to a sudden stop, he said, he braced himself and injured his arm.

Kerry's orthopedic surgeon said that following surgery his patient would have to give up shaking hands, picking up babies and other such physical activities for at least two weeks. No worse fate could befall a candidate!

Not only would the campaign be suspended for the second time in a month, but no handshaking or baby kissing? That's quite a deficit to have to make up.

Like a JFK from Massachusetts of an earlier era, Kerry has had health problems, including prostate cancer. But while reporters of John F. Kennedy's day helped to conceal his true physical condition from the public, a candidate today is under pressure to withhold nothing about his ability to serve if elected.

So what if his medical records reveal he's not part Irish, as he once claimed. They ought to be released, so voters can know all about John Kerry, from the top of his expensively coiffed head to his Gucci-clad feet.

After all, he does claim to be the candidate of the common man.

*April 9, 2004*

## Campaigning Is Risky and Someone Has To Take the Fall

Anyone running for president has to watch his step. It's so easy to get tripped up on the campaign trail, and the consequences could be injurious to the candidate's future.

Voters want someone in the Oval Office who is poised, upright and stable, a leader who can stay balanced, regardless of obstacles in his path.

With those standards, George W. Bush and John F. Kerry will have to work extra hard to get votes this fall.

They hit the ground running, but time after time both of these determined individuals have stumbled, and paid the price for their misjudgments.

The most recent occasion involved President Bush. While riding a mountain bike on his Crawford, Tex. Ranch he took a spill. Although he was wearing a helmet and mouth guard, he suffered some nasty scrapes and scratches on his face, as well as his right hand and both knees.

Bush was on mile 16 of a 17-mile course, and after the White House doctor patched him up he completed his ride. He followed his own wartime creed and stayed the course.

The president's press flacks (bicycle spokespersons?) quickly explained the reason for the fall was, "it's been raining a lot and the topsoil was loose." Democrats challenged that statement, saying it hadn't rained in the Crawford area for over a week. Thus, another round of mudslinging in the campaign.

Earlier this year Kerry took a nosedive while snowboarding on the slopes at an Idaho ski resort. He profanely accused a Secret Service agent of running into him, telling news media: "I don't fall down."

But then, not too long before the Bush flip-flop Kerry did indeed fall off a bicycle in Concord, Mass. Critics charged the Democratic senator was trying to go both left and right at the same time.

Evening the score at two tumbles each, going back to June, 2003, Bush fell from a motorized Segway scooter at Kennebunkport, Maine, where he was visiting his parents. The only pain he suffered that time was from seeing the embarrassing photographs published around the world.

Falls are nothing new for presidents or for their political challengers. Former president Bill Clinton, while visiting at golf champ Greg Norman's oceanside estate in Florida, caught his heel on a concrete step and went down. Norman broke his fall, but Clinton later had to have knee surgery.

In his 1996 campaign against Clinton, Republican Bob Dole plunged headlong from a stage into a gaggle of press photographers when a railing gave way.

War veteran Dole quipped, "I think I just earned my third Purple Heart by going over the rail."

And Gerald Ford's missteps helped launch a successful career for comedian Chevy Chase.

Candidates take warning: It's a good thing to keep an ear to the ground, but only if it's done intentionally. Voters don't want a president who might fall down on the job.

*June 4, 2004*

## If He's Going To Be In Style, The Veep Needs a Wig

The handwriting is on the wall for Dick Cheney.

The vice president's future political fate was sealed when John Kerry picked John Edwards as his running mate. The Democrats now have two white guys with lots of money and lots of hair seeking to recapture the White House in November.

The Republicans also have two rich white guys, and President Bush has a presentable head of hair. But the balding Cheney is no match for the blow-dried senator from North Carolina. If the GOP has any chance of attracting the most votes from citizens who place looks over leadership, Cheney has got to go.

The John-John ticket (has a nice Kennedy-type ring to it, doesn't it?) offers American voters two men who made their money the old-fashioned way: Kerry by marrying well and Edwards by suing doctors. Both should have a lock on the support of the country's hair stylists.

For his choice to be vice president, Kerry picked a man he had deemed unfit to be president while he was campaigning in the Democratic primaries. The Massachusetts liberal once put down his southern rival with the snide remark, "When I came back from Vietnam in 1969, I don't know if John Edwards was out of diapers then."

Why did he tap Edwards over such exciting possibilities as Rep. Dick Gephardt of Missouri, Iowa Gov. Tom Vilsack, or Florida Sen. Bob Graham? Despite their differences on issues, the two candidates do have one thing in common: they like to live well. Both have posh homes scattered around the country.

Edwards interrupted a beach vacation at one of those spots to fly to Washington for a secret meeting with Kerry, at which a deal apparently was made, with Edwards agreeing to give Kerry half of his energy and charisma.

It remains to be seen whether Kerry can embrace Edwards' theme of "two Americas"—one for the wealthy and one for the rest of us.

Kerry campaign strategists obviously recognized Edwards' potential as a fundraiser for the fall campaign. Since he lost the nomination battle to Kerry, Edwards has actively raised money all over the country. He recently spoke in Boston to a convention of well-heeled trial lawyers, the profession that made him wealthy.

As for Cheney, he apparently has been trying to remake his image to broaden his appeal to the voters. The vice president used street language on the floor of the U.S. Senate against a Democrat critic, Sen. Patrick Leahy. Some of Cheney's supporters say his rebuke was too mild and that he should have kicked the Vermont senator in the (bleep).

Edwards' favorite F-word is "fee."

Bush says he won't dump Cheney, and the longtime veteran of government and politics could give Edwards, the neophyte, a strong challenge in the debates. But before he goes before the cameras, the veep might want to go shopping for a hairpiece.

*July 9, 2004*

## The Parable of Bush and the Miracle of Charley

And so it came to pass that in the Year of Our Lord 2004, in the month of August, the ruler of the land was beset with troubles. The war in Iraq had resulted in mounting American casualties. The economy was an issue. His poll numbers were not great.

The capital city, which had survived a plague of cicadas in the spring, was in a state of high alert for terrorists.

The four-year reign of Bush, the Republican, was nearing a close. Kerry, the Democrat, was determined to deny him a second term. Kerry's followers had gathered in the city of Boston to condemn the sitting ruler, all the while preaching the gospel of the Golden Rule in politics.

Kerry traveled throughout the land telling the people of his plans to conduct wars with sensitivity, help the economy by raising taxes and end dread disease through stem cell research. His words were widely spread by adoring scribes of liberal beliefs.

As the Olympic games began in Greece, Bush was running an uphill race. His counselor, Rove, came bearing a stern message. "Verily, I say unto you, we need a miracle."

But Bush maintained a demeanor of optimism and confidence. He told the King of CNN, "I will win."

Perhaps he remembered the prophecy of Robertson, the televangelist, who in January spake these words: "I think George Bush is going to win in a walk. I really believe I'm hearing from the Lord it's going to be like a blowout election in 2004. God's blessing him."

Who could ignore the word of such a mighty oracle?

Yet Bush also recalled how he had come into power only after a difficult struggle in the state of Florida, with the final decision handed down by the highest court in the land. With that in mind, Bush had campaigned heavily in Florida, which so happened to be ruled by his brother.

Kerry, disdainfully declaring that he did not wear his religion on his sleeve, instead wrapped himself in the American flag and went about boasting of his heroism in four months of duty in Vietnam.

As time drew nigh for the Republican nominating convention, storm clouds were gathering off the coast of Florida. And lo, it became a hurricane, and the wise men of weather called it Charley.

And Charley roared into Florida with all its fury and cut a path of terrible destruction across the state. Bush responded to his brother's plea and proclaimed

Florida a disaster area, meaning the state would be flooded with millions of dollars in federal aid.

Bush made a personal visit to the stricken areas, which commanded the attention of the nation's scribes. He told them: "This is God's way of telling us that he's almighty and we're mortal."

Kerry, for once, did hold his silence.

Whether or not the oracle's prophecy was to be fulfilled, Charley did maketh for interesting speculation.

*August 20, 2004*

## Could the President Be Planning an October Surprise?

With the political conventions over, voters now turn to the serious business of deciding who should occupy the White House for the next four years.

There are many factors that could influence that important decision, not the least of which is who wears the coolest clothes: the Bush twins or the Kerry daughters.

Jenna and Barbara Bush made quite a splash at the big Republican blowout in New York, spilling such family secrets as their parents' ability to "shake it like a Polaroid picture." It remains to be seen whether voters will be more impressed with Jenna's risque remarks about her grandmother or Alexandra Kerry's tale about her father saving a pet hamster from drowning while on a family sailing trip.

President Bush came out of the convention with a sizeable lead over his opponent and the Kerry campaign has been impacted by some unexpected developments.

Former president Bill Clinton had to suspend his campaigning for the Democratic nominee because of an emergency quadruple heart bypass operation. Clinton gave the Massachusetts senator some advice in a lengthy telephone conversation, including the suggestion that he stop talking about Vietnam. Guess he figured voters don't need any more reminders about his draft dodging efforts to avoid military service.

The candidate's wife, Teresa Heinz Kerry, was hospitalized while campaigning in Iowa after she complained of lightheadedness. That's not a very desirable quality for a potential first lady.

In spite of his convention "bounce", Bush and his campaign strategists seem determined not to leave anything to chance as they head into the final phase of the election.

They're probably hatching up such ideas as a new grass-roots organization to rally support for the president: "Flip-floppers for Bush," wearing T-shirts reading, "I was for Kerry, but now I'm for Bush."

And if the tide should turn and Kerry makes a comeback and starts to pick up strength later this month, it's entirely possible the president might unveil an "October Surprise." It could take the form of an official communication:

To: LTJG John F. Kerry, USN Ret.

From: George W. Bush, Commander-in-Chief

Major gains have been made by U.S. armed forces both during and after the war to liberate the Iraqi people from the terrorist regime of Saddam Hussein.

However, in order to ensure a peaceful transition to a new way of life in Iraq, it will be necessary to maintain a substantial U.S. military presence in that country. The Department of Defense, under my direction, has assigned the necessary troops to carry out that mission, including the call-up of reservists and members of the national guard.

Although you no longer are in the Naval Reserve, you have shown by your past service in Vietnam and your more recent public statements that you are willing to serve your country whenever and wherever needed.

Therefore, by the authority vested in me, you are hereby ordered to report for active duty, no later than October 10 ...

*September 10, 2004*

## With Friends Like These, Kerry Needs No Enemies

A presidential candidate needs all the friends he can get. On some days recently John Kerry must have asked himself, "With friends like these, who needs enemies?"

Democrat campaign veteran Tony Coelho leveled a withering blast at the chaos in the Kerry camp. "There is nobody in charge," said Al Gore's former campaign manager. He criticized Kerry for having "two teams that are generally not talking to each other."

Kerry's titular campaign manager, Mary Beth Cahill, and chief strategist Bob Shrum, who has been losing elections for Democrats since George McGovern ran in 1972, are former Ted Kennedy staff members. After "black August" Kerry brought former Bill Clinton staffers Joe Lockhart and Mike McCurry on board.

The Democratic nominee has plenty of people outside the campaign staff who are eager to help him throw George W. Bush out of the White House. These friends include moviemaker Michael Moore and Clinton loyalists James Carville and Paul Begala, who provide advice while holding jobs at CNN. Matt Lauer granted not one, but three, appearances on NBC's *Today* show to discredited scandalmonger Kitty Kelley to plug her new Bush bashing book, while most other media outlets shunned her.

And then there's Dan Rather. What appears to be a coordinated effort between CBS and the Kerry campaign to ruin Bush's chances for reelection with a *60 Minutes* smear of his national guard military service blew up in the face of the 72-year-old anchorman. In his zeal to nail the Republican president, Rather rushed on the air with a story based on forged and fraudulent documents, despite warnings from experts. His source, a Texas partisan Democrat with a grudge against Bush and a record of false accusations, had been contacted by Lockhart at a CBS producer's suggestion.

A woman who might be considered Kerry's best friend continues to do him in almost every time she opens her mouth. Teresa Heinz Kerry, who once berated "putrid" Democratic party politics and said she didn't trust Ted Kennedy (when she was married to a Republican), is a fierce supporter of her husband. She makes headlines more often than Kerry's staff would like. She told a Pittsburgh newspaper reporter to "shove it", accused Bush fans chanting at a rally of wanting "four more years of hell," and called opponents of her husband's health care plan "idiots". As volunteers packed hurricane relief shipments for the Caribbean, she complained they were putting clothing ahead of other supplies. "Let them go naked for a while," she said.

Sometimes Kerry is his own worst enemy, as in a campaign appearance in Michigan where he declared his support for "Buckeye football"—an infuriating reference to rival Ohio State. Earlier he had insulted Wisconsin football fans by calling the Green Bay Packers' home field "Lambert" instead of "Lambeau."

The only thing worse would be if he went to an Oklahoma Sooners game and flashed the "hook 'em horns" gesture.

*September 24, 2004*

## Election's Over and Now It's Open Season On Lame Ducks

With thoughts turning to Thanksgiving turkeys, it's "lame duck" season in Washington.

The November 2 elections saved the president's job and gave employment to several new members of Congress, but it also turned a number of incumbent officeholders into short-timers. With their power greatly diminished because they are soon to leave office, they bear the unflattering label of "lame ducks."

*New York Times* columnist William Safire (himself a lame duck since he announced plans to retire after three decades) relates in his *Political Dictionary* that the phrase dates to the 1830s, when it was used to describe politically bankrupt politicians.

Lamest of the lame is Senate Minority Leader Tom Daschle, who lost his South Dakota seat to Republican John Thune in a race that added $30 million to the small state's economy. Even the prairie dogs must have been polled.

Voters gave Democratic presidential candidate John Kerry four more years—in the Senate, that is. But his running mate, Sen. John Edwards, did not seek a new term, so he'll have to go back to lawyering.

Secretary of State Colin Powell found himself among the flock of limping quackers as his resignation was quickly accepted while he was getting packed for a couple of overseas diplomatic missions. His chosen successor, Condoleezza Rice, put on a good face in accepting the nomination, although the job she really wants is National Football League commissioner.

All of the changes taking place—from one end of Pennsylvania Avenue to the other—were quite the buzz as Congress reconvened for a lame duck session to elect new leaders, act on some spending bills, and figure out how many congressional junkets can be taken before the new session begins in January.

The newly-elected members had to arrive early for freshman orientation where they learned the rules of Congress, how to hire staff, and where the closest bathroom is located. They had to endure a series of cocktail parties and dinners welcoming them to town. Also on the schedule were candlelight tours of the Capitol conducted by House Speaker Dennis Hastert (quite appropriate, since freshmen usually are in the dark for the first six months) and get-acquainted sessions hosted by House Majority Leader Tom DeLay and Minority Leader Nancy Pelosi (where flamethrowers might have been in evidence).

Besides a packed congressional schedule, the lawmakers had to allow time for many to attend the gala opening of the William J. Clinton presidential library at Little Rock. With President Bush and two other ex-presidents besides Clinton scheduled to attend, employees in a nearby office building were told to leave their deer-hunting rifles at home for the day.

In Washington, more changes can be expected in the days ahead. How many new faces will there be in the Bush cabinet, and who will chair the congressional committees? More importantly, will the luckless Washington Redskins be getting a new coach?

*November 19, 2004*

# Not To Be "Misunderestimated"—Bush Back For Four More

Some might say the Iraq war got George W. Bush re-elected. Campaigning as a self-described "war president," he won a new term by defeating self-styled "war hero" John Kerry. A clear majority of the electorate said they were unwilling to replace a sometimes inarticulate but determined leader with a liberal Massachusetts senator who explained his position on support of the war by saying, "I voted for it before I voted against it." Voters also might have been alarmed at the thought of Teresa Heinz Kerry in the White House after some of the off-the-wall comments she made in the campaign.

First Lady Laura Bush really came into her own in the second term. She upstaged her husband at a Washington correspondents' dinner with silky sarcastic quips. The former librarian was engaged as an advocate for education, literacy, children and women's health issues and made high profile visits to Afghanistan, the Middle East, South Africa and other parts of the world. She took an active role in seeking to resolve the human rights crisis in Burma.

Execution of the war in Iraq continued following significant first-term successes: U.S. troops and their British allies brought about the fall of Baghdad in less than four weeks and Saddam Hussein was captured. While awaiting an Iraqi trial and eventual hanging, the once-powerful dictator was subjected to humiliation by the publication of photos of him in his underwear. But violence by insurgents persisted and as the casualty count grew higher the president's poll ratings sunk lower.

Washingtonians had their spirits lifted when Joe Gibbs returned as coach of the Washington Redskins in 2004, only to resign after four seasons without matching his earlier successes.

Although the war on terror dominated the final years of the Bush-Cheney administration, there were home front crises to deal with, such as Scooter Libby, high gasoline prices and Hurricane Katrina. Bungling of the rescue and cleanup operations forced the president to eat his words after he told the director of FEMA, "Brownie, you're doing a heck of a job."

When Democrats won control of both houses of Congress in the mid-term elections, the president admitted the GOP took quite a "thumping." Rep. Nancy Pelosi made history by becoming the first woman Speaker of the House, but as for legislative achievements, she and Senate Majority Leader Harry Reid had little to brag about for their party.

George W. Bush escaped the stress of Washington by cutting brush on his Texas ranch and continued to build a legacy of conservative Supreme Court appointments and molding an "ownership society" while butting heads with Congress by vetoing spending bills.

Once accused of conducting "cowboy diplomacy," he brought opposing leaders together for a renewed Middle East peace initiative.

Meanwhile, attention was focused on the earliest presidential election campaign season ever and both Democrats and Republicans battled to see who would become POTUS 44.

## President's New Year's Resolution: To Cut the Fat

It's a demanding job, but a lot of benefits come with the responsibility of being president of the United States. For one thing, you don't have to make a bunch of New Year's resolutions.

In the case of George W. Bush, he only mentioned one. After his mid-December physical checkup, he said rather sheepishly: "My New Year's resolution has become apparent after getting on the scales. I'm a little overweight. Therefore, I fully intend to lose some inches off my waistline and some pounds off my frame."

The examination revealed that Bush had gained six pounds—going from 194 to 200 pounds—since his last checkup. "I obviously have gone through a campaign where I probably ate too many doughnuts," he told reporters.

Losing weight is a goal set by many Americans for 2005. For most of us, a gain of only six pounds in over a year is something to celebrate—with a second helping of apple pie. But it's a worry to President Bush, so if he drops in for dinner, don't be upset if he doesn't clean his plate.

Looking over a list of popular New Year's resolutions provided by First-Gov.gov, the U.S. government's "official Web portal", it's no great surprise that the chief executive made only one pledge for self-improvement in 2005. One by one, he's already got them covered.

Get Fit—The 10 doctors who performed the 58-year-old president's physical exam pronounced him "fit for duty."

Quit Smoking—Bush doesn't smoke, except for an occasional cigar.

Drink Less Alcohol—He gave up the bottle when he was 40.

Reduce Stress—Like his predecessors, Bush deals with stress by regular exercise. He enjoyed running for nearly three decades, but then his knees started to cause increasing pain. Although there's a move to bring back the hula hoop as a form of exercise, he seems to prefer mountain bike riding as a substitute for jogging.

Take a Trip—Traveling frequently goes with the job, so he doesn't need to resolve to make more trips. His favorite destination likely will continue to be his ranch at Crawford, Texas, where he also gets exercise clearing brush and evading news reporters.

Get a Better Education—With a bachelor's degree from Yale University and a master's from Harvard, Bush doesn't need any more diplomas.

Get a Better Job—If that had been his aspiration, he wouldn't have run for reelection last year.

Another reason the president doesn't need to make a list of resolutions is that there are plenty of critics who are more than willing to tell him what he ought to be doing. For example, in addition to losing pounds and trimming his waistline, many taxpayers would like to see him use the political capital he claims to have won in the 2005 election to cut more fat out of the federal government.

*January 7, 2005*

## Hillary Not Only Feels Your Pain But Hers, Too

Sen. Hillary Clinton, D-N.Y., got the jump on other Bush administration critics. She was feeling pain before the State of the Union speech was delivered.

There was plenty of bellyaching from her fellow Democrats, and some Republicans, about what President Bush said in his address to a joint session of Congress. Some typical comments:

"I just can't stomach his Social Security reform plan."

"When I saw the size of the budget, I wanted to throw up."

"His stubborn determination to stay in Iraq makes me sick."

The difference with Clinton is that she really was ill. She fainted while giving a speech at a private club in Buffalo. Rumors quickly spread. What caused her to faint? Had she been shocked to learn that her husband, Bill, had decided to become a priest? Did she receive news that her daughter, Chelsea, was thinking about running for president in 2008? Was her brother, Hugh Rodham, in trouble again?

The 57-year-old senator was not injured when she collapsed at the podium. Erie County Democratic Chairman Len Lenihan said, "She was sort of brought down gracefully."

If only Sen. John Kerry, D-Mass., could claim such an achievement, he might have a chance of making another run in four years.

Her collapse was followed by a flurry of speculation about the nature of her ailment. According to one observer, it was either the flu or a sudden need for publicity, in light of the successful Iraqi elections. Detractors also suggested it was an adverse reaction to her sudden shift to centrist positions and talk about faith-based values.

A physician attending the event checked her out and, going against the doctor's advice, she resumed her schedule. She delivered a speech about health care later that day at a nearby Catholic college, where anti-abortion protesters gathered outside to demonstrate against the pro-choice senator.

Clinton had complained about having a stomach problem. Her press secretary, Philippe Reines, said about 30 Clinton staff members who joined her in a weekend retreat in New York state also had similar symptoms.

As for her own illness, the senator shrugged it off, referring to it as "a 24-hour virus." If only her presidential ambitions were so shortlived, many Democrats would feel some overnight relief. But once you get the bug to sit behind that desk in the Oval Office, there's no cure.

Some Clinton staffers were said to be reluctant to discuss the senator's health condition. "Nobody wants to talk about a stomach problem," said one.

They had better wake up and smell the Pepto Bismol. If their boss becomes president, every cough and sneeze will be news and all her body parts will be public information. Remember Ronald Reagan's prostate surgery and the front-page anatomical drawings?

Whatever the reason for her fainting, you have to give Hillary Clinton credit for grabbing the news spotlight. Maybe it was just her gut instinct.

*February 4, 2005*

## Serious News Gets Bush-quacked By Ducks and FLOTUS

In this world news capital, war and peace got shoved to the inside pages this week. The hottest topics were two births.

The most famous duck since Donald or Daffy delivered a brood of 11 ducklings in her well-protected nest in front of the Treasury Department.

And a new comedy star was born when Laura Bush augmented her role as first lady by doing a somewhat bawdy but riotously funny stand-up routine at the annual White House Correspondents' Association dinner.

After weeks in the spotlight as Washington's newest tourist attraction, a brown mallard whose image was seen around the world decided it was time for her eggs to hatch.

She had built her nest at the Treasury's main entrance on Pennsylvania Avenue a block from the White House, a prominent lame duck's home. When hordes of springtime tourists began to take notice, the Secret Service erected metal barricades to keep her safe.

The fine-feathered fowl seemed unruffled by all the attention, as well as the bad puns. Treasury employees had offered some names for their pampered visitor: "Quacks Reform", "Duck Cheney" and "T-Bill" were among those suggested. Thankfully nobody came up with "Mallard Fillmore".

A team of government experts reported nine eggs. It turned out they miscounted, which might give a clue to why the federal budget is so out of whack. On the Saturday the downy creatures hatched, they numbered 11.

The mother and her ducklings were gently captured and caged, then transported in a four-vehicle motorcade to Rock Creek Park and placed in a holding pen. Mother mallard quickly broke free and waddled out to a nearby creek, her offspring following in a line.

As one hot news story was ending, another was developing at the Hilton Washington hotel where President Bush was starting to speak to the White House correspondents group. Laura Bush took over the podium and, with masterful timing, entertained the guests with a series of wisecracks about her husband, her in-laws and herself.

Describing a typical evening, she said: "Nine o-clock, Mr. Excitement here is sound asleep, and I'm watching *Desperate Housewives*—with Lynne Cheney.

"I said to him the other day, 'George, if you really want to end tyranny in the world, you're going to have to stay up later.'

"George's answer to any problem at the ranch is to cut it down with a chainsaw," she said, "which I think is why he and Cheney and Rumsfeld get along so well."

Referring to her mother-in-law, she quipped: "So many mothers today are just not involved in their children's lives. Not a problem with Barbara Bush."

The first lady ended her remarks on a serious note, with loving words for her husband, his family, and even the Washington press corps.

The surprise performance drew wide comment, many saying that former librarian Laura Bush showed a considerable talent for comedy. Like a duck taking to water, you might say.

*May 6, 2005*

## Who Will Be the Next Politician To Do the "Frist Twist"?

Senate Majority Leader Bill Frist's endorsement of government-funded embryonic stem cell research was a dramatic change in position on the issue. It was interpreted as a move calculated to broaden his appeal for votes in the 2008 presidential election.

Who will be the next White House aspirant to do the "Frist Twist"? Be alert for stories such as these:

Phoenix—Sen. John McCain, R-Ariz., today declared campaign finance reform "a total failure" and said he would lead an effort to repeal the law he sponsored in the next session of Congress.

He also said he will make no TV talk show appearances and grant no print media interviews for an indefinite period.

Boston—At a hastily-called news conference, Sen. John Kerry, D-Mass., announced today that he is ending his 10-year marriage to Teresa Heinz-Kerry.

The 2004 Democratic nominee for president said as soon as the divorce becomes final he plans to wed conservative commentator Ann Coulter.

"Next time I run, I need a wife who is not so outspoken," he said.

Atlanta—Newt Gingrich, who led a Republican revolution that made him Speaker of the House, revealed today that he had re-registered as a Democrat.

"I believe my views on social, economic and national security issues are more aligned with the Democratic party platform," he said.

In Texas, former House Speaker Jim Wright applauded Gingrich's decision and said he would support him for president.

Greenville, S.C.—Addressing an all-white audience at Bob Jones University, Sen. Hillary Clinton, D-N.Y., said today she agrees with the school's policy banning inter-racial dating.

She was responding to a question about a marriage proposal to her daughter, Chelsea, by a city councilman in Kenya who offered her husband, Bill, "20 cows and 40 goats" as a wedding dowry.

Clinton, who received an honorary degree, said: "I am proud to join my former Senate colleagues, Jesse Helms, and Strom Thurmond, in accepting this prestigious honor."

New York—Former mayor Rudolph Giuliani told the National Right to Life organization today he no longer opposes legislative and judicial anti-abortion measures.

"In reflecting on September 11, 2001 when terrorists destroyed the World Trade Center, I have reassessed my views on the value of human life, in whatever form it may be," he said.

Giuliani said if he were president he would continue the stem cell research policy of the Bush administration.

Washington—According to reliable sources, former Sen. John Edwards, D-N.C., got a "buzz cut" at a suburban barber shop last week.

Shunning the stylish hair salons of Georgetown, the 2004 Democratic candidate for vice president had his golden locks clipped at a shop in Gaithersburg, Md., for $15.

The barber, who prefers to remain anonymous, told this column that Edwards said he was planning to sell his expensive homes in Washington and Florida and is in the market for a small log cabin.

*August 5, 2005*

## Many New Prime Time TV Shows Have a Political Flavor

The new television season is upon us, and the fall lineup has a distinct political flavor. The schedule includes new shows as well as old favorites.

Here is a rundown on some prime time offerings that are being watched in the nation's capital:

*My Name is Earle*—A small time Texas prosecutor named Ronnie Earle has an epiphany and sets out to right all of the failures in his life, including being unable to send a Republican to jail. His first effort involves the House majority leader, Tom DeLay.

*Extreme Makeover: Court Edition*—The Republican team revamps the Supreme Court by using the tools at their disposal to install new supports for conservative ideologies. Some of the crew goes on strike after an apprentice named Harriet Miers comes on the job.

*Demander-in-Chief*—Seeing an opportunity to become the first woman president of the United States, Hillary Clinton makes demands that rankle other Democrats, including a man who thinks the office is rightfully his, John Kerry.

*The Rose Garden*—A spinoff of *The West Wing*, this new series features a canny president who holds press conferences outdoors in October, forcing reporters to endure chilly temperatures while he picks names to call from a pre-selected list. Cast in the leading role, George W. Bush makes a convincing appearance as the confident chief executive of a nation beset with problems.

*Desperate House Members*—A darkly comical drama series in which secrets and truths unfold about a group of shallow people engaged in lying and cheating, trying desperately to save their pet pork barrel projects from being killed to free up funds for hurricane disaster recovery projects.

*The Eye-Glazing Race*—Ten Republican campaign teams race around the country with their boring candidates trying to win the big prize in 2008. Starring in this unsuspenseful series are John McCain, George Allen, Bill Frist, Sam Brownback, Chuck Hagel, George Pataki, Mike Huckabee and Tom Tancredo. Rudolph Giuliani and Newt Gingrich add a touch of interest.

*CSI: New Orleans*—The newest spinoff of *CSI: Crime Scene Investigation*, this series follows the sleuthing of a team of investigators from the Congressional Hindsight Committee bent on fixing blame for the destruction wrought by hurricanes on the vulnerable Crescent City. Featured players include New Orleans Mayor Ray Nagin and Louisiana Gov. Kathleen Blanco.

*Sunday Night Live*—An irregularly scheduled series carried by C-SPAN lets the cameras roll while lawmakers perform in low comedy skits during a rare evening session in the House of Representatives. A recent highlight was the Weekend Bush-bashing Update with Nancy Pelosi and Charlie Rangel.

*The Odd Couple*—This remake of a popular series stars former presidents Bill Clinton and George H. W. Bush as two opposites who normally can't stand to be in the same room together but who join forces for humanitarian assistance and an occasional round of golf.

*October 7, 2005*

## Move Over Oprah, Here's Al Sharpton With His Own Show

Do you ever wonder what presidential candidates do between elections?

Some go back to their regular jobs, like serving in the Senate.

The 2004 loser, Sen. John Kerry, D-Mass., did take time out from his legislative duties to sit on a superior court jury in his home state. He even won an election—as foreman of the jury, which found the city of Boston negligent for a 1999 car crash involving a school principal. The jury, however, did not award damages to two people who were injured—an ambivalent decision that Kerry, no doubt, found pleasing. News reports did not say whether he received any jury duty pay (as if he needed it.)

Howard Dean captured a prize job after his primary defeat. Running the Democratic National Committee like a madman, to the delight of Republicans and the chagrin of Democrats, has given him high visibility as well as a regular salary.

Another candidate who loves the spotlight is the Rev. Al Sharpton, and he is working hard to keep his face before the public. The controversial political activist has aroused attention by becoming a TV pitchman for car title loans. In commercials he filmed for LoanMax, Sharpton stands in front of an American flag and touts the company as one "who will loan money to people the big guys won't loan to."

The practice of lending to car owners at interest rates as high as 300 percent has been condemned by consumer groups as "predatory." But Sharpton self-righteously proclaimed, "If I felt this is in any way abusive, I would stop doing the ads."

The colorful preacher is quite fond of the TV medium. During the 2004 campaign, Sharpton hosted *Saturday Night Live*. Later that year he played the role of a counselor on a reality series, *I Hate My Job*, produced by Spike TV. Just recently, he launched *Sharp Talk With Al Sharpton*, a half-hour talk show set in a Brooklyn barber shop.

Now word comes that Sharpton has been working with CBS on a pilot for a half-hour series tentatively titled, *Al in the Family* (with no apologies to Archie Bunker). He told news media the sitcom will be about a family with different social and political views.

"I don't know if I am a good actor or not," he said, "but I will be playing myself and I have been practicing that for 52 years."

Meanwhile, a potential contender for the 2008 Democratic nomination, Virginia Gov. Mark Warner, cracked jokes at a Washington Gridiron Club dinner. He recalled that eight Virginians had served as president and "we're due" for another one. He added that Virginia Sen. George Allen, a Republican, told him to say that.

Allen, who also is considering a run for president, was born in California. Warner was born in Indiana and raised in Connecticut.

Neither claims to have been born in a log cabin.

*December 9, 2005*

## Christmastime in Capital Is No Holiday for Bush Jokes

'Tis the season of goodwill, except in Washington, where there are plenty of grinches around to spoil Christmas for President Bush.

Cartoonists portray both Santa Claus and the National Security Agency as seeking to "find out who's been naughty and nice."

Comedians, both professional and those serving in Congress, are all too eager to poke fun at the man who lights the White House Christmas tree. Late night comic Jay Leno said: "The tree has over 25,000 lights—one for every indicted member of the administration."

Some local performers have built long careers on political humor.

The Capitol Steps, a troupe which got its start 25 years ago at a Christmas party in the office of Sen. Charles Percy, is doing a New Year's Eve special. It might well include their parody of the president and Secretary of Defense Don Rumsfeld on the war in Iraq, "If I Only Had a Plan" (borrowing a tune from *The Wizard of Oz*.)

Piano-playing satirist Mark Russell, who has been hurling political zingers for almost three decades, no doubt has some choice lines for both the president and Congress in his three-show performance at Ford's Theatre.

Congress offers stiff competition to the professional jokesters with some of its legislation, but some members also like to try their hand at stand-up comedy. Rep. John Dingell, D-Mich., took the floor to recite a poem which began:

"'Twas the week before Christmas, and all through the House,

"No bills were passed 'bout which Fox News could grouse;

"Tax cuts for the wealthy were passed with great cheer,

"So vacations in St. Barts soon would be near ..."

His doggerel included some partisan jibes about Iraq, gas prices and consumer confidence. That was a bit unkind, considering the president and first lady Laura Bush had hosted a White House luncheon in recognition of Dingell's 50 years in Congress.

But, as the late president Harry Truman once said, "If you want a friend in Washington, get a dog." Taking his advice, the Bush family has two dogs, which they featured in a special holiday season "BarneyCam" video available on the whitehouse.gov Web site. In the presentation, Barney, the older Scottish terrier, reveals a Scrooge-like reaction to Miss Beazley, who arrived a year ago.

Also on the Internet is a new animated political cartoon spoof by the JibJab brothers, which has a troubled president singing:

"From Katrina! FEMA! Gitmo, too! The last thing I need now is the Avian Flu."

Bush inadvertently provided some fodder for political humorists when he disclosed some of the tunes on his iPod in an interview with Fox News anchor Brit Hume. His playlist ranged from country to rock 'n roll to soul music.

He seemed to be enjoying the "high-tech stuff." He told Hume: "Put it in my pocket, got the ear things on."

Too bad he can't do that with Congress and comedians.

*December 23, 2005*

## Away from Washington, President Gets the Brush Off

It's not hard to guess what's high on the list of President Bush's New Year's resolutions: clear more brush.

Many presidents have had diversions. For Dwight D. Eisenhower and Gerald R. Ford, it was golf. Jimmy Carter enjoyed fishing, until that time a rabbit attacked his boat. Ronald Reagan liked to ride a horse and chop wood. Bill Clinton—well, we all know what he did to relieve the pressures of office.

George W. Bush claims to take pleasure in pulling on jeans, gloves and boots, getting in his pickup truck and finding a place on his ranch in Texas where some weeds and underbrush need to be cleared.

Among his favorite targets are mesquite and cedar trees, which rob precious moisture from the central Texas soil. But if there's a stand of cockleburs or any dead limbs in sight, they will not escape the presidential chainsaw.

White House aides say the 59-year-old president goes at the job with great vigor, like a man with a mission. It's his own private war on vegetative terrorists.

Even when the temperature is 100 degrees or more, Bush tackles the dusty, tiring job for hours at a time.

The activity is not strictly recreational, according to the *Washington Post*. An article quotes local experts as saying that "he will clear underbrush to preserve beautiful live oaks and pecan trees, or to prepare the 50 acres where Laura Bush is cultivating native grasses, or to help carve nature trails through the ranch's many canyons." Take that, environmental activists!

Still, many observers wonder why he does it. Some detractors say it's to show he's a man, he's tough, "he's a Texan."

"This is part of his macho image," presidential historian Robert Dallek told the *Post*.

Washington news correspondents take delight in quoting the president's critics. Many in the White House press corps hate the trips to the Prairie Chapel ranch near Crawford, Texas. They liked it better when Clinton was president, because he vacationed at places like Cape Cod. Reporters can't see the fun in weed-whacking.

If he hired a professional crew to do the work, it might cost up to $200 an hour, but that wouldn't be a deterrent to a member of the Bush family. He obviously chops away at the undesirable growth on his 1,600-acre spread just because he wants to.

When you think about it, clearing brush is one thing that Congress can't block. He's not required to ask the U.S. Senate to "advise and consent" to his choice of a spot to clear.

Except for times like now when dry conditions increase the danger of wild-fires, Bush can strike a match and burn his cuttings without having to go to court to get permission.

That kind of independence is hard to come by in his regular job in Washington. It's no wonder he likes to spend so much time on the ranch.

*January 6, 2006*

## Candidate or Not, Condi Shows Strength and Stamina

Is Condoleezza Rice getting in shape for a presidential run?

One would think so, watching her pumping iron and showing off her ab workout on Washington television station WRC.

Disclaiming any plans to be a Republican candidate in the next presidential election, the energetic secretary of state said she taped her exercise routine to promote fitness for Americans.

Political junkies are itching to see a match between Rice and Hillary Clinton. While some might say she's flexing her muscles to take on the Democratic New York senator in 2008, State Department spokesman Adam Ereli insists that his boss is focusing on the pursuit of a more "muscular and agile" U.S. diplomacy.

While it's common for public figures to sweat before the cameras when asked tough questions—and Clinton has been put on the spot about attacking the Dubai ports management deal while husband Bill has been collecting fees to defend it—Rice has a legitimate reason to perspire on TV.

In three segments airing on successive days on WRC, she was shown lifting weights and demonstrating a calorie-burning workout. Rice, a youthful 51, rode a stationary bike and talked about the importance of regular exercise.

When the segments were taped, she had just returned from a tiring trip to the Middle East. But she hadn't let that interfere with her daily routine of arising at 4:30 a.m. and getting in at least 40 minutes of cardiovascular exercise.

"When I'm on the road I absolutely schedule time to get up in the morning and exercise first," she told WRC's morning host Barbara Harrison.

In a policy decision where she and President Bush saw eye to eye, Rice decided to "speed walk and walk hills instead of running" to spare her knees. Bush, when his knees were no longer up to it, gave up jogging and took up mountain bike riding, a decision that risked producing an international incident.

During the Group of Eight summit in Scotland last July, Bush was returning from an afternoon spin on his bike and crashed into a constable, who was knocked down and suffered an ankle injury. The president had taken one hand off the handlebars to wave at some police officers and lost control of the bike. He had a few abrasions and appeared later with his left arm bandaged.

Bush joked that he should start "acting my age." Or take Condi Rice's advice and stick to stationary bike riding.

It wasn't the president's first mishap while exercising. In 2004 he had a bike accident at his ranch in Texas, and two years earlier he fell off a Segway scooter.

If it should develop that Clinton and Rice were opposing each other in the next presidential race, the Republican contender might consider challenging her opponent to a contest on the ice. Rice is an accomplished figure skater.

Can't you just see tuning in to watch *Ice Skating With the Political Stars*?

*March 10, 2006*

## As President's Ratings Sink, World Toilet Crisis Beckons

In times past, when a president saw his popularity tanking, he often would call a summit meeting where he could assert his leadership in dealing with a critical situation.

With his approval ratings at an alltime low, maybe that's an option for President Bush. The subject matter would have to be carefully chosen—certainly not immigration or Iraq.

He also should make sure Congress would support the idea and provide the necessary funding.

Perhaps the perfect solution is a World Toilet Summit.

This is an established annual event which has been held at various foreign locations. Around 400 delegates from 28 different countries attended the 2005 World Toilet Summit in Belfast, Ireland.

During a three-day discussion of the finer points of public sanitation, the delegates heard some fascinating presentations of scholarly papers with such titles as "Lifting the Lid on Washroom Problems" and "Setting Public Toilet Standards Down Under."

U.S. taxpayers helped pay for the meeting through a generous congressional appropriation of $13.5 million for the International Fund for Ireland, which was one of the sponsors. So it's only fair that this important conference be brought to the United States.

The 2006 summit already is scheduled for Moscow, but surely George Bush could persuade his good buddy, Vladimir Putin, to withdraw the Russian invitation for the sake of international relations.

An ideal site for the summit would be Flushing, N.Y., but if the Republican president wanted to deny Sen. Hillary Clinton the opportunity for a campaign speech there's always Poop Creek, Ore. or Gassaway, Tenn.

The president could expect full cooperation from Capitol Hill, if the appropriations process for the current fiscal year is an indication. Lawmakers seemed unusually keen on attending to personal needs, if not eliminating waste.

Citizens Against Government Waste, a watchdog group that takes issue with a record $29 billion in pork-barrel spending, listed in its annual Congressional Pig Book the earmarking of $4,890,000 for sewer projects in six states and $1 million for a Waterfree Urinal Conservation Initiative. The latter would allow the Navy to test these devices at sea.

Turning from urinals to pots, another project branded as a blatant example of pork was the $500,000 Teapot Museum in Sparta, N.C. Supporters of the museum said it would "expose its visitors to an unexpected art form—the tea-pot."

Also questioned was more than $6.4 million allocated to "wood utilization research" (build more privies?) and $75,000 to renovate a building for a glass-blowing museum in Lancaster, Ohio.

The waste-watchers said Alaska led the nation with $325 million in special interest spending, or $489 per capita. By contrast, Oklahoma ranked number 48 on the list with $16.55 per capita, due in part to the efforts of Sen. Tom Coburn, who has teamed with Sen. John McCain of Arizona to oppose earmarking funds for pet projects.

Bush probably need not bother inviting those two to the World Toilet Sum-mit.

*April 21, 2006*

## Bush Gets Mojo and Has Constituents Seeing Double

Will the real George W. Bush please stand up?

Loyal supporters of the president have been puzzled by some of the things going on in his administration lately. The answer might have been revealed at the annual White House Correspondents Association dinner.

Instead of one President Bush, the audience saw two. One was overly polite to the adversarial crowd, saying: "As you know, I always look forward to these dinners." The other was decidedly unrestrained. "It's just a bunch of media types, Hollywood liberals, Democrats like Joe Biden. How come I can't have dinner with the 36 percent of the people who like me?" he said.

Bush had lined up a double, impersonator Steve Bridges, who not only looked and talked like the president but had his mannerisms down pat. At the conclusion of his remarks, the real president joked that the stand-in had been the George Bush the public saw in the 2004 debates with Democratic opponent John Kerry.

It was all in fun, but events of the past few weeks make one wonder if the American people have been seeing two presidents. Consider these recent actions:

• Bowing to pressure from congressional leaders, Bush—who knows from experience what factors affect gasoline prices—ordered an investigation into alleged wrongdoing by "Big Oil" companies.

• Following a White House meeting on immigration, both Senate Democratic leader Harry Reid and Sen. Edward Kennedy—two of Bush's worst enemies—emerged spouting compliments.

• Bush replaced a protective press secretary with TV commentator Tony Snow—who once described his new boss as an "embarrassment"—and moved to become more engaged with the mainstream Washington media.

The latter development is part of an overhaul of White House operations which began with the departure of longtime chief of staff Andrew Card. His successor, former budget director Josh Bolten, is a bachelor who once escorted actress Bo Derek and cruises around on a Harley Davidson "Fat Boy" motorcycle. Bolten took over with a declaration that it is time to "get our mojo back."

Bolten wasted no time making staff changes. (At the correspondents' dinner, Bush drew a laugh when he said, "I'm feeling pretty chipper. I survived the White House shakeup.")

Presumably the "mojo" strategy includes having the president get out of Washington and engage in unscripted exchanges with citizens all over the country. The question arises: how can he be in so many places and still be in charge in the Oval Office?

In the 1993 movie *Dave*, starring Kevin Kline, an ordinary guy who could have been the president's twin was persuaded to play the role of the chief executive.

It might be amusing to speculate that a professional comedian is actually doing half the work. That might account for the scene where Bush angered the Chinese president by yanking on his sleeve to redirect him off a stage. Or maybe not.

*May 5, 2006*

## Politics Really Can Be Quite Puzzling Sometimes

We live in interesting times, when:
Hillary Clinton courts "big business;"
John McCain panders to the religious right;
Teddy Kennedy begins to look like a saint.

The "Stop Hillary" movement got a boost from an unlikely source when daughter Chelsea Clinton took issue with her Mom's remarks about young people. The Democrats' 2008 frontrunner sounded more like a Republican when she addressed the annual U.S. Chamber of Commerce meeting, saying: "A lot of kids don't know what work is. Kids ... think they're entitled to go right to the top with $50,000 or $75,000 jobs when they have not done anything to earn their way up."

Those comments must have touched a raw nerve in 26-year-old Chelsea, who landed a six-figure job in New York after getting an Oxford degree in 2003. She called her mother to complain, "I do work hard, and my friends work hard." Clinton apologized.

What prompted her to veer from her liberal ideology? Could it have been the chilling thought of going up against a Republican ticket of John McCain and Jerry Falwell in the next presidential election? McCain confounded his supporters when he made a pilgrimage to Liberty University to kiss the ring of Christian conservative leader Falwell, the man he denounced as an "evil influence" after his 2000 race for president.

Rather than worry about a prospective Republican opponent, Hillary Clinton might need to be concerned about opposition within her own party. Who knows but what Sen. Edward Kennedy might make another run, considering that he has been scandal-free for quite some time. Compared to his son, Rep. Patrick Kennedy, who was forced to admit he is a drug addict after crashing his car and not remembering it, Teddy is looking downright squeaky clean.

Of more serious concern to Hillary is the last Democratic nominee, Al Gore, according to former political strategist Susan Estrich. The lawyer who managed Michael Dukakis' failed campaign in 1988 says Gore could give her a tough challenge. "So what if he went to Saudi Arabia and criticized America?" Estrich wrote in a Los Angeles column.

If Republicans aren't cheered by that assessment, they only have to look at the plans announced by Democrats hoping to win back control of the House this fall. The prospect of Nancy Pelosi becoming speaker is scary enough, but her declared intention to investigate the Bush administration has led to speculation about a move to impeach a wartime president. "You never know what it leads to," she told the *Washington Post.*

Meanwhile, Democratic chairman Howard Dean alienated a key segment of the party's base when he incorrectly stated that the "platform from 2004 says marriage is between a man and a woman." The platform, in fact, said: "We support full inclusion of gay and lesbian families ..."

Dean made the erroneous statement in an appearance on Pat Robertson's "700 Club" show on the Christian Broadcasting Network.

Interesting times, indeed.

*May 19, 2006*

## Experts Conclude Cowboy Diplomacy Went Thataway

Ever since *Time* magazine declared an end to the era of "cowboy diplomacy" some folks have been wondering, is that a fact?

The feature article was referring, of course, to our Texan president, George W. Bush, and the manner in which he has handled America's foreign relations. The writers cited the declaration of the "swaggering commander-in-chief" that terrorist kingpin Osama bin Laden would be taken "dead or alive" and other "Wild West rhetoric."

These self-styled experts deduced that Bush had signaled a drastic change in his "grand strategy for remaking the world" when he abandoned his customary dark suit and tie for a brightly-colored Hawaiian shirt at a celebration of his 60th birthday.

This perceptive analysis prompted a review of some of the president's actions of the past and present. Bush has had a number of foreign leaders to his ranch at Crawford, Texas, including Russian president Vladimir Putin. When he accepted an invitation to visit in 2001, Bush laid on a spread of mesquite-smoked beef, southern fried catfish and pecan pie with ice cream. The two became known as "best buddies" who exchanged locker room towel-snapping jibes in their later meetings.

Bush and British prime minister Tony Blair have enjoyed a similar odd-couple relationship, sharing common goals despite the sharp differences in their personal styles.

While Bush has held fast to his basic beliefs, more recently he has done some things that set people guessing.

When the Japanese prime minister, Junichiro Koizumi, visited the United States recently, Bush accompanied him to Memphis to tour Graceland, the Elvis Presley mansion. A real cowboy would have taken him to the Bull Hall of Fame at Plain City, Ohio, which honors outstanding bovine studs.

At the G-8 meeting in St. Petersburg, Russia, Bush was caught on camera giving a brief shoulder rub to German Chancellor Angela Merkel. A real cowboy wouldn't have done that. He might have slapped her on the back and said something like, "Loosen up, little lady." (The news media have made far too much of this incident. After all, it wasn't a Bill Clinton grope. You can't blame him for being glad to see someone besides Gerhard Schroder sitting in that chair.)

Also at the meeting in Putin's country, Bush was caught on an open microphone grumbling about the U.N. secretary general and longwinded speakers, and was heard using some barnyard language. So maybe the plainspeaking cowboy characteristic hasn't totally disappeared.

Whether that incident was enough to restore the confidence of some of the president's wavering conservative allies remains to be seen. Former House Speaker Newt Gingrich, among others, was highly critical of Bush for not having a more forceful response after North Korea test-fired missiles.

According to news reports, North Korean leader Kim Jong-il has married his former secretary. If Bush sends them a set of Tupperware as a wedding present, we'll know for sure he's softening the cowboy image.

*July 28, 2006*

## Democrats' Can Do Better in Finding a New Slogan

Democrats are out to break the Republican hold on Congress—not with new programs, new policies or new ideas, but with a new slogan.

At a recent news conference, House Minority Leader Nancy Pelosi proudly displayed a red, white and blue brochure bearing the words she hopes will carry her party to victory in November:

"A New Direction for America."

As if the Democrats weren't already the butt of every other joke on late-night television, this phrase set off a new round of ridicule. The *Washington Post's* Dana Milbank commented: "Democrats have had more 'New Directions' recently than Map Quest."

They have certainly tried out a bundle of slogans. Just this year we have seen several ugly phrases aimed at Republicans, like "Culture of Corruption" and "Culture of Cronyism" (those backfired after two of their own got accused of ethical misdeeds). "Do-Nothing Congress" and "Rubber-Stamp Congress" flopped as negative assaults.

As for pro-Democrat themes, "Together, We Can Do Better" and "Together, America Can Do Better" just didn't do well. Republicans were quick to point out that Massachusetts Sen. John Kerry had used the "America Can Do Better" phrase extensively in his losing 2004 presidential campaign. This misguided idea prompted a blogger's sarcastic suggestion: "Democrats: Together We Can Be France."

Before adopting the latest slogan, Democrats gave a shot to "Six for '06", referring to six issues of critical importance. But as former Sen. Jean Carnahan of Missouri pointed out, there were only five points, "the sixth being in limbo." The "Six Pack" approach might have had some appeal to blue collar voters, but it had a short life.

When the "New Direction" slogan was rolled out, Republicans produced more than nine examples of Kerry calling for "a new direction for America" in the last presidential race. "Everything old is new again," said Texas Republican Sen. John Cornyn.

Only a short trip into political history proves the wisdom of Cornyn's comment. When John F. Kennedy was running for president in 1960, on one occasion he gave a review of the use of slogans in campaigns. "Our slogans have meaning," he said. "Woodrow Wilson's New Freedom, Franklin Roosevelt's New Deal, Harry Truman's Fair Deal, and today, we stand on the threshold of a New Frontier." And that led to Lyndon B. Johnson's "Great Society."

Republicans aren't devoting much attention to slogans because they have their campaign "Poster Girl"—Nancy Pelosi. The GOP paints her as a "horror star" because conceivably she could become Speaker of the House and just two steps away from being president, in the order of succession. It would take only a one-seat majority to put Democrats in that position.

If Republicans do decide sloganeering is a good strategy for the mid-term elections, they are likely to end up with two. President Bush will be asking voters to "Stay the Course" while GOP congressional candidates will be pleading "Save Our Ship."

*September 26, 2006*

## "Call Me Madame Speaker", Says Victorious Pelosi

A major dilemma of the post-election period is what to call the woman who will be the most powerful member of Congress. California liberal Rep. Nancy Pelosi was catapulted into the top spot by the Democrat takeover of the House of Representatives.

Republicans and conservative commentators had no problem calling her names during the campaign. Pat Buchanan tagged her as a "flamer." Some Internet bloggers ridiculed her appearance, using terms like "Popeye" and "Botox Bimbo."

Even President Bush tossed some barbs, although not as harsh as Pelosi's description of him as "incompetent" and "dangerous."

Sean Hannity of Fox News confidently predicted that only two words would allow Republicans to retain control of the House: "Speaker Pelosi." He was not entirely wrong. Democrats won in spite of her abrasive personality and leftist positions.

Probably more deserving of the highest office in the legislative branch is Rep. Rahm Emamuel, the former Bill Clinton aide who headed the Democrat Congressional Campaign Committee.

But if there's one thing Congress is good at, it's tradition. Right or wrong, when there is a vacancy in the top House post it traditionally is filled by the majority leader.

So even while votes were still being counted, Nancy Pelosi and her admirers in political circles and the news media eagerly claimed the title.

"I am the Speaker of the House," said Pelosi, in an interview right after the election, then corrected herself to say, "I will be the speaker."

The same day Katie Couric of CBS News referred to her by the odd term of "speaker-elect." The *Washington Post*, gushing in print about the "Pride of Baltimore" (Pelosi's father was a former mayor and machine politician, Thomas J. D'Alesandro Jr.), hailed the first female to shatter the congressional glass ceiling as "speaker-designate", "speaker-to-be" and "speaker-in-waiting."

That last term could be read as sexist, but the *Post* preferred to use that label against the president. In the news conference where he acknowledged his party's defeat, Bush made a joke about sending Pelosi the names of some Republican interior decorators "who can help her pick out the new drapes in her new offices." The *Post* ran quotes characterizing his remarks as "demeaning" to women and decorators.

The newspaper's fashion writer, Robin Givhan, wrote a lengthy article about the looks of "the presumptive new speaker" as she took questions attired in an

Armani pantsuit, her hair stylishly coiffed at a Georgetown salon that charges $220 per sitting.

Oldtimers in the capital will have difficulty seeing this woman occupy the same office as giants like Oklahoma's Carl Albert, who for a time was second in line to the presidency.

And when the House Sergeant at Arms announces the arrival of the president for a joint meeting of Congress, it won't be a booming "Mr. Speaker …" The way Pelosi set out to change House leadership, we might hear a soft soprano voice calling her "Madame Speaker."

*November 17, 2006*

## Hillary's No Cinch, Could Be Surprise Matchup For 2008

The 2008 presidential race is heating up to the tepid level with the entry of hopefuls from both parties onto the field of play.

Iowa Gov. Tom Vilsack became the first Democrat to make a formal declaration of a run for the presidency. He is promising to do for the country what he has done for Iowa, which is the nation's largest producer of corn.

Close on his heels was another mid-westerner, Sen. Evan Bayh of Indiana, a famous-name candidate running as the son of the long-forgotten Sen. Birch Bayh, who tried and failed in a 1976 presidential bid.

These two Democrats had incredibly bad timing in making their announcements. James Webb, the newly-elected senator from Virginia, stole the spotlight by stiffing his host at a White House reception. It was rumored that President Bush later wanted to ask Webb to be the official U.S. representative to the World Toilet Summit in Moscow, hosted by President Putin, and to "eat lots of sushi." But then someone discovered the major international event had been held in September.

Vilsack and Bayh are among the first of many to form exploratory committees and seek to become the tallest dwarf in the parade to the Democratic nomination led by New York Sen. Hillary Clinton and Illinois Sen. Barack Obama. Some cynics would say that Hillary Clinton has been exploring the dream of becoming president almost since birth. She and Obama both are now in the "testing the waters" stage of the game.

Making almost as big a splash on the national scene as the early-filing Democrats were Republicans John Cox and Duncan Hunter. Cox, a millionaire businessman from Chicago, has the double distinction of being the first formally announced GOP candidate and the most authentic political unknown since Jimmy Carter ran for president in 1976. Hunter, a House committee chairman (until January) from California, threw his hat into the ring before Republicans lost their shirts in the November 7 election.

Joining them is Sen. Sam Brownback, R-Kansas, who saw an opportunity for a conservative candidate after Sens. Rick Santorum of Pennsylvania and George Allen of Virginia were knocked out of competition by losing their seats.

While the intentions of all these White House hopefuls are no doubt sincere, it is far too early for anyone to claim that the nomination is in the bag in either party. The ultimate contest may be between two surprise candidates.

For Democrats, it could be a person with high name recognition, from a southern state—a woman who, unlike Hillary Clinton with her missing records scandals, has nothing to hide. The 2008 Democratic nominee very well could be Britney Spears.

As for Republicans, with many of the 41st president's team members playing major roles in the 43rd president's administration, don't be surprised if vice president Dick Cheney is replaced by Dan Quayle, who would be the obvious choice for the Republican nomination.

Britney vs. Dan 2008. You heard it here first, folks.

*December 8, 2006*

## Washington Holiday Parody: The Nightmare of Christmas

Twas the week before Christmas, and at the White House,
Not even Barney was stirring, it was quiet as a mouse.
The stockings were hung at Camp David this year,
In hope that Cindy Sheehan would dare not come near.
George Bush in his pj's and Laura in her gown,
It was past 9 o'clock—time to settle down.
When from the outside there came such a clatter,
The president arose to see what was the matter.
When what to his wondering eye should appear
But a great big red sleigh and eight charging reindeer.
With a little old driver, so cunning and brainy,
He knew in a moment it must be Dick Cheney.
More rapid than eagles his coursers they came,
And he whistled and shouted and called them by name:
"Now, Hunter, now, Hagel, now Cox and McCain,
"On Brownback, on Huckabee, go straight down the lane.
"On Romney, on Gingrich, through the New Hampshire snows.
"On Giuliani, the Rudolph without the red nose.
"To the top of the hill and straight through the gate,
"Now, dash away, dash away, to 2008."
The moon on Press Secretary Tony Snow
Gave a luster of midday to objects below.
And turning to go back in from the night,
The president beheld a startling new sight.
As the Republican herd went dashing away,
There suddenly appeared a shiny blue sleigh.
With twinkling round eyes and cheeks that were rosy,
In the driver's seat, sat Nancy Pelosi.
Her reindeer were really chomping at the bit,
Each one on the team wanted to be "it."
With a mischievous grin on her tight-skinned face,
She spurred them all on for the next big race:
"Now, Vilsack, now Biden, Obama and Clinton,
"On Dodd, on Richardson, and Gore, strongly hintin'
"On Kucinich and Edwards, come run and be merry,
"The race is wide open—to anyone but Kerry."
Both red and blue sleighs were loaded with gifts

For voters whose moods can take some sharp shifts.
Promises as large as the snowflakes that fall,
Tax breaks and pork barrel spending for all.
As the president finally could go hit the sack,
He exclaimed, "This nightmare is worse than Iraq."

*December 22, 2006*

## Hillary Announces, Grabs *Washington Post* Headlines

The *Washington Post* hasn't made a formal endorsement of Hillary Clinton in the 2008 presidential race, but its news columns leave little doubt of the liberal newspaper's preference for her to succeed President Bush.

When the senator from New York announced her candidacy—on the Internet, not in print media—on January 20, the *Post* played the story on Page One with a five-column headline, a large color photo and a chart showing her wide lead in a national poll. There were two sidebar stories on the inside pages, one an article gushing about the video on Clinton's campaign Web site.

"Perched almost-comfortably on a shabby-chic couch with a carefully rumpled pillow at her back," the reporter wrote, "Clinton spoke in that intimate tone befitting her rhetoric ..." It was enough to make an unbiased reader gag.

On the following two days, Clinton landed on the front page twice with non-news stories. *Post* editors apparently couldn't dream up an excuse to showcase the former first lady on the day after the State of the Union address and allowed Nancy Pelosi a day in the sun with a four-column photo of the new House speaker towering over the president. It was only a short time before Clinton was back on Page One with a heavily slanted dispatch from Iowa, where the first party caucuses will be held next January. The headline: "Clinton Begins Her Run In Earnest" (actually it was in Des Moines).

By the time this appears in print, the *Post*'s fashion maven, Robin Givhan, might well have done a feature on the front-running Democrat's attire, discreetly sidestepping a reference to her frequent wearing of dark pants suits that conceal her bottom-heavy figure. Givhan previously had written about the 1994 "pink press conference" in which she "wrapped herself in sugary innocence" by dressing in a pink suit to answer questions about Whitewater, her family's finances and the $100,000 in profit she'd made trading cattle futures. That was before she became the *Post*'s supermodel candidate.

There likely will be a syrupy *Post* Sunday magazine article about the Clinton mother-daughter relationship. The woman who once sneered that she "could have stayed home and baked cookies" instead of pursuing a career now is trying to project a softer image of a devoted mom. Chelsea Clinton, now 26 and drawing a six-figure salary on Wall Street, could be a liability, however. Her boyfriend's father is serving a six-year prison term for fraud.

Hillary Rodham Clinton is the only candidate using her middle name (Sen. Barack Hussein Obama certainly doesn't) and that might make a good feature if it weren't for the fact that her two brothers, Tony and Hugh, brought shame to the Rodham name by taking large sums of money to lobby for presidential pardons in the Clinton administration.

With all of his wife's history, Bill Clinton might be the shiniest asset of the *Post*'s favorite candidate.

*February 2, 2007*

## News Correspondents' Musical Review of Politics

Presidential politics took center stage at the annual satirical review of the Washington Gridiron Club. News correspondents lampooned Republicans and Democrats alike, and even took a few digs at themselves.

Melodies from the '60s were parodied as the Gridiron chorus echoed the Beatles singing, "We're the bleedin' lib-ral press corps band" and "getting by with a little help" from White House sources: "So, we played ball with the President's men, no, can't recall our conversations with them."

Hillary Clinton was portrayed as a former "flower child" now marching to a military tune:

"I am the perfect candidate, Bill taught me to triangulate,

"I'll stand up and be a man, better than Obama can."

Syndicated columnist Clarence Page, as Sen. Barack Obama, D-Ill., belted out a show-stopping version of "I'm a Soul Man" to, as the Gridiron writers said, "convince some of his critics that he's black enough for the job."

On the Republican campaign trail, a stand-in for former New York mayor Rudy Giuliani pleaded for support from conservatives:

"Do not forsake me, Jerry Falwell, before election day.

"Do not mistake me for a lib-ral, wait—I can pray!"

The fickle Fourth Estate depicted its former favorite GOP candidate, Sen. John McCain, R-Ariz., as a "leader of the pack" who rides his scooter offstage and crashes.

High-flying fundraiser Mitt Romney took the spotlight as the Mormon candidate "pre-ordained to be president." As the former Massachusetts governor eager to leave the liberal state behind, Gridiron associate member Joe DiGenova sang:

"Fly me up to Mars, and let me change my point of view,

"Gun rights, abortion, these positions ain't that new.

"A flip, a flop, some will say, I can't win this race any other way."

The show benefited from lyrics written by two byliners familiar to readers of *The Oklahoman*. Washington correspondent Chris Casteel penned a global warming parody to "Summer in the City": "Hot time! Summer in the Arctics, condos rising in the polar tropics ... It's an inconvenient truth, or a hoax—that's Inhofe's view ..." Retired capital bureau chief Allan Cromley skewered arrogant House committee chairman Charles Rangel ("All hail the power of ways and means, let fat cats prostrate fall") and put words to "Pagliacci" for a lament by California Gov. Arnold Schwarzenegger that the presidency "could be mine, but the Constitution says 'nein'."

House Speaker Nancy Pelosi was put on the griddle for demanding a gas-guzzling large airplane ("she'll pollute, won't give a hoot") and trading political favors for donations from lobbyists ("got a little system, always sees me through, if you're good to Nancy, Nancy's good to you").

Washington columnist Robert Novak appeared as Vice President Dick Cheney. Costumed as Darth Vader, he growled, "It's not that easy being mean ..."

The newspaper-oriented Gridiron Club, which now admits television news personalities, closed the show with a nod to changes in news media but proclaiming, "everything old is new again."

*April 6, 2007*

## With Historical Perspective, Is It Time For a President Fred?

Is this country ready for a president named Fred? That's a question that begs for an answer as former Sen. Fred Thompson moves toward an active campaign for the Republican nomination.

The United States has never had a Fred as president. In fact, the name can't even be found in the list of forgotten vice presidents. There's a Teddy, but no Freddy.

Another former senator, Oklahoma's Fred R. Harris, made two tries at the White House—a shortlived campaign in 1972 and a more intensive effort in 1976—but his liberal positions denied him a place on the ticket.

Running as a conservative, Thompson might have a better chance. The GOP frontrunners—Rudy Giuliani, John McCain and Mitt Romney—all have taken stands that don't set well with the party's right wing.

But many voters base their decision not on political views but on personality. And there Fred Thompson has a distinct advantage.

Well known to the public through his roles as a character actor in movies and television, the hulking six-foot-six Tennessean already has found a welcome in many homes from his appearances on the screen.

He has played a White House chief of staff, a director of the CIA, an F.B.I. agent, an admiral, a senator and, in five seasons on NBC's *Law and Order* a New York district attorney. While not yet a real president, he plays one on TV. He was cast as Ulysses S. Grant in HBO's *Bury My Heart at Wounded Knee*.

The *New York Times*, in a profile of Thompson, said: "When Hollywood directors need someone who can personify governmental power, they often turn to him."

Whether he can transfer that image to a performance as a presidential contender remains to be seen. He's being compared favorably with another former actor turned politician, Ronald Reagan. One of his throwaway lines is quite reminiscent of the popular Republican president.

When asked why he left the Senate after serving two years of an unexpired term and one full term, he responds: "After eight years in Washington, I longed for the realism and sincerity of Hollywood."

Regardless of whether his views on immigration, terrorism and taxes appeal to the masses, Thompson has one good thing going for him: his name. Who could dislike a guy named Fred?

When you think of such figures as actor Fred MacMurray, dancer Fred Astaire, children's TV personality Fred Rogers, sitcom favorite Fred Mertz (Lucy and Desi's neighbor), and cartoon character Fred Flintstone—well, Thompson fits right in.

Besides all that, he looks presidential. In fact, he has the countenance of a president who already has served one term—the eyes of experience, the wrinkles, the graying, thinning hair.

Another valuable asset is his wife, Jeri, a lawyer and political media consultant with blonde movie star glamour. One look at her, and who wouldn't rather see her as first lady than Bill Clinton?

*June 8, 2007*

## As a Candidate for President, Richardson Flunks Too Often

If Bill Richardson has any hope of winning the Democratic nomination for president and replacing George W. Bush, he had better not be a contestant on that *Smarter Than a Fifth-Grader* show on television.

The New Mexico governor, who served in both the legislative and executive branches of the federal government, is having a hard time giving the right answers to questions on the campaign trail.

In a recent speech in southern Nevada, a member of the audience had to remind him that France is a member of the United Nations Security Council—an embarrassing misstep for a candidate who was ambassador to the U.N. in Bill Clinton's administration.

Asked by a student in an elementary school in Las Vegas how much salary a president receives, he hesitated, then guessed $250,000. The correct figure is $400,000.

Both amounts are more than the $110,000 he earns as governor. But, of course, people don't run for president for the money. Most of those who are in the race are pretty well off financially.

Financial disclosure reports filed with Congress show, for example, that Sen. Hillary Clinton is worth from $10,460,000 to $51,050,000. (Congress wrote the rules to allow members to fudge a little on how wealthy—or poor—they really are.)

Clinton's fellow Democrat, Sen. Barack Obama, listed assets ranging from $456,000 to $1,142,000. On the Republican side, Sen. John McCain tops his congressional colleagues who are running with holdings valued at $36,632,000 to $53,430,000.

These reports don't include major GOP contenders Rudolph Giuliani or Mitt Romney, but neither would have to get by on a paltry $400,000 annual income. In fact, Romney has said that if elected he would give the money to charity.

Why is Richardson in the race anyway? It was hard to tell from his appearance on NBC's *Meet the Press*. He stumbled badly on questions from Tim Russert regarding his conflicting positions on Iraq, immigration, gun control and other issues.

Russert put him on the spot about supporting attorney general Alberto Gonzales because he was Hispanic, then calling for his resignation a few days later. He had also said his model Supreme Court justice was Byron White but backpedaled when reminded that White wrote the dissent in Roe v. Wade. Then came the baseball questions.

Richardson, who was born in southern California and spent his early childhood in Mexico City, played baseball in college. But he finally had to retract a claim that he was drafted by the Kansas City Athletics in 1966 after an Albuquerque, N.M. newspaper exposed the untruth.

After admitting his mistake on the broadcast, he was asked about a statement that his dream job would be playing for the New York Yankees. It seems he also had stated publicly that his favorite team was the Boston Red Sox. Pressed by an incredulous Russert, Richardson said he was a fan of both teams.

A fifth grader would have had better sense than to say that.

*June 22, 2007*

## Washington Version of New Prime Time TV Lineup

Reality shows, game shows and situation comedies are still big in television, as the new fall schedule indicates. The nation's capital is all of those wrapped into one. Take a look at the Washington version of this season's prime time lineup:

*P-Ville*—(P stands for politics, which impacts this city with hurricane force in all seasons of the year.) In an uneasy campaign climate marked by posturing and mudslinging, polar opposite federal election law enforcers are assigned to investigate violations together. The explosive give-and-take between the two often reaches the intensity of the Sunday morning televised debates.

*Dirty Sleazy Money*—A competitive offering, this nighttime soap stars Norman Hsu as a shady character who became a fugitive from justice after pleading guilty to grand theft in the 1990s, then resurfaced as a political fundraiser for Hillary Clinton. Will the return of $860,000 from 260 donors "bundled" by Hsu satisfy wary voters, or revive suspicions of large sums of money from overseas pouring into Clinton campaign coffers?

*Are You As Smart As Alberto Gonzales?*—While controversy might not swirl about Michael B. Mukasey, nominee for attorney general, his Senate confirmation hearing could provide some excitement for C-SPAN viewers if he is peppered with the kind of questions his predecessor couldn't answer properly.

*Limopoolers*—With gasoline prices soaring as high as Gucci loafers, four K Street lobbyists decide to share a limousine for their daily commute from the suburbs. Their eternal complaining about administrative roadblocks and legislative gridlock is apt to get tiresome.

*Budget Deal or No Budget Deal*—Congressional appropriators seek to take home big pork barrel prizes without losing to a presidential veto.

*McCain*—One of the most-hyped shows of the new season, this saga features John McCain as an ambitious U.S. senator who must overcome numerous obstacles in his bid for the presidency. How he faces the challenges of funding his campaign, recapturing the appeal of his 2004 race and winning votes from a war-weary electorate should keep viewers guessing.

*The Greenspan Report*—Premiering to coincide with publication of his new book, Alan Greenspan's business newscast reveals a new facet of the former Federal Reserve chairman's fascinating personality: his masterful use of hindsight on matters ranging from the global economy to the current home mortgage crisis.

*Samuel Who?*—President Bush is tested on his ability to remember names of cabinet members like energy secretary Samuel W. Bodman.

*Dancing With the Candidates*—This popular series opens with a group of contestants that includes these sexy matchups: Barack Obama and Oprah Winfrey,

Rudy Giuliani and Sally Field, John Edwards and Rosie O'Donnell, Chris Dodd and Barbra Streisand, and Joe Biden and Cher. In an extraordinary pairing, Hillary (Two Left Feet) Clinton has for her partner a talented musician—her husband, Bill (Hot Sax) Clinton.

*Craig's Anatomy*—New episodes explore the mystery of a conservative lawmaker's use of his hands and feet.

*September 21, 2007*

## Hillary Laughs (Cackles) Her Way Through the Campaign

It began with hairstyles ... or was it her legs? Hillary Clinton's appearance has been the topic of discussion ever since she became a public figure. Political observers have scrutinized her from top to, uh, bottom.

She has come a long way since the "Headband Hillary" days as the wife of then-Gov. Bill Clinton, when her hippie dress and feminist views irritated Arkansas voters. After the Clintons took over the White House, she adopted a black pants suit look, which some critics said was to conceal her "hippy" figure.

More recently, since New York's junior senator has become a candidate for president, attention has been directed more to her upper body. The *Washington Post* devoted considerable space to a sighting of her on the floor of the Senate wearing an outfit with a plunging neckline that showed (gasp) some cleavage.

Currently the focus is on her throat—or rather what comes forth from that region during town meetings and media interviews. It's her laugh.

When Clinton is asked a question she doesn't want to answer, she responds with a vocal outburst that has been variously described as a guffaw, a caterwaul, a bray, or most commonly, a cackle.

A video was posted on YouTube under the title, "The Cackle That Killed 1,000 Ears." Comedy Central's *Daily Show* with Jon Stewart presented a "laugh track" of examples of Clinton cackles." Radio hosts play sound recordings on their shows. For those without access to these sources, one story spelled it out in a headline: "Bwah-ha-ha!"

Fox News host Bill O'Reilly produced a body language expert who said Clinton's responses were contrived and that she exhibited "evil laughter."

Even the *New York Times* was critical. An article by Patrick Healy described how she laughed her way through recent interviews on all five major Sunday morning talk shows. "I don't know what she had for breakfast," Healy said, "but her laughter was heavily caffeinated at times."

The *Boston Globe* came down harder. Columnist Joan Vennochi wrote: "Hens cackle. So do witches. And, so does the front-runner in the Democratic presidential contest." She quoted former Bill Clinton adviser Dick Morris as saying her laugh was "loud, inappropriate and mirthless ... a scary sound that was somewhere between a cackle and a screech."

A London newspaper, *The Independent*, weighed in with an observation that "deployment of the full belly laugh is the latest weapon used by the leading Democratic presidential candidate when she is being pummelled by reporters or rivals."

Howard Kurtz of the *Washington Post*, in a piece headlined "Chucklegate", raised the question: "Do we want to listen to that laugh for the next five years?"

America's voters will make that decision. In the meantime, Clinton leads in the polls and in fundraising for the quarter. She's getting almost as much good press as her husband. Clinton adversary Newt Gingrich predicts a Hillary victory.

She could have the last laugh yet.

*October 5, 2007*

## Some Candidate Might Win By a Hair in Next Election

Forget about Iraq, immigration, children's health and other issues. The next presidential election could turn on something as simple as hair.

According to the *Washington Post*, Democrats Hillary Clinton and Barack Obama are competing fiercely for votes in South Carolina, which holds a primary in January. Their battleground: beauty salons. Both are strategically targeting black women.

A *Post* article quoted Clinton's state director, Kelly Adams, as saying, "we have to go where the voters are." One ploy being used by the Clinton campaign is a countertop poster featuring photos of the candidate with seven different hairdos and a line from her speeches: "Pay attention to your hair, because everyone else will."

Obama has a poster that shows him getting his hair trimmed by a black barber in a Marion, S.C. shop. His campaign workers also are making the rounds of hair dressers urging them and their customers to support the only African American in the race. Maybe they should reprint his high school yearbook picture—when he had an Afro haircut and went by the name of Barry.

Meanwhile, John Edwards, who is running a distant third in polls of black women in South Carolina, is still trying to disassociate himself from hair salons. The former North Carolina senator was branded by news media as a "pretty boy" who gets high-dollar haircuts.

Farther back in the Democrat pack is Sen. Joseph Biden of Delaware, who got a hair transplant in the 1970s. He also had a facelift and got his teeth capped.

If voters decide to pick the next president on the basis of hair, Republicans are at a distinct disadvantage. Of the four leading GOP candidates, three have very little head covering.

When Rudy Giuliani was mayor of New York City, he used a "combover" in an attempt to conceal his baldness. But in 2002 after leaving office he allowed his pate to shine in all its glory, with the encouragement of lady friend Judith Nathan, now his wife.

Arizona Sen. John McCain appears to be "follically challenged" (to use a politically correct phrase) because his hair is white and thin. But as Doodles Weaver once said, "Who wants fat hair?"

The newest Republican contender, former Tennessee Sen. Fred Thompson, has lost the dark wavy locks shown in revived video footage of his days as a Watergate hearing counsel.

Mitt Romney could be a model for shampoo ads. His campaign advisers worry that his hair is too perfect, and the former Massachusetts governor had to deny using dye.

A bald or balding president has not been elected since Dwight Eisenhower, and he defeated an equally bald Adlai Stevenson. But Democrats shouldn't count on the pattern continuing.

In the last election, the "big hair" ticket of John Kerry and John Edwards lost to George W. Bush, whose hair is unexceptional, and Dick Cheney, who needs a comb like a barracuda needs water wings.

*October 19, 2007*

## Voters Like Fruitcake Better Than President or Congress

President Bush doesn't seem to be bothered by polls showing that less than one-third of the electorate gives him a favorable job approval rating. He summed up his disdain in a comment last April in Tipp City, Ohio. "I've been in politics long enough to know that polls just go poof at times," he said.

Congress rates even lower in public opinion surveys.

Since the president claims he doesn't pay any attention to polls, he might not be disturbed at all by a CBS News finding that more people like fruitcake (40 percent) than him. So don't think too unkindly about someone who gives you a fruitcake for Christmas.

Some other things that surprisingly drew higher ratings than Bush or Congress in the CBS poll were "the dentist" (45 percent), brussels sprouts (51 percent) and in-laws (68 percent). Bear in mind this data comes from the network that had to fire a producer for Dan Rather because of unsubstantiated allegations about Bush's national guard service.

Nobody could blame the president much for not being upset by such outrageous comparisons as these. But how would he react to this shocking revelation: The "Talking George W. Bush Doll" which formerly headed the Top Ten List of Political Toys has been replaced by the "Barbie for President Doll."

That's the official word from *TD Monthly*, a trade magazine published by Toy Directory, Inc. The Bush doll had been a best seller since it was introduced in 2002 by John Warnock, a California Republican. But now Barbie, clad in a red pants suit and patriotic scarf, is first on the list of "Top 10 Most Wanted Political Playthings." She's a candidate of the "Party of Girls." (Has that news reached Hillary Clinton? By the way, check out the "bobblehead" version of her.)

There's also a talking Osama bin Laden doll, but a better choice might be the chewable model from Political Pet Toys. This company also offers the president of Iran, Karl Rove and Michael Moore.

These novelty gift items in a way are like polls. They provide an opportunity for citizens to express their feelings about certain personalities on the political scene.

But whether it's doll purchases or poll figures, President Bush apparently is able to take the results in stride. He elaborated on his attitude toward polls in a *Meet the Press* interview in 2004. Host Tim Russert posed the question: "Why do people hold you in such low esteem?" Bush answered:

"I don't know why people do it. I believe I owe it to the American people to say what I'm going to do and do it, and to speak as clearly as I can, try to articulate as best I can why I make decisions I make, but I'm not going to change because of polls. That's just not my nature."

You won't find those words coming from the mouth of a talking doll.

*November 30, 2007*

## Theme For Next Inauguration: Obamarama, Hucklebuck or Coronation?

Anyone passing by the campaign headquarters of Democrat Barack Obama in early December might have heard some different words being sung to a familiar tune:

"OOOOOprahbama,
"When the 'O' comes sweeping down the plain,
"With Barack in tow, the Oprah show
"Gives a mighty boost to his campaign.
"OOOOOprahbama,
"What a keen political machine.
"She's got so much clout,
"The crowds turn out.
"They all want to see the TV queen.
"He knows she's the best thing he's got.
"Hillary doesn't have anyone that hot (not even Bill).
"So when we say, YOW! We're sweeping Ioway,
"And marching on to South Carolina and New Hampshire,
"Oprahbama, make way!"

With both Democrat and Republican races tightening, candidates are geared up for a torturous drive toward the November election. Along the way they'll face many challenges: surviving the primaries, winning the nomination, and making a choice for vice president.

This time next year some busy people will be knee deep in planning the inauguration of a new president. The actual swearing-in on the Capitol steps is pretty much the same every four years. But that ceremony is only a minor part of the festivities that will draw the world's attention to Washington in January 2009.

It will be a time of joyous celebration for the victor and it might be fun to guess what it will be like, depending on who wins.

Traditionally, in addition to the many inaugural balls around the city, the event includes a spectacular entertainment gala keyed to the president-elect's personality and background. After raising what it takes to get elected, by that time money is no object.

If the Obama-Winfrey ticket is triumphant, the imagination could run wild. We know from the Ellen Degeneres show that the Illinois senator can dance, so he is sure to attend all the balls. And it wouldn't be surprising if Oprah gave a new car to everyone at the Obamarama gala.

Should voters choose the "faith-based" Republican team of Mitt Romney and Mike Huckabee, the Mormon Tabernacle Choir certainly would add a special perspective to the occasion. Huckabee, the former Southern Baptist preacher, could display his skill in playing the guitar as Bill Clinton did with the saxophone at his first inauguration in 1993. And surely he knows how to do the "huckle-buck" on the dance floor.

Rudy Giuliani could call on ample talent to stage a Broadway production for his gala, but John Edwards might have the inside track for the cast of *Hairspray*.

Fred Thompson's inaugural entertainment featuring stars of Hollywood and the Grand Ole Opry might include former lady friend Lorrie Morgan. Let's hope his running mate, John McCain, doesn't sing like he did on *Saturday Night Live*.

As for the Clinton-Clinton ticket, it could be a repeat of their first two inaugurations. But chances are if Hillary becomes the first female president, you'd better prepare for a coronation.

*December 14, 2007*

# Attitude and Gratitude

Writers of political humor tend to exhibit a cynical attitude toward Washington, D.C. and the institutions of government. It's nothing new.

In 1897, Mark Twain wrote: "There is no distinctly American criminal class—except Congress."

Will Rogers said in the 1930s, "I don't make jokes. I just watch the government and report the facts."

More recently, P. J. O'Rourke observed: "Giving money and power to government is like giving whiskey and car keys to teenage boys."

Mark Russell, in his nightclub act at the Shoreham Hotel, extended a special Washington welcome to out-of-town visitors, "because this is your capital where your laws are made and broken, by the same people in many cases."

In today's world, late night TV comedians are brutal in their ribbing of presidents and lawmakers. Blogs, the modern outlet for criticism of public officials, often read like no holds are barred.

So if my work is tinged with cynicism, I come by it naturally. But that isn't to say that I am a confirmed cynic. I'm actually quite fond of politics and its breeding ground, Washington.

Having worked in the capital for many years, I find it is unlike any other city in the United States.

Only in Washington is there a New Year's Eve celebration on September 30. That's the end of the fiscal year. Bureaucrats put on funny hats and throw red tape out the window.

Washington has more lawyers than the whole state of Texas. The city's largest single employer is the Government Printing Office.

My Washington experience convinced me that we truly live in a great country. It's a country that guarantees wrinkled old men and women in wheelchairs can go naked on a beach in Florida—the government built a special ramp. We have a government that spends almost $200,000 to study "social organization through poker." (Using an army barracks for a lab?)

In this free society we can, and do, poke fun at Washington and the silliness tht goes on there. But if you look past the human foibles of those who govern, the nation's capital really is a symbol of what's good about this country. Its museums and memorials tell the story of America and the dedicated men and women who built this nation and made it great.

It's still a thrill to walk past the U.S. Capitol, or the National Archives where the Constitution and other precious documents are displayed. And, yes, the White House, too. They are symbolic of a hard-won freedom that no other nation enjoys quite as much.

As for concerns about the current state of affairs, just remember what Will Rogers said in 1932: "We have been staggering along under every conceivable horse thief that could get into office, and yet, here we are, still going strong. That we have carried as much political bunk as we have and still survived shows that we are a supernation."

Also bear in mind the words of the Greek philosopher Plato, one of history's first standup comedians: "One of the penalties for refusing to participate in politics is that you end up being governed by your inferiors."

Now, some thank yous. In addition to POTUS 41, 42 and 43, as well as many politicians and bureaucrats who made this book possible, my gratitude goes to *The Oklahoman*, which published the *Potomac Junction* column from 1989 through 2007. The selections in this volume are reprinted with permission. I am especially indebted to the newspaper's editor, Ed Kelley, my former colleague in the Washington bureau.

Words cannot properly express my heartfelt appreciation to my wife, Mary, for her encouragement and support of my writing efforts. Combined with insider knowledge about national politics, her keen eye and her background as a corporate magazine writer were invaluable in proofreading and editing the manuscript.

I am grateful to fellow newspaper columnists in many parts of the country for their friendship and advice.

Last but not least, I treasure the thought of readers who took time out of busy lives to peruse my commentaries, and often offered comments that were most welcome.

My thanks to all.

Robert L. Haught

# About the Author

For a good portion of his long and varied career in journalism, politics and government, Robert L. Haught was a part of the Washington scene.

A former UPI correspondent who took a detour to work for two Oklahoma governors, Haught helped elect one of them (Henry Bellmon) to the U.S. Senate and served as a senior staff member for 12 years. He then became top aide to Sen. Charles Mathias (R-Md.) before establishing a self-owned business firm specializing in editorial services.

In 1987, Haught returned to journalism, becoming the first Washington-based editorial writer for *The Oklahoman*, Oklahoma's largest newspaper. He also originated a column, *Potomac Junction*, a commentary on events and personalities in the nation's capital, which he wrote for 18 years. In 2003, he began writing a self-syndicated column, *Now I'm No Expert*. He is the author of a book based on that column, *Now, I'm No Expert on Cats and Other Mysteries of Life*, published in 2006.

As a member of the National Society for Newspaper Columnists, Haught organized the 2007 Will Rogers Writers' Workshop in Oklahoma City. He is responsible for creation of the Will Rogers Humanitarian Award, honoring a columnist whose work best exemplifies the ideals of Oklahoma's beloved cowboy-philosopher. He held offices and served six years on the NSNC board of directors. He also is a member of the National Conference of Editorial Writers.

Haught has been recognized for his achievements by induction into the Oklahoma Journalism Hall of Fame. He is an Army veteran and an elder in the Presbyterian Church. He and his wife, Mary, live on a 40-acre farm in the foothills of Virginia's Blue Ridge Mountains.

978-0-595-47154-6
0-595-47154-4

Printed in the United States
106876LV00003B/1-90/P

9 780595 471546